Read SAP PRESS online also

With booksonline we offer you online access to leading SAP experts' knowledge. Whether you use it as a beneficial supplement or as an alternative to the printed book – with booksonline you can:

• Access any book at any time
• Quickly look up and find what you need
• Compile your own SAP library

Your advantage as the reader of this book

Register your book on our website and obtain an exclusive and free test access to its online version. You're convinced you like the online book? Then you can purchase it at a preferential price!

And here's how to make use of your advantage

1. Visit www.sap-press.com
2. Click on the link for SAP PRESS booksonline
3. Enter your free trial license key
4. Test-drive your online book with full access for a limited time!

Your personal **license key** for your test access including the preferential offer

eg7z-v8fm-psw5-u4ha

Outsourcing SAP® Operations

 PRESS

SAP PRESS is a joint initiative of SAP and Galileo Press. The know-how offered by SAP specialists combined with the expertise of the Galileo Press publishing house offers the reader expert books in the field. SAP PRESS features first-hand information and expert advice, and provides useful skills for professional decision-making.

SAP PRESS offers a variety of books on technical and business related topics for the SAP user. For further information, please visit our website: *www.sap-press.com*.

Boris Otto, Jörg Wolter
Implementing SAP Customer Competence Center
2009, 169 pp., hardcover
ISBN 978-1-59229-258-5

Martin Riedel
Managing SAP ERP 6.0 Upgrade Projects
2009, 362 pp., hardcover
ISBN 978-1-59229-268-4

Gerhard Oswald, Uwe Hommel
SAP Enterprise Support
ASAP to Run SAP
2009, 339 pp., hardcover
ISBN 978-1-59229-302-5

Snabe, Rosenberg, Møller, Scavillo
Business Process Management – the SAP Roadmap
2009, 411 pp., hardcover
ISBN 978-1-59229-231-8

Luc Galoppin, Siegfried Caems
Managing Organizational Change during SAP Implementations
2007, 364 pp., hardcover
ISBN 978-1-59229-104-5

Yosh Eisbart

Outsourcing SAP® Operations

Galileo Press

Bonn • Boston

Galileo Press is named after the Italian physicist, mathematician and philosopher Galileo
Galilei (1564—1642). He is known as one of the founders of modern science and an advocate
of our contemporary, heliocentric worldview. His words *Eppur si muove* (And yet it moves)
have become legendary. The Galileo Press logo depicts Jupiter orbited by the four Galilean
moons, which were discovered by Galileo in 1610.

Editor Florian Zimniak
Copyeditor Jutta VanStean
Cover Design Nadine Kohl
Photo Credit Getty Images/Paul Eekhoff
Layout Design Vera Brauner
Production Iris Warkus
Typesetting SatzPro, Krefeld (Germany)
Printed and bound in Canada

ISBN   978-1-59229-284-4

© 2010 by Galileo Press Inc., Boston (MA)
1st edition 2010

Library of Congress Cataloging-in-Publication Data

Eisbart, Yosh.
  Outsourcing SAP operations / Yosh Eisbart. -- 1st ed.
    p. cm.
  Includes bibliographical references and index.
  ISBN-13: 978-1-59229-284-4 (alk. paper)
  ISBN-10: 1-59229-284-4 (alk. paper)
  1. Information technology--Management. 2. Contracting out. I. Title.
  HD30.2.E387 2010
  004.068'4--dc22
                        2009033087

Contents at a Glance

Contents

Section 3: Best Practices, Insights, and Lessons Learned

Foreword by Bridgette Chambers, ASUG CEO

Since the Americas' SAP Users' Group's (ASUG) was founded in 1991, it has consistently strived to provide a platform for its diverse and passionate user community. As a result, it has grown into the largest independent community of SAP professionals in the world. Its passion for helping customers reap the most value from their technology investments fuels its mission of not only ensuring that members can influence SAP product and service strategy, but also that they have the education and training they need to be successful.

Accomplishing this mission — not unlike carrying out any given SAP implementation — is a truly collaborative process. Each component of the greater SAP ecosystem — SAP Americas as the software provider; customers as users and consumers; and partners as subject matter experts and facilitators — all play key roles within the community. Without each group working in concert with the others, it is difficult for customers to align their IT and business concerns and realize the full value of their investments. Thus, productive collaboration between customers, partners, and SAP cannot be an afterthought; rather, it must be a daily requirement. This three-way symbiotic relationship is truly codependent, rooted deeply in shared goals and complementary objectives. As the collective voice of the customer in North America, ASUG plays a critical role in this collaboration.

Collaboration

ASUG's relationship with SAP is a rich alliance in which ASUG works closely with SAP in multiple capacities, including user community education, joint programs such as the Benchmarking and Best Practices initiatives, and the Influence program. This strategic alliance drives innovation and user adoption and provides true, measureable value to ASUG's member community.

ASUG's partnership with SAP

As *the* single voice representing SAP's North American user community, ASUG is tremendously proud of this relationship and the shared collaborative commitment toward making SAP customers successful.

That being said, although ASUG deeply values its close relationship with SAP, it is committed to maintaining its independence. This objective position enables ASUG to act as a trusted advisor worthy of serious dialogue. Furthermore, this careful balance between collaboration and objectivity is crucial to ASUG's effectiveness as a voice for its members.

ASUG's partnership with its Associate Members

As stated earlier, each member of the ecosystem plays a pivotal role — none more important than the other. This is clearly true for ASUG's Associate Member community, which plays a crucial role in supporting not only SAP in its ability to deliver SAP solutions but also customers in terms of implementation and education. Although this partner community brings great value to the SAP ecosystem, its greatest contribution is the knowledge and experience it can bring to a project when engaged as part of an implementation team. In this age of budget cuts and downsizing, it's a rare company that can afford to hire — in-house — all of the full-time employees required for project preparation, blueprinting, development, and go-live. Rarer still is the circumstance in which all of these permanent positions make sense. Many times, it's much more cost-effective to outsource critical aspects of an implementation, and doing so often brings the added benefit of acquiring leading-edge, experienced resources who — quite literally — have "been there" and "done that." Augmenting an internal team with external resources can also trim implementation cycles and speed time to value — a critical factor as IT departments strive to be seen as a true business partners and not just a fulfillment arm. Although outsourcing may not be the appropriate delivery model for all scenarios, environments, or clients, it is prudent to explore this alternative as one of many options. Simply stated, the outsourcing and consulting services available via the SAP partner community provide valuable resource alternatives for the customer base.

The topic and importance of this book

Yosh Eisbart — a leading technology expert in the SAP community — has over 15 years of in-depth, hands-on SAP implementation experience. His extensive global SAP project and production support experience has provided him with a deep understanding of the potential challenges inherent in SAP projects and how to drive these projects successfully.

Based on his expertise and extensive research, Yosh has been able to create an objective and balanced overview of SAP outsourcing and its various aspects. Far from delivering a rallying cry for the necessity of external resourcing, Yosh presents both its advantages and disadvantages, respective to its major determining factors. Delving deep into both the strategic and tactical, Yosh provides an excellent framework for both those interested in the possibilities of outsourcing and those already actively involved in conversations with potential partners. One of the primary themes throughout the book revolves around the importance of partnership. Yosh emphasizes the criticality of customer and partner collaboration, along with the need for a shared vision and understanding. This point resonates specifically with ASUG's true mission and evokes the spirit on which ASUG was founded. In some respects, ASUG acts as the bridge and facilitator between all parties, encouraging teamwork and mutual respect. Yosh highlights the importance of this again and again.

As with most things in life, SAP is a team sport and we are all team players. I highly encourage you to approach this book with the spirit of ASUG as well as with the writer's intention in mind — an intention steeped in the goal of deeply productive partnerships where all parties end up winning.

Bridgette Chambers
Chief Executive Officer
Americas' SAP User Group

Preface

In his 2005 award-winning book, *The World Is Flat: A Brief History of the Twenty-First Century*, Thomas Friedman describes the then current (and still accurate) state of affairs for the world of outsourcing and the truly global nature of business today. This New York Time's thinker, columnist, and author stated it bluntly when he declared that customers are now afforded many more options for IT outsourcing than ever before; or more concisely: "the world is now flat." Through thoughtful discussion and insight, Friedman broke down various industries and highlighted in particular the use of information technology and its service-oriented provider. He cites that since 2000, corporations — whether driven based on lower cost modeling or internal resource constraints — have broadened the delivery spectrum to rely on alternative services models.

The SAP world not only recognizes this reality but is embracing this philosophy. Outsourcing SAP operations as a viable option both from a strategic and tactical execution perspective has become a commonly adopted practice within the industry.

Embraced by business, the "flavors" (i.e. methods of leveraging external SAP consulting services) range from a single resource on a point SAP solution (strategic staffing) through to fully-outsourced comprehensive technical production support (ABAP custom development, SAP NetWeaver Basis operations, Security Administration support, etc.) and functional production support (SAP core business process functional configuration support of Financials [FI/CO], Materials Management [MM], etc.) and everything in between.

This book tackles this complex topic, addresses the fundamental questions asked by those involved both strategically and tactically, offers actionable recommendations, and provides real client case studies and examples. The book is divided into three distinct sections:

Structure of this book

1. Strategy

2. Application

3. Best Practices

Section I —
strategy Many SAP organizations — varying in size from midmarket to global multinationals, spanning complexity from simple business models to multifunctional/dimensional organizations, and ranging in application from targeted point solution to complete business process outsourcing (BPO) — leverage outsourcing in some way. These companies are attracted to the outsourcing operations and delivery options for a multitude of reasons, all unique to their specific business needs, corporate strategy, and environment.

The five w's In this book, we will explore the five fundamental "w's" behind outsourcing:

1. **Who** implements outsourcing?

2. **Why** do organizations choose to leverage outsourcing?

3. **When** is the appropriate time for an organization to leverage outsourcing?

4. **What** are the decision factors behind the breadth/scope of BPO?

5. **How** should an organization implement outsourcing for their environment?

This book will not provide a one-sided rally cry as to the benefits and necessity of outsourcing. Instead, it will provide an objective and critical look behind the outsourcing phenomenon that will delve deeply into both the positives *and* negatives, as well as some of the common challenges encountered.

Furthermore, no valuable resource is effective without testimony. Therefore, this book will provide "real world" examples from client case studies; lessons learned from actual experiences; interviews with key decision makers behind their unique situations; and step-by-step decision trees on how these organizations came to choose BPO as a strategy, along with their ultimate execution. Throughout the book, client outsourcing experiences (and adventures) are cited and discussed, each speaking specifically to a particular outsourcing aspect.

This book is intended for three audiences:

1. Those responsible for deciding on an outsourcing strategy (decision makers, executives, influencers, etc.)

2. Those responsible for the strategy's execution (project managers, directors, team leads, etc.)

3. Those interested in outsourcing as a potential alternative for SAP services.

The narrative's approach will be that of a workbook meant to empower. The book's focus will be to provide a valuable and actionable resource guide to those involved in this complex discussion. While theory is important, ultimately, application is where organizations fail or succeed.

Section I will set the stage from a strategic perspective, focusing on the strategic pillars involved in outsourcing (i.e., the first four "w's" of who, what, where, and when). This section will be geared towards the *decision makers* involved in the outsourcing decision making process such as CIOs, CEOs, and so on. **Chapter 1** (Who) sets the discussion around who are the best candidates for SAP outsourcing and what kind of organization is best suited based on numerous factors (e.g., size, strategy, geography, location, corporate culture, etc.). **Chapter 2** (Why) delves deeper into the rationale why an organization might benefit from outsourcing and conversely, why an organization might not benefit. **Chapter 3** (What) defines the various designations across the myriad of models and **Chapter 4** (When) explores timing, transitioning, and communication.

Moving from the strategic view to the tactical view, **Section II** shifts the focus from theory to practice. Although this section will also be relevant to those targeted in the previous section (i.e., decision makers), its target audience is those responsible for implementing the selected strategy (e.g., production support managers, global delivery management, service leads, etc.). Despite not being heavily utilized for implementation purposes, **Chapter 5** (Implementations and Upgrade) discusses the ever-growing practice of leveraging outsourcing for project work. **Chapter 6** (Production Support) discusses the more frequently thought of use of BPO, the maintenance and ongoing operations of an SAP environment. This chapter will discuss this type of model and its various flavors. Following the evolutionary growth into broader utilization (and associated market buzz), **Chapter 7** (Global Delivery) discusses the latest iteration of outsourcing, including implementation and subsequent production support. Regardless of scope, depth, and lifecycle stage, the proper integration model is paramount. **Chapter 8** (Engagement Construct) provides an overview of the primary engagement models and their respective pros and cons. Rounding out Section II, **Chapter 9** (Selecting a Partner) discusses the process and objective criteria for those organizations who decide to partner with a third-party outsourcing firm.

Section III — best practices To provide tangible and actionable value, **Section III** presents insight and practical lessons learned behind some of the special areas around BPO that might not be so obvious. Nuances between the different challenges faced by midmarket as compared to larger organizations, the role and value of integration management, and so on, will be featured in this section. **Chapter 10** (Large Enterprise) highlights some of the afforded luxuries (and associated alternatives) of Fortune 100 companies and the global organization space, whereas **Chapter 11** (Midmarket) breaks down some of very different challenges and opportunities faced by the companies at the other end of the size spectrum. However, regardless of an organization's size, **Chapter 12** (IT Standardization) and **Chapter 13** (Integration Management) discuss the importance of how to partner with your outsourcing provider, including standardization methodologies as well as the new integration models. Completing section III, **Chapter 14** (Service Level Agreements) discuss the importance of service levels along with response times, risk management, escalation management, change control, communication protocol, and so on.

Objectivity Regardless of the noblest of intents and how objective a viewpoint one attempts to pursue (and profess), every person has a somewhat subjective perspective. I, the author of this book, am no different. Having spent most of my career working for SAP consulting organizations and service integrators, including many focused on selling SAP outsourcing services, I might be viewed as less than neutral. Those claims are understandable. Nonetheless, I have done my best to provide a candid and unbiased perspective, providing examples of both positive *and* negative client experiences. In fact, to go even further, one might argue that my experience provides the reader with a unique "insider's" angle and affords a "behind the curtain" vantage point. Without question, the reader will find the book to be candid in nature, and without any sales or marketing propaganda. The intent for this book is that it will become a trusted reference for those interested in outsourcing SAP operations.

This book tackles a broad range of outsourcing topics, from organization size, to SAP lifecycle stage, to corporate culture impacts, and so on. In turn, some of the content will be more relevant (and interesting) to certain audiences based on their respective unique scenario. To provide the most valuable reading experience, feel free to use this book as more of an interactive workbook meant to be used in conjunction with your unique situation *rather than* a step-by-step manual providing a linear and authoritative guidebook.

Workbook construct

Working with SAP outsourcing providers might be an organizational paradigm shift for some. This approach is not for every SAP organization or every SAP initiative. It is simply one option out of many. For those unfamiliar with this delivery method, it requires a mind shift or transformation in thinking. I challenge you to, while reading this book, approach SAP outsourcing with an open mind and an objective approach. It just might work for your SAP scenario.

Transformation theme

Finally, it is of note that SAP and their ecosystem speak their own language. This language is known as SAPanese (pronounced similarly to Japanese). Consisting of many acronyms and insider lingo, SAPanese provides those who speak it a concise and expressive language far richer than simple IT speak.

SAPanese

Although this book is not meant to be an SAP language or SAPanese course, it is impossible for the reader to not pick up some phrases, words, or terminology along the way when dealing with such a complex subject. This beautiful language, rich in flavor, will provide you with unique insight into the SAP world.

Acknowledgements

I always wondered who, aside from the author and the author's mother, actually reads the acknowledgements. So, for those curious souls beyond me and Sharon (hi mom), I would like to take the time to acknowledge those who were fundamental in the development of this book.

However, there are truly too many individuals to thank individually, including my wonderful network of customers, and my deep, rich pool of SAP colleagues. But although the overall number of people involved in the development of this book is too large to list, I would like to mention several key individuals who have blessed me with their knowledge, experience, and support. Without this group, this book would simply be a hollow shell.

Professionally speaking, I have had the honor of working with some of the strongest, brightest, and most experienced SAP professionals. My over fifteen years of SAP experience has afforded me the luxury of working with subject matter experts both within SAP America and the larger SAP consulting world. This group of thought leaders has been pivotal in sharing their extensive personal implementation experiences as well as their vast wealth of knowledge. Colleagues such as Joshua Baillon (pave), Sumit Manocha, Vlad Eydelman, and Ravinder "Sunny" Masuta have gifted me with their SAP knowledge over the years. I am grateful for their patience, knowledge, and friendship.

As you will see throughout the book, I have attempted to provide as many real-world experiences as possible. I strongly believe that although theory lays a great foundation, it is real-world experiences that show where the rubber meets the road. I am grateful to all of the clients who have been willing to share their specific SAP outsourcing experiences — whether positive or negative — with the greater public. This client "case study" material provides real value and insight into how theory has been applied and how organizations such as your own have experienced the SAP world, and I would like to acknowledge some of the individuals who have provided me with this material.

Guillermo "Bill" Garcia of Altoviento Solutions provided invaluable insight, vision, and clarity with respect to the relevance and importance of standardization when dealing with SAP outsourcing (Chapter 13). Bill's Altoviento methodology for both overall SAP project management and the optimization of SAP production support environments raises the bar to set a new standard for SAP projects. He is a leader within the SAP space and I am humbled that he was willing to contribute so much of his tremendous knowledge and experience to this book. Chapter 13 is a testament to his depth and breadth within the overall SAP project methodology arena. Muchas gracias, doctor.

I have also been fortunate to have been working closely with one of the rising technical stars within the SAP industry over the past five years, Michael Pytel, and even luckier to have him as a business partner. They say that a business partnership is like a marriage — in that case, I am lucky to be Michael's second wife. His incredible support throughout this process (including tremendous contribution to the book), his deep understanding of SAP systems' capabilities and sharing his insights, the countless hours worth of research and heated discussion, and his willingness to assist in any way he could was truly amazing. I am very lucky to have Michael as a business partner. Thanks, Mike.

On a personal level, I want to thank my mother and father for all of their support, and the wisdom and drive they instilled in me from day one. Although my pop is not proofreading this book as he did for me throughout college, it was not for a lack of willingness. I am the man I am today because of my parents and no gratitude is sufficient to thank them. It all started at Shapiro's over a corned beef sandwich in Indy. Thanks tata and mama.

Finally, I want and need to thank my incredible wife Orly. For those of you who have embarked on a similar journey (writing a book), you understand the necessary support, love, encouragement, and patience required of your loved ones. My Orly has been incredible in her gifts of understanding, wisdom, guidance, invaluable input, and again patience (to name only a few). Thanks so much, motek, for your support of this dream and your ability to keep me focused. This book is because of and for you, and baby Maya. All my love.

I hope that those of you reading this book enjoy the content, the humor, and the intent behind the creation of this book. I welcome the opportunity to exchange ideas directly if you are interested; you can reach me at *yosheisbart@benimbl.com*. I look forward to discussing outsourcing SAP operations with you.

Happy reading!

Taking a new step, uttering a new word, is what people fear most. ~ Fyodor Dostoevsky

Introduction

The phrase "outsourcing SAP operations" holds different meanings for different audiences. Depending on the beholder, this ambiguous term — and the topic of this book — can conjure up differing definitions, emotions, and images. In Chapter 1 (Introduction), the stage is set to discuss this topic objectively to maximize this discussion. Also, some background information and a brief history is provided to place this topic into a greater context. Next, the construct of the discussion is provided, laying out the path followed throughout the book. Furthermore, defining outsourcing is imperative to embarking on a discussion on the topic and thus, although the definition is written about in great detail in Chapter 3, a foundation is laid from the onset by defining the term in the introduction to provide a reference point. Finally, the chapter closes with a few comments on the book's goal of objectivity and limiting bias.

Everyone has heard horror stories about outsourcing — whether with respect to SAP or another technology. (In fact, some readers might have experienced such challenges firsthand.) Perceptions of communication issues, reactive support (versus proactive resolution), "you get what you pay for" commentary, potential recycling of issues and increased solution response, correlations between lower cost equating to lower quality and non-local based operations resulting in less than ideal support all color the perception of outsourcing. But, as the idiom goes, perception *is* reality. As with any service, the end result is only as good as the supporting people and processes; and both positive and negative experiences exist depending on previous events and their unique circumstances.

Debunking the outsourcing myth

Don't generalize!

Unfortunately, almost everyone has dined at a restaurant at one time or another and had a bad experience. Whether it was the food, the service, or the ambience, some aspect of the meal was less than ideal, perhaps even downright awful. Conversely, everyone has experienced the exact opposite — an amazing or perhaps even sublime dining experience. In either case, it would be foolish to declare that all restaurants reside completely in either camp. The same holds true for outsourcing. Therefore, to get the most out of this book, the reader is advised to suspend judgment and approach the topic with an open mind.

Real-world examples

Theory provides an excellent example of "ideal-world" potential. However, as we are all aware, theory doesn't always translate into reality. In the text that follows, you'll find several real-world outsourcing examples from clients having real-world impact. First, one of the world's largest consumer products companies (CPG), responsible for many of the products we find in our kitchens, recently embarked on one of the biggest and most complex SAP implementations to date. Attempting to replace a significant portion of their existing legacy systems across the world, this multinational "blue chip" with headquarters in Switzerland had a demanding roadmap ahead and various multi-dimensional SAP outsourcing challenges. Rom Kosla, senior manager:

> *"Without question we knew from the onset, that this project presented interesting outsourcing scenarios both with positive and negative attributes. Our company was faced with rarely-presented challenges involved in such an SAP project of this magnitude. Depending upon a wide range of factors such as the phase of the project, time zone considerations, complexities of technologies being implemented, corporate brand, partner capabilities, etc., different outsourcing solutions were required."*

Presented with a wide range of strategic as well as tactical outsourcing decisions, Kosla and his colleagues chose a unique path that is still followed and modified today.

As another example, after recently implementing SAP ERP 6.0, Scorpion Offshore Limited (Scorpion), an international ultra-premium jackup offshore drilling construction and operating company, was faced with the outsourcing dilemma. In many respects, Scorpion sits on the opposite end of the spectrum than the previously mentioned CPG conglomerate; from an organizational size and corporate outsourcing strategy perspective, Scorpion's landscape and challenges are much less complex. Scorpion operates multiple offshore drilling rigs in the middle of the ocean across the world (as well as multiple office locations throughout the globe) and these rigs all require end-user SAP support. Facing a much less complicated set of SAP challenges, Scorpion's outsourcing approach was laser-sharp and clearly understood. Determined to focus on its core business, Scorpion had little difficulty in coming to a rapid decision on outsourcing SAP operations: they outsourced everything completely. Pam Thompson, Scorpion's corporate controller and sponsor of the outsourcing option, felt that this was definitely the right approach. "Based on our business needs, outsourcing a non-core competency to a specialized provider was the logical approach." Faced with the challenges of a mid-market company (e.g., small-to-no internal IT staff, limited internal SAP knowledge, a strategic plan to not build an SAP support organization, etc.), Scorpion chose to outsource their entire SAP application support needs and their around the clock (24x7x365) level I/II/III help desk to a third-party SAP outsourcing firm.

Outsourcing SAP operations has been utilized in a multitude of ways by organizations varying in size from that of Scorpion Offshore Limited to Fortune 50 multinational conglomerates. The effectiveness and applicability of outsourcing has moved from novelty to standard practice when exploring alternative delivery and support options and the SAP world is no different. No longer is the struggle focused on the question: "Is outsourcing a viable support strategy?" Instead, the question now is: "Is outsourcing the right strategy for *my* organization?" This paradigm shift has opened the discussion and possibility of outsourcing to organizations for whom it was previously not an option.

Outsourcing in its broadest sense — obtaining outside resources for internal corporate needs — has been around since the caveman. According to Rob Handfield's "A Brief History of Outsourcing" (SCRC; May 31, 2006), during the industrial revolution, third-party resources were frequently leveraged for the production of products and/or services. In the last century, initially within the manufacturing space in the 1980s, large organizations attempted to gain a competitive advantage by exploiting

History

29

lower production costs outside of their home country. Eventually, other industries such as IT (including services) found that similar potential benefits could exist within their respective industry space. As a result, SAP outsourcing services — using external consultants to deliver on client needs — began to flourish.

During the 1990s, outsourcing (both onsite and offsite) within the SAP space began to gain popularity and pick up momentum. Global corporations rolling out major SAP platforms (or "templates") began to recognize the benefits of using *SAP offshoring*; in essence, outsourcing large development, testing, and implementation efforts to offsite SAP outsourcing centers. However, a major initial constraint existed. For a variety of reasons (lack of offshoring providers, offshoring vendors who focused only on the Fortune 500 segment, etc.), SAP offshoring was limited to only large corporations Therefore, smaller organizations — particularly midmarket and small and medium enterprises (SMEs) of $1.0 billon and below — were unable to even consider this option due to its unavailability. Eventually, with an increase in demand coupled with the growing number of Asian (especially Indian) SAP offshoring companies able to provide support, SAP outsourcing became readily available. Today, customers view SAP outsourcing as a commodity, and rightfully so.

4.1   Outsourcing Definition

The term *outsourcing* was not formally defined within the business world as a strategy until 1989 (Mullin, 1996). Since then, the definitions of SAP outsourcing run the gamut. Furthermore, the derivatives of outsourcing — ranging from "onsite consulting," "partners-in-projects" (PIP), "offshoring," "offsiteing," "global sourcing," "rightshoreing," "near-shoring," and others — can all be interpreted as outsourcing offshoots influenced by various factors (location and/or proximity being a primary factor). Each of these outsourcing models is described in detail in Chapter 3, "What is Outsourcing?" However, from a high level viewpoint, the outsourcing spectrum is driven by both location and number of resources. The following are the main categories, beginning with minimal resources and moving towards a more robust delivery mechanism:

- **Staff augmentation**
  This offering covers consultant ability to augment client teams with quality contract resources. It is included to show where it falls in the spectrum of offerings in the consultant service delivery model.

- **Staffing solution**
  With this offering, consultant assists with the definition of a solution approach during the early stages of the engagement and provide additional value-add during engagement execution.

- **Partial project outsource**
  With this offering, the client expects the consultant to provide a solution while the client maintains control of the overall effort; the consultant is responsible for some aspects of the project execution and the delivery of contracted deliverables.

- **Full project outsource (turnkey solution offering)**
  With this offering, the client expects the consultant to provide a full and complete solution. The consultant is responsible for all aspects of the project execution and the delivery of contracted scope and deliverables, often using a fixed-cost commercial arrangement

- **Global delivery**
  This is the most comprehensive outsourcing delivery model.

For the purposes of this book, outsourcing is defined as *any outside SAP service provided to a customer*. This definition is broad in scope. However, the rationale behind defining outsourcing so broadly is intentional. Due to the nature of how outsourcing is leveraged in the market place today — ranging from a single resource at the client site for implementations services to complete, offsite multi-team support organizations for operational production support services to everything in between — no other definition provides the required depth or scope.

Definition of outsourcing for the purposes of this book

However, to be clear: SAP is the focus. Although some of the concepts discussed in this book might be applicable to outsourcing in general, all of the topics are centered on supporting SAP as an ERP platform, on its product suite, on the specific nuances surrounding outsourcing SAP operations, and on specific client examples experienced through the SAP lens.

The only way to start is to start.
— Unknown

Section 1: Strategy

Section I delves into SAP outsourcing from a strategic perspective. Chapters 1, 2, 3, and 4 focus on the basic strategic pillars and the components involved in the decision making process, deciding whether SAP outsourcing is the proper tool for an organization, and if so, what the fundamental decision making components involved in its modeling are.

These fundamental strategic "w's" of who, why, what, and when all provide the necessary framework required in determining whether outsourcing — in any of its forms — make sense for your organization depending on your unique circumstances.

Because these chapters focus on high-level executive type discussions and circles (COOs, CIOs, CTOs, etc.), the material will be presented with this audience and their respective concerns in mind.

The easier it is to do, the harder it is to change.
— *Eng's Principle*

1 Who — Determining Whether Outsourcing is Right for Your Organization

Outsourcing is not right for all organizations. Determining whether to use external resources for internal SAP requirements (whether short-term project based or longer-term operational) should be decided on a case-by-case basis. The purpose of this chapter is to provide insight into and guidelines for the myriad of factors that influence this decision. Unfortunately, covering *all of the possible factors* involved is not possible; however, by tackling several major themes, an organization can better assess whether they are primed for an outsourcing relationship.

Some organizations lend themselves to working with external partners while other do not. Whether the decision revolves around the type of work performed (operations vs. bleeding-edge new SAP technology), corporate culture (an "us against the world" vs. a "we are the world" mentality), internal capabilities ("you can handle it" vs. "there ain't no way"), cost (external is cheaper vs. internal is cheaper), and so on, a different answer can be obtained for the same question for different organizations.

Do you fit the bill?

Table 1.1 highlights several pervasive determining factors and themes surrounding whether your organization is positioned for leveraging SAP outsourcing.

Determining Factor	Favorable	Might not make sense
Corporate culture	Open to leveraging external resources	Vehemently opposed to leveraging outside resources
Internal capabilities	Capabilities do not exist within existing resource pool	Internal resource pool possesses deep expertise within respective skillset(s)
Type of work*	Bleeding-edge technology	Repetitive, operational efforts
Type of work*	Repetitive, operational, commoditized efforts	Bleeding-edge technology
Short-term vision	Focus on quick execution	Focus on internal execution
Long-term vision	No interest in building skillsets within respective area	Interested in eventually obtaining given skillsets internally
Cost	Internal costs exceed leveraging external resources	Not an issue and/or internal resource cost is more cost effective
Volume	Large amount of effort; and leveraging internal resources is a waste of time, talent, bandwidth, and so on	Effort size is irrelevant and internal resources have the ability, time, bandwidth, expertise (or willingness to train), and so on
Skillset(s) available	"Purple squirrel," that is, the given required skillset is very specialized and difficult to find	Skillset(s) readily available and/or internal resources are easily trainable
Service level	Required service levels (e.g., in operational work or tight project timelines) are greater than internal resource availability, desire, or bandwidth	Required service levels are acceptable for internal resources either because they are low or the agreed on levels fall within internal resource responsibilities

* Notice how the same determining factor can result in completely different answers.

Table 1.1 Key "Who" Outsourcing Factors

Depending on how you responded to each of the factors mentioned, your organization might be a candidate for SAP outsourcing. Let's take a closer look at several of these factors.

1.1   Corporate Culture and Executive Influence

Corporate culture and executive direction weigh in heavily on an organization's SAP outsourcing strategy. Ironically, the direction does not swing consistently and paradoxically, it swings wildly and broadly from "forced strategic mandate" to "vilification". Again, the final opinion depends entirely on the company. (Do you see a common theme/trend unfolding here?)

Based on the "cost is king" mentality of the past several years, some executives have dictated to outsource their internal SAP skillsets to take advantage of economies of scale and specialized SAP outsourcers. (During the writing of this book, the 2008—2009 global financial crisis was unfolding. The United States was experiencing one of the worst financial situations since the time of the Great Depression. The run-up to this once-in-a-lifetime event began in earnest in the 2nd quarter of 2008 and was solidified when the U.S. Department of the Treasury put into law the "Troubled Assets Relief Program" (TARP) on October 3, 2008.) However, although cost was a major factor in driving organizations to look to outsourcing as a lower-cost delivery alternative, it drove neither the rationale nor the relationship. Filippo Passerini, CIO and global shared services officer at Proctor and Gamble (P&G), knew that executive sponsorship and stewarding was fundamental to its success. Passerini states:

> *"12 months, four contracts, nearly $4.2bn — on both sides of the table we knew that the stakes were high. For P&G, [our outsourcing partners] would come to support 140,000 employees in 86 countries and work that is core to our company's daily operations and long-term success. For each partner, P&G quickly became either their largest, or one of their largest, services customers. Success of our partnership model was a mandate."(www.the-chiefexecutive.com/features/feature172/)*

As with everything in life, differing executive viewpoints and in turn, corporate SAP outsourcing strategies exist. Whereas Man Mohan Goyal,

CIO of Philips Carbon Black (PCB), found value in outsourcing other technologies, SAP was not one of them, and PCB followed suit. (*http://dqindia.ciol.com/content/industrymarket/ciospeak/2008/108111001.asp*)

> *"Initially, there was a lot of discussion on whether we should have our own people manage SAP, which we implemented in 2004. Finally we decided in favor of our own people managing the data center... while outsourcing other non-SAP components."*

1.2   SAP Components Best-Suited for Outsourcing

Assuming that your executive management buys into outsourcing some component(s) of your SAP operations, the next logical step in determining whether BPO makes sense is to perform an inventory of your SAP suite. Not all SAP components are best-suited for external outsourcing. In fact, depending on a whole range of factors, outsourcing very complex areas (such as industry-specific business processes, poorly designed and cumbersome custom built ABAP developments, etc.) could prove fatal.

1.2.1   SAP Operations

Perhaps the easiest (and least painful) place to begin contemplating whether your organization is primed for SAP BPO is within the operations space. Many organizations running SAP "cut their teeth" with SAP outsourcing within day-to-day operations. This might include behind the scenes technical activities such as SAP NetWeaver Basis operations, system tuning, SM37 job scheduling oversight, and the like. Beginning within these areas, allow IT (and business executive management) to gain trust within the process instead of jumping in head first, using almost a "try-then-buy" approach.

Table 1.2 shows several areas typically used most frequently for SAP outsourcing.

Typical Outsourcing Area	Specific Areas
NetWeaver Basis	System performance tuning
	Transports
	Hot packs/OSS application
	System backup and restore
	Job scheduling
Custom development	Break/fix
	Low priority enhancements (reports, interfaces, developments, etc.)
	OSS/service marketplace application
	ABAP and Java programming maintenance
Functional/business process	Level 1 end-user support (menu flow, how-to inquiries, etc.)
Security administration	User password reset
	User profile and authorizations
Operations	Standard cross SAP technology SAP maintenance tasks

Table 1.2 Typical "First-Timer" SAP Outsourcing Areas

1.2.2 Project Work and SAP Staff Augmentation

Another common practice within organizations — whether implementing or having implemented SAP or another technology — is leveraging external consultants to augment implementation and/or specialized SAP efforts. Working with outside SAP expertise is widely accepted, and therefore extended discussion isn't required. However, several key points surrounding this practice are worth mentioning.

Outsourcing SAP project consulting work has become commoditized — even more so than offsite SAP operational services. (This is because it is far more difficult to set up offsite support services than it is to set up onsite services.) With the influx and popularity of SAP within the marketplace, the resource pool is both vast and deep for most SAP special-

Vendors in the driver's seat

39

ties. Therefore, within most SAP areas — and although SAP is still considered a "hot skillset" — clients are at an advantage and can demand higher quality at lower price points.

The only exception to this rule is the "purple squirrel," that is, those SAP skillsets that are highly specialized and thus low in supply. As with any supply and demand model, SAP skillsets in high demand with few resources are able to demand higher rates, with potentially less experience. Beginning in April 2006, with the acquisition of Virsa Systems, SAP started a targeted growth strategy of purchasing several best-of-breed financial software companies. Shortly thereafter, in May 2007, SAP acquired Outlooksoft Corporation to strengthen its integrated planning, budgeting, forecasting, and consolidation products, and it also acquired BusinessObjects in October 2007. With this "recent" set of acquisitions of best-of-breed products such as Outlooksoft (rebranded as Business Planning and Consolidation, aka BPC), Virsa (rebranded as Governance, Risk, and Compliance, aka GRC), and BusinessObjects, supporting skillsets have generated an unsustainable demand. Additional, highly sought-after SAP skillsets — whether within SAP's "All-in-One" series, industry-specific SAP business process expertise such as Oil and Gas Joint Venture Accounting (JVA), or bleeding-edge SAP technologies such as SAP NetWeaver Process Integration (PI), SAP NetWeaver Master Data Management (MDM), and others — all are highly sought-after skillsets because of their unique specializations.

SAPanese — SAP All-in-One (A1)

In collaboration with SAP's partner ecosystem, SAP provides a series of "business-flavored" ERP 6.0 products known as All-in-One (A1). These preconfigured SAP ERP products are designed and developed by SAP partners (vendors) to address specific market verticals and their respective industry requirements. A1 example solutions are focused on medical device manufacturers, high-tech, wholesale distribution, retail, and others to provide an incentive for organizations to leverage an SAP product. These A1 versions of SAP ERP are meant to meet the needs of the midmarket rather than larger, more complicated organizations.

One caveat with working with A1 products is that they are very partner-centric because a vendor owns the intellectual property. Thus, if an organization is interested in purchasing and implementing the product, they must work with its creator.

1.3　SAP Components not Best-Suited for Outsourcing

Later chapters dig much more deeply into which components might not be best-suited for SAP outsourcing; however, this topic is also relevant when your organization is at the stage of deciding whether outsourcing makes good business sense. This is especially true if your company is only interested in outsourcing within the limited SAP space. If this limited area doesn't easily lend itself to BPO, then the decision is quite easy.

Several key factors play a large role in affecting SAP outsourcing. These aspects are discussed in greater detail in the following sections.

1.3.1　Data Sensitivity, Security, and Compliance

Some organizations might find it challenging to outsource their SAP operations if they deal with highly sensitive data. Examples include personal information such as social security content, financial data such as banking details or credit card information, or highly-classified information. This is especially true within the financial segment and the government sector (specifically at the state and federal level). Depending on the level of sensitivity and the respective legal regulations involved, these organizations might simply not be legally allowed to leverage external parties for SAP services. In other cases, the outsourcing options might be less restricted but companies might still be limited to outsourcing alternatives applying only to citizens of the same country.

Another potential complication can be with where the data physically resides, that is, where the database servers holding the SAP data are located. For example, if an organization is required either by law or corporate policy to maintain their data domestically, international hosting with an SAP hosting provider might not be an option.

1.3.2　Home-Grown SAP Environments

Another potential challenge to outsourcing SAP services can arise based on the crude growth of your SAP environment. If your SAP environment grew organically, with little vision or strategic direction, and your organization never had a chance (or desire) to clean up the resulting "mess," your environment might not be in a good position for SAP outsourcing. (It would, however, be in an *excellent* position for a major reengineering initiative!). Handing over a highly customized environment with custom development on top of custom development to those not intimately familiar with the original design and/or logic (whether outsourced internally or externally) could not only pose tremendous challenges but also increased risk. Because this danger exists with even the cleanest SAP environments, overly complicated customizations exacerbate this challenge even more.

> **Warning: Handing over "spaghetti logic" could be dangerous to your organization's health!**
>
> Overly complex and poorly designed and developed SAP customizations ("spaghetti logic") given to an outsourced provider who is unfamiliar with the original design presents obvious challenges. This is not to say that it is impossible or not recommended. However, if you choose to do so, patience and understanding are required. Taking responsibility for others' code is a daunting task and patience should be exercised while your outsourcer is brought up to speed learning the logic.

1.3.3   Services Providers/Service Level Agreements

Another area where outsourcing might not make the most sense revolves around service level agreements (SLAs). If your organization is responsible for direct SLAs with your end client, engaging a third party for its delivery might be risky.

For example, let's assume that your business provides SAP hosting services to your clients limited to the infrastructure layer (networking, operating system, database, etc.) and NetWeaver Basis application services. It's quite possible that based on the outstanding level of service you provide, a client inquires about expanding the scope of services to include core SAP functional services (i.e., Financial/FICO, Order-to-Cash/SD, etc.) for 24x7x365 Level 2 support. If such additional opportunities arise, it might be tempting to expand beyond your core competencies to support your client.

If these new skillsets do not reside within your expertise (and you don't plan on brining these skillsets in-house), you will be forced to leverage a third-party partner to deliver on your behalf. *However, layering SLAs in which you have little control increases risk and could potentially jeopardize your reputation!*

1.4   Limits of Full-Time Employee Hiring/Quick Hit Temporary Project Work

You won't always be able to bring in full-time employees (FTEs) for your SAP initiatives or production support environment. Whether your ability as a hiring manager is limited for internal reasons (e.g., a hiring freeze, budget decrease, etc.) or external reasons (e.g., talent unwilling to convert to FTE, a market that's too hot for a specific SAP skillset, etc.), these real-life challenges arise from time to time in any business environment. Therefore, you sometimes are given no alternative but to look externally for SAP resources.

What about strategic "quick-hit" project work? This is another common example of where leveraging SAP outsourcing might make sense. Instead of hiring new full-time employees or investing in additional required training (if necessary), leveraging third-party resources might be a less expensive and quicker alternative.

1.5   Organization Size

An organization's size can definitely have an impact on obtaining and retaining SAP talent; therefore, size affects both the who (determining whether SAP BPO is right for your company) and how (inherent challenges based on an organization's size) of outsourcing.

To provide a common set of baseline definitions for corporate size to be used in the context of this book, we'll remain consistent with what SAP uses for its market bandwidths.

Figure 1.1 shows a pictorial representation of how SAP slices up the market place in terms of organization size.

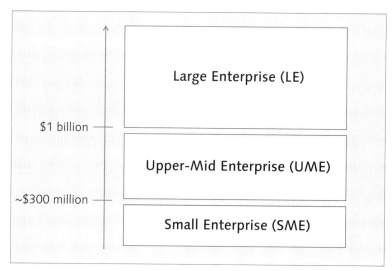

Figure 1.1 SAP's Slicing of Market Size

1.5.1 Small Enterprise (SME)

This book doesn't speak to the market segment known as small enterprise (SME). From SAP's perspective, this segment begins at the first revenue dollar up to approximately $300 million. Attempting to provide more flexible on-demand and subscription-based product offerings for this segment, SAP offers two types of products: Business One and Business by Design. Jumping on the software as a service (SAAS) bandwagon, SAP offers these easy-to-install and easy-to-use products that require minimal setup, configuration, and support. Almost a "Quicken on Steroids," these two products are available for as little as $149/user and are focused on smaller organizations not interested or willing to invest in SAP's more robust ERP products.

1.5.2 Upper Midsize Enterprise (UME)

For the upper midsize enterprise (UME) space (small to mid-sized businesses or SMB's loosely defined between $300 million and $1 billion of yearly revenue), looking externally for SAP talent (whether for temporary project work or longer-term SAP production support) might be the easiest approach. Whether real or perceived, SAP resources typically find this market segment less attractive. Due to less visibility and, in turn, less name recognition, businesses within this space usually don't carry as much weight as those within the Fortune 500 such as Nestlé or T-Mobile. Because of this challenge, finding full-time resources can be more difficult for these organizations than for larger organizations. Of course, this is a generalization — one can always find exceptions.

Case Study: Scorpion Offshore Ltd. and the midmarket space

Scorpion Offshore Ltd. — a Bermuda-based corporation founded in 2005 to own and operate state-of-the-art offshore drilling rigs — recently implemented an SAP system. Challenged by the task of supporting an SAP ERP 6.0 global implementation, Scorpion chose to partner with an SAP consulting firm for their "production support plus" services. Similar to many mid-sized organizations, Scorpion neither possessed nor desired to fully staff a comprehensive set of SAP resources. Tailored to Scorpion's needs, their partner provided a 24x7x365 production support model, covering both functional and technical requirements.

Many on Scorpion's management team came from much larger corporations and were prepared to adjust their expectations regarding the availability of high-end services and solutions, as well as the degree of attention they might receive. However, according to Scorpion's Controller, Pam Thompson, "[Our outsourcing provider] has made the implementation and use of SAP possible for us on our scale in a very painless way — our solution is all upside." Referencing her service level concerns, Ms. Thompson stated "Our entire experience has made us feel like big fish...; we have been nicely surprised at every turn. This has opened up a whole new range of possibilities for mid-sized business."

1.5.3 The Fortune 500

While the converse doesn't always ring one hundred percent true, larger organizations don't typically find themselves as challenged to find internal talent. However, this doesn't mean that the Fortune 500 don't leverage external SAP talent; to the contrary, this group is undoubtedly the largest consumer of external SAP resources. What it does mean is that the options for Fortune 500 companies are more diverse and that these companies aren't limited by the same constraints as those encountered by companies in smaller market segments.

1.6 SAP as Software: Its Complexity, Integration, and Inherent Challenges

One would be remiss to not ask the obvious question: as software — with its complexity, tight integration, and associated challenges — is SAP truly a viable candidate for outsourcing? Doesn't the very nature of SAP software either warrant closer scrutiny or outright rejection of outsourcing? Or more specifically, is a given *component* perhaps too complex or new to risk external delivery? Clearly, the answers to these questions are subjective and the questions themselves both reasonable and necessary.

> **Case Study: A major retailer and its SAP implementation struggles**
>
> According to a court filing, in January 2009 a national retail jewellery chain based in the Mountain West filed for Chapter 11 bankruptcy protection due to rampant cost overruns on an SAP implementation. This organization chose to outsource their SAP implementation and came up short financially.
>
> Based on court documents, in 2005 the company entered into a contract with SAP for a "highly sophisticated point of sale and inventory management system" at an originally projected cost of $8-10 million and a one-year project schedule. However, the retailer did not find themselves going live until September 2007, 32 months and $36 million later.
>
> Of course, outsourcing their SAP consulting services was not the only reason for the cost overrun (or their filing for bankruptcy!); however, a 300 % project overrun doesn't help any organization.

Key Points to address

Depending on your business, your SAP expertise, your risk-tolerance, and so on, embarking on an SAP initiative might be the prudent solution, independent of the specific SAP complexity (whether technical, business process/functional, or other). However, several key points must be addressed to define a strategy:

▶ **Specific SAP component**
How complex is the given SAP component? Is the component inherently complex, as is the case with MDM or PI? Or is it relatively straight forward, as is the case with Solution Manager Product Administration?

- **SAP product version level**
  Is the given SAP product still in an early version or are you dealing with a new SAP acquisition product such as Business Planning and Consolidation (aka Outlooksoft)? Or is the product a tried and true, tightly integrated component, such as an SAP ERP 6.0 Financials component?

- **Corporate risk tolerance**
  From an internal business perspective, coupled with the component's complexity, is the risk too great to consider outside assistance? For instance, if your company specializes in RFID (Radio Frequency Identification) technology, does an outside provider possess the necessary knowledge to deliver services?

- **Initiative's level of impact**
  Is the given SAP initiative a major corporate reengineering program such as a complete redesign of your point of sale process? Or is it "just" an additional bolt-on or enhancement meant to improve solid internal SAP driven-processes?

The answers to all of these questions, along with additional factors, paint a much clearer picture of SAP as a software and its potential impact within your organization. Still, as mentioned before, any decisions you make are very personal to your organization and quite subjective.

1.7   Summary: The Perfect Organization Best-Suited for SAP Outsourcing

After all of this discussion, including probing into key factors and their potential impacts, identifying nuances between different market segments, and looking at several client case studies that reflect both positive and negative experiences, the question still remains *who* is the perfect candidate for SAP BPO? The answer lies within another question:

Who is the perfect candidate for SAP BPO?

Can your organization:

- Successfully deliver on the given SAP initiative...
  - ...on-budget
  - ...on-time

  ▸ ...with internal component resources

  ▸ ...at the necessary level of quality

  ▸ ...without compromising competing projects or timelines

  ▸ ...and with support from executive management?

If you are able to answer yes to every one of these question components, then your organization is poised to tackle your SAP initiative on your own. However, if you found yourself either scratching your head or answering no to any of these question components, read on.

It doesn't work to leap a twenty-foot chasm in two ten-foot jumps.
— *American proverb*

2 Why — Potential Reasons why Outsourcing Might Make Sense for Your Organization

After determining whether your organization is a potential candidate for leveraging third-party SAP resources, another fundamental step is figuring out why you should do so. Your business rationale could run the gamut from lack of internal capabilities through cost pressures as dictated by strategic initiatives. Understanding the *why* assists in providing the necessary framework in deciding whether to engage external support.

This chapter probes deeper into the *why* and provides additional non-traditional rationale beyond the standard talking points of cost, expediency, timeframe, etc. (these fundamental reasons are touched on briefly as well).

2.1 Cost

It would be negligent to have an honest debate involving outsourcing without first discussing cost. As with most business discussions, while not always *the* most important factor, cost frequently is *one* of the most important factors.

Cost is king!

Depending on an organization's unique situation and its cost/benefit analysis, external consulting costs may come out to be less expensive. However, depending on the initiative and the skillset, although the work is performed quickly, the knowledge remains with the external provider and knowledge transfer and internal resource aptitude rank low in importance. With cost pressures always a factor in any environment (regardless of the strength of the economy, or whether the company is prosperous or struggling, etc.), the short term goals of minimizing overall project expenditures outweigh the long term goal of in-house knowledge capture.

> **Discussion point: Cost-benefit analysis — external vs. internal**
>
> Although it's difficult to generalize costs associated with internal employees ("loaded" cost must include benefits such as health insurance, vacation, training, etc.), it's quite easy to determine accurate costs associated with external consulting (an hourly or daily fixed rate, plus expenses if applicable). After an organization quantifies the costs associated with leveraging internal resources, an "apples to apples" comparison can be performed. This cost-benefit analysis must also include intangibles such as the benefits associated with having internal resources gain or further enhance their knowledge and hands-on experience with the given SAP application(s) and/or process(es).

2.2   Objectivity

In addition to experience, one of the perceived benefits of leveraging outside assistance is objectivity. Working with an outside SAP consultant frees you and your organization from internal politics, personalities, bias, predispositions, history, and other unproductive constraints.

As Einstein once said, "insanity is defined as doing the same thing over and over again and expecting different results." Thus, internal experiential bias can act as a hindrance when tackling SAP initiatives.

One of SAP's strongest selling points revolves around its great flexibility. While many applications provide several choices as to how to configure something, SAP allows you to construct an almost literally endless number of scenarios, each providing your organization with options as to how to best leverage SAP software. However, undoubtedly, this feature also creates a potential challenge.

Proper design needs experience

Therefore, due to their complexities and the array of available choices, SAP systems must be designed, developed, and configured "properly" to make your business sing. But what does "properly" mean? Enter the

50

expert. By leveraging a resource that has previously implemented your given SAP component(s) — ideally, *multiple* times —your organization has the advantage of experience, including an understanding of what is truly possible.

For example, if your organization wants to implement SAP's new general ledger (G/L) functionality as part of SAP ERP 6.0's new and improved financial reporting capabilities, new G/L ERP 6.0 experience is fundamental. Assuming that your organization had the necessary experience to perform this "upgrade," wouldn't it make sense to look to outside assistance for direction? Most SAP components can be implemented in many ways; therefore, working with someone who has experience with multiple ways of implementation provides your organization with alternatives perhaps not previously understood or identified. As has been said: *"If you only have a hammer, everything looks like a nail!"* Thus, this scenario holds true across many SAP applications and processes.

2.3 Expertise

One of the primary driving factors behind bringing in external resources is expertise. Although many organizations cringe at this reality, experience and knowledge is sometimes more easily obtained via outside parties. Looking for outside help is not a sign of weakness but rather a strong and confident move and sophisticated organizations understand this. Whether driven by new, bleeding-edge SAP technology such as Manufacturing Execution (ME) or lack of internal client knowledge, reaching out for external support and expertise can make sense depending on your specific situation.

Knowledge is power

A major reason *why* organizations leverage SAP outsourcing is to gain immediate expertise that was previously unavailable. Although this statement is not prophetic, this is the most widely cited reason.

Partnering with external SAP consulting resources enables your organization to immediately access a wealth of experience, SAP software know-how, best-practices, an understanding of what functionality is available, and so on. (Of course, all of this implies that the resources leveraged are highly experienced, professional, knowledgeable, articulate, and able to impart their expertise.)

Knowledge transfer
Another method of maximizing external SAP outsourcing is via knowledge transfer. Although some initiatives call for rapid deployment and, in turn, do not facilitate the luxury of knowledge sharing, many times knowledge transfer does take place. Whether via "osmosis," partnered delivery, hand-off delivery, and so on, using another's SAP expertise is an excellent way of internally building a missing skillset.

Building a knowledge base
Formally capturing this knowledge is also another excellent method for cultivating SAP skillsets within an organization. In some cases, a business might ultimately wish to drive all SAP initiatives internally, either via SAP project teams or via a center of excellence (COE). By either holding formal knowledge transfer workshops or sessions or requiring your external resources to construct comprehensive user manuals or how-to-guides (see Figure 2.1), you begin to build your knowledge base. Doing so empowers your organization and provides an internal, value-added mechanism for reference material, training, and continued education.

SMD & Wily Agent Installation

SMD Agents
The SMD agent is installed once per system, not per SID. One agent on the system will be able to connect to multiple SIDs. The same is true for hosts which have a mixture of J2EE and ABAP instances. The SMD Agent is an independent Java program which is run in the background and communicates to the SMD system. The installation is run using SAPInst, the setup of SAPInst is the exact same as you would configure for any Netweaver based install.

The installation which was completed in 04/08 was based on the attached configuration guide.

SMD SPS06
Supportability Guide.j

The agent only needs to be installed on systems running NW04s SR2 or below. As of SR3, the SMD Agent is part of the Netweaver installation.

Download the agent
1. Navigate to **service.sap.com/swdc** → Download → Support Packages and Patches → Entry by Application Group → SAP Technology Components → SAP SOLUTION MANAGER →SOLUTION MANAGER 4.0→ Entry by Component → Agents for Satellite Systems → SMD AGENT 7.00 → <choose OS>. The file smdagent06_0-<version>.sar contains the SAPinst package.

Figure 2.1 Example of a How-to Manual

If it isn't already, documentation should be standard practice within any SAP initiative. Whether omitted, ignored, or simply not valued, documentation is an often overlooked component that shouldn't be neglected. Regardless of whether an SAP project is delivered by internal or external resources, thorough documentation should be part of the end deliverables. (This should hold true even more if you're using external resources and should be included as part of the statement of work [SOW].)

2.3.1 Shadowing (Premeditated Osmosis)

Another effective method of obtaining valuable SAP functional and technical knowledge is via "shadowing". This partnered approach allows your internal team to co-deliver on project deliverables or operational support by working in concert with your external SAP provider(s). The knowledge transfer can be performed using several methods, as follows:

▶ **Watch-and-learn**

The SAP expert performs the given work product (i.e., SAP functional configuration such as setting up the financial G/L; technical development such as the construction of a Portal iView for employee self-service [ESS]) while the internal resource observes. After several iterations of the SAP expert performing the given task, the internal resource performs the task with the ability to ask for guidance as needed.

▶ **Back and forth**

With this method, activity responsibilities are more cleanly defined, with direct responsibility for a given phase assigned to one party. For example, in a Business Warehouse (BW) 3.5 to BW 7.0 technical upgrade, each of the installation boxes will be the specific responsibility of either the consultant or an internal resource. A typical example includes consultant responsibility for the installation of the development and production systems and internal NetWeaver resource responsibility for the quality assurance and regression systems.

▶ **Smooth transition**

Another take on the knowledge transfer method relates to how the transition occurs. To make the transition more seamless and less disruptive to the business, in some cases, an internal production support team is formed during the realization phase of the implementation (construction and testing phase). While the project is underway and the project team is busy implementing the given SAP functionality or technology, the production support team begins ramping up — learning the newly implemented functionality.

▶ **Clean break**
The last knowledge transfer method is usually invoked via a project and then executed during the production support transition. This handover approach assumes that external consultants are responsible for the implementation and internal resources either do or do not shadow the work being performed. After the implementation go-live, the on-going SAP production support responsibility resides with your internal SAP production support mechanism.

2.3.2 Emotional Component

While this book isn't meant to focus on the emotional impact involved in outsourcing SAP services, the topic does deserve mention. According to Cesar Chavez, "you are never strong enough that you don't need help." Clearly, external SAP resources are brought into an organization to provide different types of expertise not available internally. This practice within the SAP, IT, and non-IT space has been employed for centuries. Inherent in this process is the potential for personal insecurity and, as a result, drama.

Reaching out for assistance isn't an admission of failure but a sign of strength
It should be acknowledged that for some, asking for assistance doesn't always come easy. Coupled with (or exacerbated by) the stereotype of the arrogant and wealthy consultant, an already defensive client is provided with a recipe for emotional fireworks.

Therefore, interacting with defensive or insecure clients requires a delicate approach rich in patience and building trust.

2.4 Inherent Standardization Advantage

One point inherent in outsourcing SAP operations is the built-in standardization processes that result from migrating an SAP process from inside the castle to outside its walls. When dealing with an external partner, your organization is, by default, forced to conform to a series of standards simply to engage with your chosen partner. Some of these components include:

▶ **SAP Best Practices**
Outsourcing any of your SAP processes should improve and implement SAP Best Practices. If your organization has either failed or chosen not to implement SAP Best Practices, your SAP outsourcing partner should provide you with opportunities to improve on your existing SAP functionality, both functionally and technically.

SAPanese — Best Practices

Within the SAP world, the term "Best Practice" can mean two distinct things:

▶ Industry-common, proven methods for running a business in the best way possible.

▶ SAP preconfigured functionality (actual SAP functional configuration) that can be implemented within an SAP environment.

The first definition is more generic and its concept spans across software products and industries. Conversely, the second definition is SAP-specific and deals directly with how the software is implemented and, in turn, behaves. Typically, within the SAP world, when people talk about "Best Practices," they're referring to the SAP-specific definition of preconfigured functionality.

▶ **Methodology**
Every SAP outsourcing vendor should follow an SAP proven methodology. Whether it's Accelerated SAP (ASAP), Run SAP, an industry recognized methodology, or a partner-specific SAP roadmap, your SAP outsourcing partner must follow a formal project framework.

▶ **Toolset**
To facilitate outsourcing services and provide the best services possible, your SAP outsourcing partner should be leveraging a suite of tools to improve your given area. Ticket tracking, work assignment, and Solution Manager's suite of "bag of tricks" all exist as potential toolset improvement options.

▶ **Communication**
With outsourcing, delivery is removed from direct internal responsibility. Thus, a communication process must be implemented to

ensure proper delivery. This should be provided by and be the responsibility of your partner.

▸ **Management**

The overall process for managing change and service level reporting to the business can also potentially be improved by shifting direct ownership from internal to external resources. Because your SAP outsourcing provider works with multiple clients on concurrent SAP initiatives, they should provide improved overall management direction.

▸ **Streamlining**

One of the value propositions for working with third-party SAP specialists is their SAP expertise. Working with an organization that sees and potentially even follows different SAP paths depending on their client's unique needs provides your organization the ability to leverage your partner's experience and knowledge. Streamlining and performing process improvement is another key standardization opportunity when dealing with outsourcing your SAP operations.

Optimizing internal organizations

As a by-product of the outsourcing process, your organization and the corresponding SAP services provided to the business should theoretically be improved and made more efficient. Without the outsourcing initiative, this optimization activity could also be achieved but it would need to be a separate initiative. However, with outsourcing, instead of performing this optimization activity, your SAP environment is improved by default.

> **Thinking outside the box — Bringing SAP delivery back in house**
>
> Although the focus of this book is on exploring the world of outsourcing SAP operations, the last discussion about the inherent standardization advantages in outsourcing brings up an interesting and "radical" outsourcing approach: bringing SAP delivery back in house.
>
> If your organization has been outsourcing an SAP component for some time (e.g., SAP Security Administration) and has been working with an SAP outsourcing partner that is "worth their weight in gold," there is a high probability that simply via the outsourcing process, your overall SAP delivery services have improved and even been streamlined.

For example, Best Practices around profile construction will have been implemented, strong security strategies are now being employed, and previously non-existent documentation has been created. If this is the case (it should be considered standard with any SAP outsourcing provider), the process improvement framework and foundation has been perfectly laid. What an ideal time to bring back this service in-house! Of course, there is whole array of factors to consider; however, this possibility should be explored. And although it might not necessarily result in letting go of your partner for these services, it will definitely initiate interesting discussion.

2.5   Specific SAP Initiatives

Another reason for potentially looking for external SAP consulting relates to specific, laser-focused SAP initiatives. Although leveraging outsourcing for full-blown SAP projects (such as ERP upgrades and new SAP NetWeaver BW installations), or operational activities (such as production support, SAP NetWeaver Basis COE, Service Desk, and level 2 and above SAP functional support) is standard outsourcing practice, the following SAP initiatives might also be potential opportunities.

2.5.1   Assessments

Within the SAP space, an assessment is typically defined as an initiative focused on either scoping desired subsequent programs (such as implementing new functionality or an SAP application such as SAP Business Objects) or identifying areas to improve (such as a technical SAP NetWeaver audit or functional optimization initiative, as described later).

Assessments typically are short-term in nature and are performed almost universally as a prerequisite step for a subsequent SAP endeavour. Therefore, *one advantage of conducting an assessment lies in its investment.* Because assessments are typically designed to act as "quick hit" appraisals of larger, more complicated modifications to your SAP environment, the associated investment of both resources and funds pale in comparison to the grander initiatives they're exploring. Funding a two-week, $10,000 assessment exploring the potential implementation and

Short term, quick hit, and high value

integration of SAP's GRC Access Controls tools is far more palatable to executives than diving head-first into a four-month, $100,000 implementation.

> **Case Study: Integration Assessment**
>
> After acquiring another company of comparable size in the fall of 2008, a manufacturer of vitamin, mineral, and herbal products found itself faced with the challenge of integrating a non-SAP based company into their existing productive SAP environment. Not only was the acquiring company challenged with combing two distinct and separate IT environments but also two distinct and separate business processes.
>
> "We knew that we were about to embark on a major challenge of integrating two unique environments — one SAP and one not" remembers the company's IT director. "Our best bet was to perform an assessment capturing what work lay before us and the path to get us there." To best understand and, in turn, plan for the integration project, the company chose to reach out to external consulting partners for an assessment focused on scoping the given effort, timeline, and cost. This week-long assessment gathered all of the necessary stakeholders for a series of discovery workshops. The final result was a concise solution mapping, detailing the schedule, activities, responsible parties, and associated costs.

2.5.2 Optimization

Optimizing your SAP environment (and investment) is crucial to the long-term success of your organization. Clearly, no matter how successful, not every SAP implementation accomplishes what it intended to; or if it does, most likely there are additional opportunities to further enhance its functionality. Optimization initiatives tackle this prospect.

Optimization projects look for methods of improving on, redesigning, or replacing existing SAP technologies or functionality. When performed properly, optimization initiatives assist your organization in better understanding how to maximize existing SAP functionality by providing recommendations for areas of improvement.

These types of projects focus on better understanding the potential opportunities that exist to improve (or optimize) what has been previously implemented.

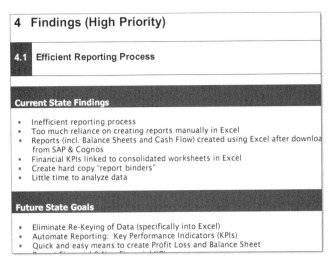

Figure 2.2 Sample Optimization Report

What follows are examples — both functional and technical — of the optimization initiatives typically performed. Note that multiple optimization initiatives can be combined within a larger optimization program.

Typical initiatives

- ▶ Financial business process (financial month-end close, financial reporting, financial consolidation)
- ▶ Purchase-to-Pay process (procurement, banking/treasury, invoicing)
- ▶ Order-to-Cash process (sales process, billing, account processing)
- ▶ Hire-to-Retire process (talent management, workforce, HCM processes)
- ▶ Production planning (MRP, discrete manufacturing)
- ▶ Warehouse management (inventory, inbound/outbound logistics, transportation)
- ▶ Security (audit, profile retuning/reengineering, compliance)
- ▶ Integration services (MDM, XI/PI, IDoc/ALE, EAI)
- ▶ Business intelligence (BusinessObjects, BW)
- ▶ SAP NetWeaver (Solution Manager, system recovery, tuning)
- ▶ Custom development (ABAP, portal, Java)

Optimization initiatives typically provide recommendations but stop before implementation; therefore, the corresponding end deliverables

Define scope and deliverables

tend to be more conceptually and strategic rather than tangible. This could lead to unrealized client expectation. To ensure that no disconnect exists between your organization and your external partner, a clearly documented SOW must be defined with a strict scope and mutually agreed on set of end deliverables.

Finally, just because most optimizations stop prior to implementing their recommendations, this doesn't necessarily have to be the case. If you wish to include execution as part of scope, go for it. However, the execution phase must be clearly defined within the SOW. Otherwise, this initiative will end at only identifying future state.

Case Study: Tuthill Corporation — Financial optimization initiative

Tuthill Corporation — a diversified global manufacturing company developing and supplying industrial products in over 150 markets — had been a productive SAP customer since 1998. After completing an upgrade in the spring of 2008, Tuthill's finance department reached out to Dan Amend, Tuthill's SAP director. "As an SAP internal support mechanism, our end client is the business. Based on the finance team's need to further bolster their capabilities via SAP, we chose to perform a financial optimization project to define the ideal future state, code named 'Project Grandslam'." Amend and his team partnered with an external SAP consulting firm to define and map out where Tuthill needed to be. After four weeks of research, discovery, design workshops, and in-depth discussion, Tuthill defined three major initiatives:

▶ Upgrading to SAP ERP 6.0's new G/L

▶ Implementing a training program for the finance team to reinforce some of SAP's FI/CO reporting capabilities

▶ Implementing SAP BusinessObjects for in-depth financial reporting

Project Grandslam was not without its challenges, however. Competing priorities and a difference in end-result deliverables led to a disconnect between the business and IT. While IT was focused on identifying future state, the business thought that IT was also planning on implementing the recommendations. Ultimately, the business and IT regained alignment and Project Grandslam highlighted areas of optimization.

2.5.3   Audits

Audits — whether of technical or functional purpose — provide objective, third-party, "cold eyes" review services. These services are meant not to poke holes or identify flaws within a given process but to review and provide observations. Areas of improvement can undoubtedly be identified as part of an audit; however, this isn't the audit's intention. If anything, an SAP audit is meant to act as a validation of what is being reviewed.

For example, a technical SAP landscape audit might be performed to ensure that for an SAP ERP 6.0 environment sitting on top of a SAP NetWeaver platform, SAP NetWeaver System Landscape Directory (or SLD) is being leveraged properly for maximum system efficiencies.

Another common SAP audit exercise revolves around security and compliance and multiple SAP security auditing activities can be implemented. Whether they're "simple" internal SAP Security Administration authorization profile and role reviews or more intense GRC Access Controls-compliant user provisioning and role remediation projects, all security audits are meant to accomplish the same goal: provide the needed access to the user community without compromising risk. For example, should your procurement manager be able to create a one-time vendor and pay invoices? Most likely, the answer is "no."

Performing an audit not only ensures that your SAP processes or technical components are performing as they should (i.e., to their fullest potential and as designed) but also acts as an internal safeguarding and protective measure. The audit process is an often used and much needed "CYA" (cover your assets) initiative.

2.5.4 "GO — No GO" Gate Review

Prior to a *go-live* decision within any SAP initiative, the all important "press forward" decision must be made. In any responsible organization, this decision is not taken lightly and a systematic decision making process should be employed. Although called by multiple names such as "gate review," "go — no go," "go-live," "quality assurance review," and so on, the focus is always on the same end result: ensuring that the given initiative has met all of the project's deliverables and timelines and is ready to move into productive mode.

> **Expert panel: The role of the gate review**
>
> According to Tom Mochal of the Tech Republic (*www.techrepublic.com*), gate reviews are excellent and important processes as part of any prudent IT initiative. "In the past, it wasn't uncommon to gain a commitment to start a project and then never look back again. Over the past ten years, however, it has become more common to set up specific points in the schedule where the project could be evaluated to ensure things are on track and to determine whether the work should continue." Focused on quality assurance, the gate review looks at whether processes have been completed rather than reviewing any specific deliverables. (For expanded discussion around the role of the gate review and Mochel's take on this type of initiative, refer to *http://blogs.techrepublic.com.com/tech-manager/?p=406.*)

2.5.5 "Bulldog" Services — SAP Project Management Oversight

SAP Project Management Services enable your business to take advantage of years of SAP consulting experience. Whether your business is embarking on a new SAP initiative (full life-cycle implementation or ERP upgrade), is adding new SAP modules to an existing installation, or is expanding your current SAP Business Suite (adding CRM or BW), highly competent SAP project managers can assist in delivering your project on time and within budget. Leveraging the knowledge and experience of "bulldog" services affords you the ability of leveraging real-world, relevant experience.

Benefits   Potential benefits include:

▶ Expertise and proven SAP project management track record

▶ Development of a risk management plan that addresses common SAP project shortcomings and pitfalls

▶ In-depth experience with a variety of project management methodologies such as SAP ASAP, PMP, Six Sigma, and so on

▶ Project management quality assurance

▶ Measurable results to gauge project success

Safeguarding   Furthermore, as the "bulldog" label implies, SAP project management oversight can also be used as a safeguard in various capacities. More and more frequently, clients are looking for a third-party project management safeguarding mechanism to ensure that their main SAP services integrator is delivering as promised. This especially holds true in cases where the client has either little or no SAP experience. By employing a third-party, objective SAP project manager to look out for the company's best interest, clients are ensuring that their SAP initiatives run more smoothly and within budget. Although some clients might balk at the additional "unneeded" expense, others might feel that the investment is well worth it.

Case Study: Gulfmark Offshore — Project management oversight

In the spring of 2007, Gulfmark Offshore — a premier niche participant in the international offshore marine services industry — embarked on a new SAP ERP 6.0 implementation. Due to their relative inexperience with SAP either as a software or business process enabler, Gulfmark employed the services of both a third-party services integrator (SI) and independent, experienced SAP project manager to work together with Gulfmark's chosen SI. Via this partnered approach, Gulfmark was able to deliver the project on time and within budget. Sam Rubio, the corporate controller at the time, had a front row seat to the implementation. "Our collective efforts including our SI, Gulfmark, and third-party project management oversight enabled us to effectively implement SAP. While our implementation did have its challenges, utilizing additional third-party project management oversight assisted us greatly. I highly recommend the practice."

2.6   Focus on Internal Core Capabilities

As businesses evolve, two separate and distinct paths emerge regarding their overall IT strategy and how SAP fits into the greater puzzle. These diametrically opposite positions are as follows:

▶ Choosing to support all SAP project and support functions internally

▶ Complete outsourcing of all SAP project and support functions

(A hybrid approach does also exist and is commonly used; however, by discussing the two extremes, we inherently cover this "middle of the road" option.) The factors involved in determining which of the two primary strategies to employ are numerous and are the essence of this book.

For those who choose to internally support all SAP functions (as discussed later in Chapter 7), the corporate strategy is one focused on empowerment, that is, on building the core competencies within the company. This strategy accepts the investment in training, cost, and resources and believes that this approach will pay off long-term. Building such core competencies in house is not seen as "taking one's eye off the ball" or as deviating from the organization's core business.

Focus! However, the opposite approach adheres to a completely different philosophy, one of "do what we do best," and "focus, focus, focus." This school of thought believes that SAP services should be provided by those specialized within this space. Driven by a business strategy focused on core values, these organizations believe strongly that just as they excel within a given business model (i.e., building offshore oil rigs, providing the tastiest beverages to the public, or providing best-in-class professional legal services), they are better off leaving SAP services to specialized SAP providers.

Again, the decision of which option to exploit (including the hybrid approach) is personal to each company and determined by a myriad of factors unique to each organization. However, the two main approaches are clear choices, with both advantages and disadvantages.

> **Case Study: Gambro Renal Products — The perfect outsourcing combination**
>
> Gambro Renal Products — a global medical technology company specializing in dialysis technology — recently began a major global SAP implementation. Choosing to partner with a tier one SI for the implementation, Gambro was insistent on bringing in SAP experts for the implementation component. However, having the vision to think beyond the implementation, Gambro wished to also cultivate the internal skillsets necessary for long-term operational SAP support. Thus, Kirk Schamel — Gambro's director of business solutions and in-house program manager responsible for the SAP implementation — chose to use and bring up to speed in-house SAP functional and technical resources for an internal COE. "While Gambro knew that the SAP implementation was outside of our existing core competencies, we strategically chose to augment our outside provider with Gambro employees for the project. Ultimately, Gambro will be responsible for maintenance; therefore, we needed to build that missing expertise in conjunction with our partner."

Therefore, as part of the project plan, Schamel and his team shadowed the SI to facilitate knowledge transfer. While Gambro's core competencies were not SAP and never will be, they chose to focus on their core business while simultaneously support their SAP operations with a small COE. Schamel reflects that "the blend of core business focus and strategic SAP COE support is the best of both worlds for us."

2.7 Reasons Why NOT to Outsource your SAP Operations

Along with all of the potential opportunities associated with outsourcing your SAP services come contradictory reasons not to do so. Not every organization is suited for leveraging external partners for SAP services. Challenges associated with outsourcing exist abound and for those of the weak heart, be weary.

Word on the street: CIO response to outsourcing

In January 2008, Robert Half Technology — a leading provider of information technology professionals — conducted a survey of 1,400 CIO's across a wide spectrum of company size and industries. Contrary to its perceived ubiquity, outsourcing (as defined as utilizing offsite resourcing) isn't as pervasive as one would think. In fact, the survey showed that the majority of U.S. companies actually do *not* leverage this practice and 94 % of the CIOs surveyed said their organizations do not outsource outside of the U.S. Furthermore, among those companies that previously used offshoring, 59 % cited management challenges as the reason why they discounted the practice. For firms contemplating offshore outsourcing, the survey highlighted four important factors an organization must take into account:

- ▶ Outsourcing organization stability
- ▶ Related setup time and cost
- ▶ Offshore management challenges
- ▶ Potential security concerns

Several of the main challenges associated with SAP outsourcing have been highlighted in the previous section; however, here are several of the main reasons as to *why* organizations might not find value:

Reasons not to outsource

65

▶ **Strong internal skillsets/existing COE**
If your organization is a mature SAP organization and possesses extensive in-house SAP expertise, you might not need to leverage external help. Typically, larger organizations (such as the Fortune 500) fall into this category. Mature and sophisticated SAP client organizations exist as exemplary models or standards for any consulting organization; these clients have no need for external assistance.

▶ **Cost constraints**
Although "cost is king", the old adage rings true from both perspectives — including the expense associated with paying for high-priced SAP consulting. If an organization — regardless of size — is limited financially, hiring external resources regardless of need is simply not possible.

▶ **Strong philosophy of in-house delivery**
Some organizations prefer to deliver SAP solutions via their own resources. In cases where internal resources do not possess the needed skillsets, organizations send their resources to either SAP education classes (*http://www.sap.com/services/education/index.epx*) or to other leading SAP education providers such as TerraFirma or Teksoft.

2.8   Summary

Several key themes have been highlighted as to *why* organizations might find outsourcing a strategic option for supporting their SAP initiatives. Whether driven by specific initiatives best suited for third-party objectivity such as gate reviews and audits or out of a simple cost rationale or lack of internal capabilities (either by design or accident), outsourcing exists as a viable and frequently leveraged alternative for many companies.

After defining the *who* (whether your organization is a potential candidate) and the *why* (whether your company is positioned to benefit) of outsourcing, the next logical area to look at is *what*, that is, digging into your company's SAP functionality, business areas, and technology to determine what components or areas might be a good fit. This topic will be covered in the next chapter.

The industrial landscape is already littered with remains of once successful companies that could not adapt their strategic vision to altered conditions of competition.
— Ralph Abernathy

3 What is SAP Outsourcing? The Various Flavors

To define outsourcing is quite simple: Outsourcing is the contracting of external resources, regardless of length of contract, skillset, type of role, implementation or services, location (onsite or offsite), and so on. All constitute some manifestation of SAP outsourcing. Because SAP outsourcing, by definition, casts a wide net, this section will assist in defining the myriad of models ranging from a single onsite resource to full "wall-to-wall" outsourcing. However, beyond the obvious flavors of leveraging external SAP support, there are additional, perhaps not as widely utilized, approaches to SAP outsourcing. This chapter will focus and delve into some of these more specialized SAP outsourcing strategic flavors (such as SAP Administration and Infrastructure COE) and their respective SAP-centric productivity tools (such as Solution Manager's Central System Administration and Business Process Monitoring).

3.1 Baseline: The Various Flavors of SAP Outsourcing

As is the case with any technology, SAP as a product uses a standard set of outsourcing models that are typically leveraged in some form or another. The models are impacted by two primary factors: location and size (see Figure 3.1). As the permutations increase, so do their challenges. This section describes each of the fundamental SAP outsourcing integration methods in detail.

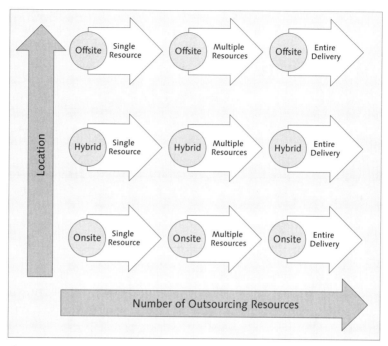

Figure 3.1 SAP Outsourcing Continuum

3.1.1 Onsite Resources

The most basic example of outsourcing in all of the possible combinations is a single, client-located resource. Whether this is a single SAP consultant who is physically located at the client site or an entire 100-person plus SAP outsourced implementation team, onsite resourcing provides yields that other delivery models simply do not. The bottom line is that on site consultant presence affords your organization several primary advantages over offsite landing. First and foremost is communication. Not being able to work side-by-side with your fellow project team members increases miscommunication potential. This is true regardless of distance, culture, or language. As with the classic child's game of "telephone," simple messages can be potentially misinterpreted. Because, according to leading physiologists, the vast majority of communication is non-verbal, the ability to work with onsite resources is not a luxury but almost a necessity. (Of course, all of the benefits do not account for potential and common financial issues.)

For complex SAP initiatives, if your organization has the opportunity to utilize onsite resources instead of other outsourcing models, *take it*! For more operational or routine SAP projects, the advantages of onsite resources are not as pronounced; however, for highly complex developments requiring heavy communication and discussion or complicated industry-specific expertise, onsite design and development are ideal. Leveraging onsite resources for most development expedites the entire deployment and reduces unneeded recycling.

Complex technical or business process work

3.1.2 Offsite Resources

Moving along the SAP outsourcing continuum (and farther away from the client) you will find offsite resources. As the term suggests, offsite resources are SAP resources that don't reside at the client delivery location. Offsite is often misinterpreted to equate to offshore or nearshore but this isn't accurate. Offsite resources could mean resources sitting across town in another client facility (i.e., corporate headquarters vs. a slightly out of town distribution center), across the country within the same country (i.e., corporate headquarters vs. a regional office), or out of the country (i.e., corporate headquarters vs. an out of country SAP global delivery center).

Offsite resources are typically used for delivery in the place of onsite resources for two main reasons: cost or convenience (or both). Let's assume that your organization has multiple manufacturing plants across the U.S. Although assembling the entire SAP implementation team in a single delivery location is frequently the most ideal scenario, it isn't always possible. As in many SAP implementations and post-production support models, resources — including employees — typically wear multiple hats. Thus, if a highly valued client resource sitting in Green Bay, Wisconsin is needed for subject matter expertise for your project being delivered in San Jose, California, this offsite alternative may be the only option.

Reasons for offsite outsorcing

3.1.3 Nearshore Resources

As the onslaught of India-based offshore delivery centers became omnipresent, clients began requesting similar alternatives but closer to home.

Depending on geographic location, this originally translated into either Eastern European locales (Ireland, Poland, Hungary, etc.) to support Western Europe or South American locales (Brazil, Argentina, etc.) to support North America. The value proposition for nearshore delivery vs. other offsite models is multi-fold: time zone and equivalent quality.

Time zone

The name and branding of "nearshore" is obviously intentional; it equals closer to home and thus, more aligned with the client. Clients choosing to leverage a nearshore outsourcing consultant work during the same business hours and/or time zone. The time difference between an eastern U.S.-based client (such as a company located in New York City) and a Brazilian nearshore facility is only one hour — the same time difference as that between Boston and Chicago! The same holds true for countries in Western Europe and Eastern Europe.

Stronger culture alignment

Beyond time zone, another nearshore advantage resides in stronger culture alignment. Again, due to the geographic proximity between client and consultant, there tends to be a more closely aligned cultural fit. Whether this relates to the Americas' understanding between North and South, or Europe's overall cultural meshing, accent, shared overarching values, language, and so on, outsourcing your SAP operations to a nearshore partner might be a viable — and more easily adaptable — alternative to other outsourcing options.

Case Study: Nearshore SAP delivery leader — Politec

Politec is one of South America's leading nearshore (in relation to North America) IT services provider with over US $300 million in revenue (fiscal year 2008), 5,500+ FTEs, and 22 global development, testing, support, and delivery centers (Brazil, Argentina, and Chile). Anointed in 2006 as SAP's first certified Application Maintenance Services (AMS) partner in the region, Politec provides a multitude of SAP global delivery services supported by over 130 dedicated AMS consultants.

Well known within South America, Politec and its service offerings have continued to gain momentum as they began to expand their sales growth efforts into the U.S. "Our strong SAP expertise of over 20 years, plus a strong reputation within the SAP ecosystem, has allowed us to focus growth efforts into the U.S. as a trusted nearshore partner" said John Edwards, Politec's VP of sales and alliances. "We are excited about the nearshore models and their advantages."

3.1.4 Rightshoring

"Rightshoring" is a Capgemini term and outsourcing model originally coined in 2008 by three Senior SAP consultants: Anja Hendel, Dr. Wolfgang Messner, and Frank Thun. Rightshoring, according to its authors, is more of a methodology than a specific model, as follows:

> *"[Offsite] delivery creates the opportunity to improve quality and to allocate resources in a better way. It is not a question of 'yes' or 'no' to [offshore locations]; it is about organization of a distributed delivery process that embraces onsite, nearshore, and offshore services."(Hendel, Messner, Thun: Rightshore! Successfully Industrialize SAP Projects Offshore, Springer 2008. p. v.)*

The main difference between a hybrid SAP outsourcing delivery model and rightshoring is that certain Capgemini-specific implementation strategies and methodologies are built into this outsourcing mechanism. For more specifics around this unique approach, refer to their book titled "Rightshore! Successfully Industrialize SAP Projects Offshore."

3.1.5 Offshore Resources

The most common — and perhaps most often misused — term surrounding outsourcing SAP operations is offshore. This term has most often been equated to using India-based SAP resources. Although the origins of SAP offshoring does have its roots in India, offshore SAP outsourcing no longer means using only India-based resources. However, as they say, bad habits die hard, and therefore, this perception still remains prevalent.

Offshore SAP outsourcing is defined as using any foreign international location. While India still remains a leading delivery and operations center throughout the SAP world, many other well-established and newly emerging offshore locations exist. Countries throughout Asia, including Malaysia and the Philippines, as well as the new economic powerhouse China also have been providing SAP outsourcing services for quite some time.

Any foreign international location

The value proposition cited for offshore delivery models primarily relates to value. Due to their large supply of SAP expertise, coupled with a lower cost of living, these local markets are ostensibly able to provide high quality resources at lower costing models.

3.1.6   Hybrid Resources

Of all of the outsourcing models, the hybrid approach is the delivery vehicle most commonly used. This model combines the utilization of multiple types of outsourcing models, including all of those described previously. Typically, the hybrid SAP outsourcing model employs both onsite and offsite resources. Usually, the offsite resources come from the same offsite delivery mechanism (i.e., nearshore, offshore, or offsite locally). Although it is not uncommon for large SAP implementations to potentially leverage multiple offshore delivery centers for different components within the implementations (Bangalore for SAP NetWeaver Basis operational support, China for SAP WRICEFP Development, and Budapest for SAP functional configuration), it's rarer to mix offshore and nearshore outsourcing. Typically, organizations select one over the other for specific client reasons.

SAPanese — WRICEFP

WRICEFP is the SAP acronym meant to capture all of the custom development categories typically required for an implementation. A breakdown of what each of the initials represent follows:

▶ **W — Workflow.** Any SAP-specific workflow configuration.
▶ **R — Reports.** All custom SAP reports developed within ABAP (whether interactive, static, ALV, etc.).
▶ **I — Interfaces.** All ABAP-developed programs designed to integrate SAP with other systems. The other systems could be SAP or non-SAP systems. Likewise, SAP NetWeaver XI/PI sometimes also falls under this category.
▶ **C — Conversions.** Data conversions developed within ABAP or the Legacy System Migration Workbench (LSMW) to load SAP systems with vital information.
▶ **E — Enhancements.** Any ABAP custom development used to enhance existing functionality. This could include user exits, field exits, module pools, GUI enhancements, and so on.
▶ **F — Forms.** This includes Smartforms and SAPScript.
▶ **P — Portals.** All portal development for any of the SAP portal-driven products. This could be the creation of iViews and other portal custom development.

Another SAP delivery mechanism being used more and more within the marketplace is the deployment of offsite resources onsite for critical phases within the initiative. Let's take a look at two common hybrid SAP delivery practices for two different scenarios:

Full Lifecycle Implementation

Following the SAP ASAP implementation methodology (see Figure 3.2), specific phases within the lifecycle typically require heavier business user and project team interaction than others. Specifically, the phases of "blueprinting" (requirements gathering, analysis, and design) and user acceptance testing within the "realization" phase are critical segments usually requiring face-to-face interaction.

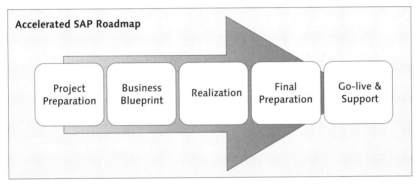

Figure 3.2 SAP's ASAP Methodology Roadmap

Therefore, in this approach, offshore resources are deployed onsite during the entire business blueprint phase to work together with the client business process experts. During this lifecycle segment, the offshore resources collect business process requirements via a series of workshops, meetings, and so on and then design the specific SAP solution (whether technical such as customized ABAP reports, interfaces, and data conversion programs or functional such as SAP business process configuration — company code structure, G/L construct, and sales order types). After the business blueprint has been completed, these offshore resources return to their "home base" to continue working on development and construction.

Blueprint

User acceptance testing

Moving along the systems lifecycle, after completing unit and string testing, the offshore resources are again deployed to the client location for user acceptance testing, only to return after successfully testing. (In some cases, offshore resources continue to remain onsite or are deployed back to the client site after go-live for a production support warranty period. This onsite/offsite hybrid model for implementation is a cost-effective way of ensuring that the business requirements are properly captured and translated into SAP functionality.)

Post-Production Support

Another common hybrid SAP outsourcing strategy revolves around productive SAP environments. In cases where external consulting is utilized for SAP production support, a combination of onsite/offsite delivery is sometimes employed. This approach is leveraged in two methods: "SWAT" team absorption deployment and continued onsite presence. (For those unfamiliar with the term, "SWAT" is a special forces elite police squad assigned to the most difficult situations.)

SAP SWAT team "absorption"

In the SWAT team absorption model, key individuals within the production support team (production support manager, team members supporting complex technical and/or business functions, team leads, etc.) are deployed to the client site to "absorb" as much SAP environment knowledge and functionality as possible. As a rule of thumb, the deployment of this SWAT team should occur during the "realization" or implementation phase during critical testing phases.

It is during this "realization" phase that the core design is built. Any modifications will begin to be discovered during this phase as part of unit testing. During this timeframe, the SWAT team shadows the implementation team to understand the SAP design. After absorption is successfully accomplished, these onsite deployed offshore resources return home for on-going SAP production operations.

Benefits

If your organization plans properly, the SWAT team will actively participate and not just observe during the testing phases of the project (i.e., during integration testing and user acceptance testing). Key takeaways captured in this hybrid model include:

▸ **Knowledge transfer**

Bringing in your SWAT absorption team members during the project's implementation allows them to "learn on the job." By integrating the team members during testing phases, they can better understand the core functionality that was implemented and, in turn, gain a deeper understanding of what they will ultimately be responsible to support or enhance.

▸ **Practice**

Similar to knowledge transfer, the more exposure the SWAT team has to the system, the greater its in-depth understanding of the system's functionality will be. Some organizations use their SWAT team prior to go-live for project related support. This allows the production support mechanism to practice while on the job *prior* to supporting the end user community after the system goes live.

▸ **Organizational acceptance**

During the project's implementation, end users and super users are typically most familiar with their project team implementation counterparts and strong bonds are created. In some cases, these project team members transition to the production support team, making the end-user support seamless and painless. Not in this case. Leveraging an offshore SAP production support partner forces end users into looking to new contacts for production support. Integrating the SWAT team/production support into the later phases of the implementation assists in this transition and facilitates end-user acceptance.

▸ **Training**

Mobilizing the SWAT team prior to go-live can assist in building logistical operational experience. Phone system operation, ticketing tool system run-through, triage procedures, communication etiquette, and so on are all fundamental givens that must be mastered before ever working on SAP issues. Working with the SWAT team to make these procedures second nature enables the production support team to focus on resolving end-user SAP issues as opposed to carrying out production support functions.

▸ **Responsibility transition**

To empower the production support team to be seen both externally (by end-users) and internally (by production support and the project team) as the system gate keepers, it is imperative that the formal handing over of the keys to the "kingdom" is performed. Prior to go-live, the production support team should be formally anointed by management that they now have the authority to manage and protect the system's integrity. The responsibility transition from project team (and project mode) to SWAT team/production support team (and production support mode) is crucial for long-term system stability. There is nothing more dangerous and morale-deflating than the "never ending" project. Transitioning the responsibility ensures that there is a clear understanding by the entire organization that a "new sheriff is in town."

Onsite integration management with offshore production support

Another very successful hybrid SAP delivery model involves the use of an onsite integration manager. Although this role and corresponding responsibilities are discussed at length in Chapter 14, it is important to touch on this hybrid outsourcing approach at this point. Figure 3.3 describes the onsite/offsite interaction.

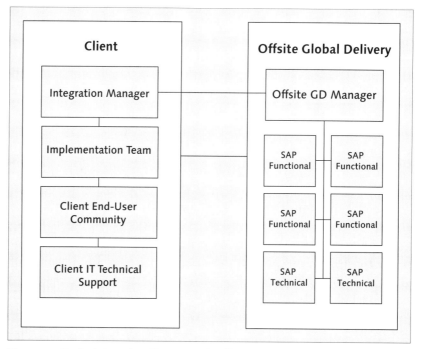

Figure 3.3 Onsite Integration Manager with Offsite Production Support Model

Per this delivery model, a full-time integration manager resides onsite at the client location. The integration manager performs many tasks (described in detail in Chapter 14); however, his primary role is to act as the human interface between the client team and the offsite delivery mechanism. The integration manager's onsite presence assists in facilitating quicker issue resolution and proactive prevention. Although most of the "heavy lifting" is performed by the offsite delivery team, the integration manager not only can aid in ticket resolution but also provide direction for priorities and escalation.

3.1.7 Collocation

Popular within the technical infrastructure and networking world, data center collocation is an established practice. Based on its popularity, a recent client trend has arisen focused on bringing this infrastructure model into the personnel realm. Whether limited on physical office space or focused on eliminating the investment costs of office space, equipment, computers, telephones, and so on, clients are looking to their partners to shoulder this burden. This phenomenon, known as collocation, shifts the logistical responsibility to the outsourcing partner, where the partner "houses" the client's consultants for the duration of the SAP initiative. This model provides great flexibility to the client.

Another unique advantage to the collocation model lies in client proximity. Typically, in these scenarios, the collocation location is very close geographically to the client site. Different from the nearshore and offshore models, where resources reside time zones or continents away, the collocation model purposely locates resources near the client site. This proximity advantage gives the client the ability to work more directly with the outsourced partner (face-to-face meetings, in person interaction, etc.).

Client proximity

These "burdened" costs are built into the outsourcing pricing; however, clients are afforded the luxury of scalable resourcing from a physical space and equipment perspective.

3.1.8   Partners-in-Projects

Somewhere between outsourced strategic staffing and complete turnkey outsourcing lies the "partners-in-projects" (PIP) model. This outsourcing delivery model provides the client with flexibility around consultant deliverable ownership. This model is utilized the most when clients wish to return some level of project management and deliverable ownership without completely "handing over the keys." Think of it as "co-PM'ing." Many clients are simply not comfortable with having external partners completely own the SAP initiative with little more than business process subject matter expertise involvement from their own side.

> ### Spotlight: PIP — a successful implementation
>
> The PIP model was originally introduced in the late 1990s as a delivery alternative to full outsourced project responsibility. Clients looking for more than staff augmentation but still unwilling to relinquish project management control found a void within the partner alternatives. The unique approach of the PIP model provides flexible project management modelling specific to the client's desire and threshold. It has successfully supported hundreds of SAP clients and continues to provide a viable alternative to customers looking for SAP subject matter expertise, a strong and scalable resource pool, and logistical and administrative resource support.
>
> For more information regarding the PIP methodology and its application, contact COMSYS IT Partners (*www.comsys.com*).

Client/outsourcer collaboration
In the PIP model, the client and the outsourced SAP partner work together in managing the SAP implementation, ERP upgrade, production support mechanism, and so on. This approach gives the customer a single vendor who provides a qualified consultant team, allowing the client to maintain co-project management responsibility. In addition to leveraging the partner for traditional staff augmentation, PIP provides the SAP process tools and knowledge (Solution Composer, Solution Manager, Project Administration), methodologies (ASAP, Run SAP, PMI, etc.), and specific SAP needed know-how while maintaining control over the strategic direction of the SAP program.

Additionally, the PIP outsourcing delivery model can also lean more towards a model of "staffing on steroids." If the client wishes to maintain total delivery responsibility and wants to leverage an outsourced partner strictly for resources, the PIP model provides additional value-added services beyond bodies. This may include engagement oversight, pre-screening of candidates, creating status reports, providing subject matter experts, and access to a consultant knowledge base. Figure 3.4 represents the PIP model.

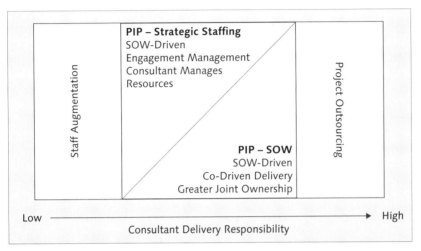

Figure 3.4 PIP Delivery Model

3.2 Specific SAP Outsourcing Models

There is a multitude of SAP outsourcing models that provide clients with either commoditized or variable SAP offerings. The commoditized option of "one-size-fits-all" typically works most effectively for the more routine, highly-repeatable, SAP services such as NetWeaver monitoring, transports, and so on, while the variable option is more of a "grocery list" model enabling clients to pick and choose services as appropriate for their needs. Let's look into several of the widely utilized SAP outsourcing models and how your organization might be able to use them.

3.2.1 SAP NetWeaver Basis Operations

One of the most widely leveraged SAP-specific outsourcing models is found within the NetWeaver Basis area. Perhaps due to its logical proximity to other widely-used non-SAP outsourced services such as networking and infrastructure, Microsoft Exchange, Application hosting, and the like, this natural extension into the SAP world has been embraced by the market place. In many cases, the manager responsible for the NetWeaver Basis area also manages the other infrastructure and system landscape areas. (To see it from their perspective, think of NetWeaver Basis as another infrastructure component sitting on top of an Oracle database and Microsoft operating system!)

> **Case Study: A leading office furniture manufacturer and its outsourced Basis COE**
>
> An industry leading office design and manufacturing company has been an SAP customer since 1996. Since that time, they've installed over 23 different SAP systems in their landscape, across the SAP product suite. In 2006, this company began to explore leveraging an external partner to support their NetWeaver Basis operational needs. The focus was to complement and not replace their existing internal Basis resources. According to the organization's NetWeaver manager, "our goal was to offload some of the more operational activities to a vendor in order for our team to focus on more strategic Basis activities." Working in tandem throughout the day, the internal Basis team would focus on strategic activities such as landscape optimization and supporting the business lines, while the offshore partner would handle maintenance and operational activities during the evening. "Our model provided us with a more responsive and strategic approach to the business."

When working with an outsourced Basis model, the client typically engages their partner in a commoditized manner, meaning that the partner has a tiered structure of support packages. Whether the partner model is setup as a minimal, enhanced, or premium suite of services, all Basis packages cater to a client's NetWeaver operational needs.

Services included   Basis services within this model will include system monitoring (batch processes and dialog processes), batch scheduling within SM37, printer setup and maintenance, connectivity (RFC, ALE, and EDI), Service Marketplace (the old OSS) Note and hot pack/patch application, and potentially even transports. As the partner model package moves up the food chain, additional NetWeaver services may be delivered, including upgrade services and new SAP product installations. (Depending on your partner, some of these services might even be included in the "basic" package.)

Table 4.1 shows examples of some of the services that might be provided by an outsourced SAP NetWeaver provider.

1	NetWeaver Support Services	Standard Service	Add-on Service
1.1	Installation of packages for basis support packages	X	
1.2	SAP upgrades installation		X
1.3	SAP additional module installation	X	
1.4	Application development transport requests		X
1.5	Monitoring update log and information of customer		X
1.6	Analysis of update errors within SAP Basis	X	
1.7	Processing update errors	X	
1.8	Go-live check		X

Table 3.1 Sample SAP Outsourcing NetWeaver Support Services

3.2.2 SAP Hosting

Another common outsourced SAP utility service is SAP hosting. In some respect, this outsourced offering is an extension of the SAP NetWeaver operations model above. A multitude of SAP hosting providers exist throughout the globe, including Freudenberg IT, Secure-24, IBM, and Kanbay. As with many SAP offerings, SAP certifies hosting providers within their partner system with a special accreditation. As of this print, there were over 15 certified SAP hosting providers globally.

Figure 3.5 SAP's Global Hosting Partner Accreditation

Scope

SAP hosting provides customers with the ability to outsource their SAP hardware and corresponding infrastructure support needs. These include not only the SAP NetWeaver stack and corresponding applications such as ERP, CRM, BI, and so on but also the underlying operating system and database. As part of the SAP hosting offering, the outsourcer provides consultant services supporting the entire infrastructure system needs necessary for your SAP landscape.

Key factors involved in choosing a hosting provider

When exploring this SAP outsourcing alternative, there are several important factors to consider because you are entrusting your SAP environment completely to an outsider. Think about the following:

▶ **Experience**
How long as the SAP hosting provider been in business? Do they focus on a specific SAP market segment such as the SME space or only Fortune 100 companies?

▶ **Certification**
Is the SAP hosting provider certified as an SAP global hosting provider? Are they SAS-70 type II or tier IV certified?

▶ **Geographic location**
Where are the hosting provider's facilities located? Along an earthquake fault line or hurricane path, or are they located in a safe environmental location? Also — if your organization requires global reach — does the hosting provider possess hosting facilities close to your important locations?

▶ **Number of existing clients**
Are you customer number two or 200?

▶ **Service level**
What are the service levels promised, down to the most basic hosting service offering?

▶ **Customer defection**
Does the SAP hosting partner keep all of their existing clients or do clients switch to competitors often?

▶ **Disaster recovery strategy**
What is the provider's system recovery backup and data storage strategy? Do they run a dual data center concept? What is their recovery point objective?

▶ **Historical system availability**
What is the provider's historical uptime level? Or conversely, how often over the past year has the system been down? 99.998% up or down?

▶ **Customer support**
What customer support mechanisms does the hosting partner provide? Do they have 24x7x365 hotline support?

As discussed previously, every hosting provider offers different types of hosting packages ranging from the most basic services to "Rolls-Royce" packages. Table 4.2 shows an example suite of hosting products:

Sample SAP
hosting models

Features	Eco-ERP	Pro-ERP	Advanced-Pro ERP	Advanced-Plus ERP
Customer Profile				
Company Employee Size	< 1,500	< 6,000	< 6,000	< 6,000
Named SAP Users	< 300	300–2,000	300–2,000	300–2,000+
Database Storage Required	< 0.5 TB	> 0.5 TB	> 0.5 TB	> 0.5 TB
Platform Features				
Hardware Platform	HP Proliant series	IBM p-series	IBM p-series	IBM p-series
OS Platform	Linux	AIX	AIX	AIX
Database Platform	MaxDB	SQL Server/Oracle	Oracle	Oracle
Storage	Local-Attached with RAID	Local-Attached or SAN	SAN	SAN
Cold Standby Servers Option	Yes	Yes	Yes	Yes
Synchronous Data Mirroring	No	No	Yes	Yes

Table 3.2 Sample SAP Hosting Options

Features	Eco-ERP	Pro-ERP	Advanced-Pro ERP	Advanced-Plus ERP
Passive DB Shadow	No	No	No	Yes
Landscape Features				
ERP Landscapes Supported (All SAP Landscapes)	SAP ERP, SAP Business Suite, BW, HR, APO, NetWeaver	SAP ERP, SAP Business Suite, BW, HR, APO, NetWeaver	SAP ERP, SAP Business Suite, BW, HR, APO, NetWeaver	SAP ERP, SAP Business Suite, BW, HR, APO, NetWeaver
Landscape Architecture Options	2 or 3-system (DEV, QAS, PRD) and 2 or 3-server, customer-dedicated	2 or 3-system (DEV, QAS, PRD) and 2 or 3-server, customer dedicated	2 or 3-system (DEV, QAS, PRD) and 2 or 3-server, customer dedicated	2 or 3-system (DEV, QAS, PRD) and 2 or 3-server, customer dedicated
Service Levels and Support				
Contract Period	3 or 5 years	3 or 5 years	3 or 5 years	3 or 5 years
Theoretical System Availability	99.5 %	99.5 %	99.5 %	99.85 %
Recovery Point Objective	4 hours	4 hours	< 1 hour	< 1 hour
Recovery Time Objective	24 hours	24 hours	4 hours	< 1 hour
24x7x365 Support	Yes	Yes	Yes	Yes
Managed Service	Hardware, OS, DB, and Basis Administration	Hardware, OS, DB, and Basis Administration	Hardware, OS, DB, and Basis Administration	Hardware, OS, DB, and Basis Administration
Network Line Provisioning (Point-to-Point, VPN, MPLS)	Customer or Provider	Customer or Provider	Customer or Provider	Customer or Provider
SAP and DB Licenses	Customer	Customer	Customer	Customer

Table 3.2 Sample SAP Hosting Options (cont.)

Features	Eco-ERP	Pro-ERP	Advanced-Pro ERP	Advanced-Plus ERP
SLAs and Penalties	Yes	Yes	Yes	Yes
Data Center Infrastructure (UPS, Generator, Security, etc.; SAP Hosting Certified)	Yes	Yes	Yes	Yes
Dual Data Center DR Concept (Distributed Landscape and Tape Backup in Other Data Center)	Yes	Yes	Yes	Yes

Table 3.2 Sample SAP Hosting Options (cont.)

One final point regarding SAP hosting: SAP and database licenses are most often the customer's responsibility. Therefore, if your organization is embarking on a new SAP initiative requiring additional SAP software or underlying database licensing, don't forget to factor in these additional costs.

3.2.3 Custom Development

SAP custom development services are another widely leveraged outsourcing strategy. Whether employed for full lifecycle SAP implementations, mini-projects or enhancements, or incremental "piece-meal" services, outsourcing SAP development has long been a go-to service. And due to its availability within the market place, both the pricing and commoditization are well established.

Outsourced custom development services could be utilized in multiple ways including: ABAP WRICEFP (workflow, reports, interfaces, conversions, enhancements such as user exits or module dialog programming, and forms including SAPScript and SmartForms, PI/XI, Portal/JAVA), or bolt-on integration.

Scope The scope and breadth of SAP custom development outsourcing can range from "break-fix" services (as described later in Section 3.2.6) all the way to full, comprehensive enhancement development. Depending on the amount of custom development activity within an organization, budget, and internal resources (as well as many other factors), outsourced SAP ABAP work and the like differ dramatically from customer to customer.

3.2.4   SAP Centric Help Desk/Service Desk

Depending on the size and needs of your organization and the amount of SAP users, some form of SAP-centric help desk facility might be required. For larger organizations with a large number of end users or expected call volume, a dedicated tier I and tier II Service Desk might be in order. For smaller companies — with a smaller pool of end users or call volume — a smaller SAP Service Desk (or perhaps an integrated SAP Service Desk mechanism within a larger shared services help desk) or centralized help line might be sufficient.

Scale A standard measure for whether to build an SAP-centric help desk is the number of end users. As a rule of thumb, if your SAP end user community is over approximately 50 users, then some form of SAP help desk is in order, even if it is a small one to two person operation. In addition, call volume per user is relevant (because one user could make 100 calls while conversely 100 users might only make one call); however, typically 50 users has been shown to be a critical threshold.

> **Case Study: A leading Biotech company and their 24x7x365 internal SAP help desk**
>
> In 2006, one of the world's leading biotechnology companies embarked on an SAP global implementation. With more than 10,000 users spanning over 20 countries, this company needed to build a support COE, including a level 1, 2, and 3 SAP help desk. Their SAP Service Desk supports their SAP roll-out and consists of a multitude of SAP experts (both functional and technical) and service desk specialists located both in the U.S. and Western Europe.

Building a responsive and competent global SAP production support center was imperative to the overall success of the client's global SAP implementation. To support their user base effectively, this company designed a robust 24x7x365 "follow the sun" model, where North American-based service desk personnel supports the user community and hands off responsibility to their European counterparts as the workday started there and ended in North America. This level 1 SAP Service Desk provides basic SAP support including user password resetting and basic SAP navigation. Consisting of over 20 SAP service desk specialists, including multiple service desk leads, the overall help desk includes additional level 2 and 3 resources supporting more involved SAP issue resolution.

3.2.5 Implementation

To lower SAP implementation costs, clients now look to offsite outsourcing as a delivery alternative in implementation projects. Unheard of during the initial days of SAP projects due to the newness of the software and outsourcing in general, leveraging outsourcing mechanisms are now touted as not only a viable alternative but a great value. Although more complicated and involving escalated risk, implementations of lesser complexity with highly repeatable components can be executed mostly or entirely offsite. Some projects can even be driven completely offsite.

A perfect example is a technical upgrade. Technical SAP upgrades such as upgrades from SAP R/3 to SAP ERP 6.0 or basic upgrades from SAP BW 3.5 to BW 7.0 are excellent candidates for complete offsite delivery. The IT director of a previously mentioned company was at first sceptical of such an approach. However after a rapid six week, lower cost, and successful technical ERP 6.0 upgrade delivered 100 % offsite, this seasoned SAP customer is a believer:

Technical upgrade

> "After understanding the work effort involved, the approach, and the cost differential, I was comfortable with the model and after successful delivery, I am a believer."

Another option is an onsite/offsite delivery mix. For some efforts, complete offsite delivery is not feasible whether due to complexity or timeline. In these cases, onsite representation is the answer. Commonly leveraged in SAP America's own consulting delivery model, project management and critical business process functional expertise is deployed onsite (as discussed in Section 4.1.1). The less complex, less business-heavy interaction resources, however, work remotely, receiving direction and business process requirements via the onsite resources.

3.2.6   The Break/Fix to Global Delivery Services Pyramid

Break/Fix   In the break/fix model, the extent of SAP outsourced services is minimal. In essence, the partner's sole responsibility is to "keep the lights on." This means that the break/fix model addresses only critical production support. *No enhancements are supported.* As end users identify flaws in the system, the break-fix support team addresses and repairs them. Depending on the volume, sophistication, control measures, and so on, issues are identified, tracked, prioritized, and resolved. Again, this model does not address enhancements or modifications to the system beyond error resolution; these types of SAP requests are either handled by another team or they are not done. For some mid-market organizations, the break-fix model is the only appropriate model. The determining factors for employing the break/fix model are internal resource bandwidth, assuming that an internal IT staff performs these services, and budget.

The following are several break/fix type issues covered by this model:

- ABAP short dumps
- SM37 job scheduling
- Mandatory business-critical modifications (e.g., new company code creation, or adding a plant)
- Legal-related modifications (e.g., new tax or financial regulations)
- Security authorization profile issues
- NetWeaver operations
- Service Marketplace OSS Notes, hot packs, and enhancement package application

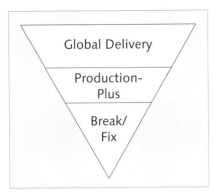

Figure 3.6 The Break/Fix to Global Delivery Services Pyramid

Moving up the services food chain lies the "production-plus." In the production-plus model, the SAP outsourcing's scope of services is expanded beyond error resolution. How much, you ask? This depends entirely on your organization's needs. For example, one organization might choose to use its production-plus outsourcing for smaller enhancements only, whereas another company might task its partner to drive more involved SAP enhancements such as new business custom reports or interfaces. The bottom line is that the production-plus model provides expanded SAP support, moving beyond basic break/fix services.

Production-plus

As the name itself implies, production-plus is geared towards productive SAP environments and not brand new implementations (for this, see the discussion on global delivery that follows). Therefore, the services and breadth tend to more tailored to live installations. It would be difficult to provide production-plus services without a productive SAP environment!

At the top of the pyramid sits global delivery (sometimes also called application management services [AMS]). Global delivery expands SAP outsourcing services beyond the production-only type customers and reaches into all forms of SAP required services. While the possible SAP global delivery services are infinite, the following are example offerings that highlight the magnitude of its reach:

Global delivery

► Production-plus services (as described earlier)

► ERP upgrade

- New core ERP module implementation
- New ERP 6.0 G/L
- PI/XI system integration
- New SAP product installation (e.g., CRM 7.0, or SAP BusinessObjects)
- Security authorization audit

3.3 Summary

As you can see throughout this chapter, there are many ways to describe what outsourcing is depending on the type of SAP consulting service. Whether a single resource, a team of resources, the use of SAP hosting, or everything in between, there is an overall thread connecting all of these permutations: the external delivery of an SAP service.

Change is inevitable. Change for the better is a full-time job.
— Adlai E. Stevenson

4   When — Timing and Transition

"Timing is everything;" thus, both choosing when to engage an outsourcing organization and when to begin thinking about outsourcing is very important. As discussed previously, although some organizations choose to only engage BPO as an operations/production support mechanism, there are potential great benefits to explore implementation/delivery as well. Regardless of the engagement vehicle, bringing in external support at the appropriate point in time is fundamental to its executable success.

Another key timing element when leveraging SAP outsourcing is transition. Transition is very important to the overall success of any SAP outsourcing initiative. Thus, this section will discuss all of the necessary steps involved in handing over "the keys" to an outsourcing partner, including planning, communication, proper structure, and so on, as well as how prominent SAP methodologies (including ASAP and Run SAP) play into timelines and the communication and change management procedures used during the transitional phases.

4.1   Choosing the Proper Timeframe

The timing for when to bring in external SAP resources is dependent on a multitude of factors, including urgency, knowledge transfer, ramp-up timing, use of resource, and so on; however, most the important factor is need. If the demand is paramount, timing becomes irrelevant. (Think of the time when your project was approaching a critical deadline and you simply didn't have the resources to deliver! Bringing in the cavalry was the only viable solution.)

But let's assume that your organization drives SAP projects properly and plans appropriately for the number of resources; that's one problem solved. The next challenge is bringing them in with enough time to ramp-up without too much time for idle activity. When dealing with non-post production SAP support (a topic to be discussed shortly), that is, strategic staffing, you must factor in several elements regarding timing (most of which have little to do with SAP as a product). Here is a subset:

Timing factors to consider

▶ **SAP initiative ramp-up**
Is it critical that the consultant is deeply aware of the overall intent of the initiative (i.e., the global SAP roll-out's purpose, impact, reach, etc.), the players (it's a global roll-out and the players will work with a global delivery center halfway around the world), business process (the specific reasoning behind why a given SAP functionality has been developed), and so on?

▶ **Industry/corporate culture**
Does the resource need time to be indoctrinated into your organization's culture? Does your company have industry-specific requirements such as good manufacturing practices (GMPs), HIPAA compliance, or other requirements that every consultant must learn? Does the resource have to potentially take an exam?

▶ **System administration**
Having a consultant sit idle without the appropriate system access, including all of the appropriate SAP environments (development, quality assurance, sandbox, etc.), email (Outlook, Lotus Notes, etc.), and environments (Windows, Intranet, etc.) is a waste of time and money.

▶ **Background check**
Some organizations require thorough background checks, which take time. External and lengthy background checks for criminal activity, drugs, and so on, can add extra time to your onboarding.

4.2 Timing for Post-Production Support Outsourcing

Bringing in resources for SAP post-production support is a different animal. (The same holds true whether building a post-production support organization, aka COE, internally or leveraging an external provider.) Although it's never too early to begin thinking about how your organization should implement the post-production support or COE, building the COE too early can result in COE team burnout and waiting too long can result in production support problems.

As a rule of thumb, an organization should begin seriously discussing their SAP post-production approach sometime during the "realization" or implementation phase. Following the ASAP methodology systems lifecycle, the "realization phase" immediately follows the "blueprinting" or design stage (see Figure 4.1).

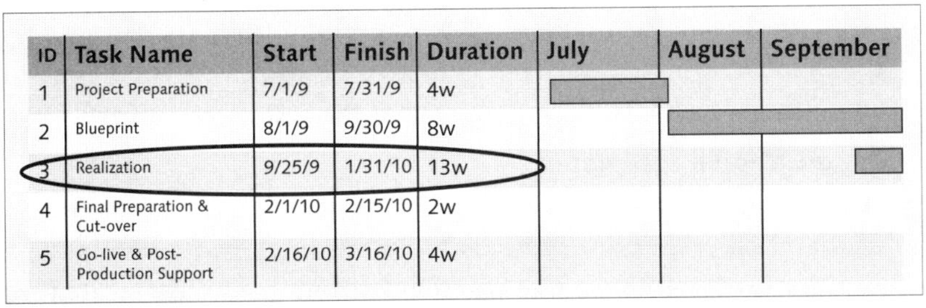

Start during the implementation

ID	Task Name	Start	Finish	Duration	July	August	September
1	Project Preparation	7/1/9	7/31/9	4w	▬		
2	Blueprint	8/1/9	9/30/9	8w		▬	
3	Realization	9/25/9	1/31/10	13w			▬
4	Final Preparation & Cut-over	2/1/10	2/15/10	2w			
5	Go-live & Post-Production Support	2/16/10	3/16/10	4w			

Figure 4.1 Realization Phase Within ASAP

It is during this "realization" phase that the core design is being built and any modifications are beginning to be discovered as part of unit testing. During this timeframe, the integration manager can be assigned, enabling him to begin conceptually modelling what scope, services, SLA's, and so on, should be the building blocks of the COE. Furthermore, the integration manager can begin to "straw man" the organizational structure, ensuring that all of the appropriate SAP skillsets are represented on the team. The topic of the integration manager is discussed at length in Chapter 14.

Integration Manager

If organizations plan properly, ensuring that your production support SAP resources are aligned in some form should be well in place *prior* to the planned *go-live*. Ideally, the core of your COE should be mobilized during the testing phases of the project (i.e., integration testing and user acceptance testing). This strategy helps provide the best circumstances for a successful production support model for several reasons:

COE go-live during testing

▶ **Knowledge transfer**
Bringing in your core SAP production support team members during the project's implementation allows them to "learn on the job." By integrating team members during testing phases, you allow them to better understand the core functionality that was implemented. This, in turn, provides them with a deeper understanding of what they will ultimately have to support and/or enhance.

▶ **Practice**
Similar to knowledge transfer, the more exposure your production support resources have to the system, the greater an in-depth understanding of the system's functionality they will have. Some organizations utilize their production support mechanism prior to go-live for project-related support. This allows the COE to practice while on the job *prior* to supporting the end-user community after the system goes live.

▶ **Organizational acceptance**
As mentioned previously, during the project's implementation, end users and super users are typically the most familiar with their project team implementation counterparts and strong bonds are created. In some cases, these project team members transition to the COE, making end-user support seamless and painless. However, if the project team continues to move forward with additional roll-outs and changes their focus, end users must look to new contacts for production support. Integrating the COE into the later phases of the implementation assists in this transition and facilitates end-user acceptance.

▶ **Training**
As also mentioned previously, mobilizing the production support team prior to go-live can assist the COE in building logistical operational experience. Phone system operation, ticketing tool system run-through, triage procedures, communication etiquette, and so on, are all fundamental givens that must be mastered before working on SAP issues. Working with the team to make these procedures second nature enables them to focus on resolving end-user SAP issues as opposed to carrying out production support functions.

▶ **Responsibility transition**
As discussed before, to empower your production support organization to be seen both externally (by end users) and internally (by the

production support team and project team) as the system gate keepers, it's imperative that the formal handing over of the keys to the
"kingdom" is performed. Prior to go-live, your production support
mechanism should be formally anointed by management that they
now have the authority to manage and protect the system's integrity.
The responsibility transition from project team (and project mode) to
post-production support team (and production support mode) is crucial for long-term system stability. There is nothing more dangerous
and morale-deflating than the "never ending" project. Transitioning
responsibility ensures that there is a clear understanding by the entire
organization that a "new sheriff is in town."

Case Study: Novolyte and the timing of its post-production transition

"Our SAP post-production support transition was most likely a bit different
than most," remembers Rick Watkins, Novolyte Technologies' corporate controller. Spun off a larger company in the fourth quarter of 2008, Novolyte
inherited their parent company's robust SAP environment. With little time
and little internal SAP expertise, Novolyte scrambled to find a way in which to
support their small but important SAP user base. "From a timing perspective,
we were under the gun, so to speak. We had a productive SAP environment
and end users across the globe (U.S. [multiple locations] and China) dependent on SAP working properly." As opposed to having the luxury of a meticu-
lously planned transition plan, Watkins and his company needed to setup an
SAP production support mechanism yesterday.

Although the situation was less than ideal for Novolyte, it's a common situation for many midmarket SAP environments. Novolyte continues to run
smoothly and leverages SAP every day for critical business process needs.

4.3 SAP Methodologies' Impact on Timing

As part of SAP's standard methodologies for project and operational initiatives, resource allocation and ramp-up are integrated into the overall
strategy. During specific phases, SAP typically recommends bringing in
different skillsets to support the given SAP program. Let's take a look at
the two primary SAP methodologies and how SAP recommends allocating resources.

4.3.1 ASAP

Until recently, SAP's only codified implementation methodology was ASAP. This SDLC (see Figure 4.2) approach was SAP's version of the common analysis, design, construction, testing, and implementation methodology.

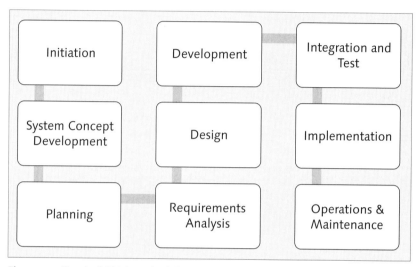

Figure 4.2 Standard SDLC Methodology (SDLC Model from Information Resources Management, 2003; U.S. Department of Justice)

Resource strategy   Based on SAP's standard ASAP approach, SAP chooses a somewhat sequential and hierarchical deployment of resources. Of course, every project differs dramatically but more often than not, SAP recommends the resource strategy shown in Figure 4.3, by ASAP phase. (Again, this is a broad generalization regarding how to allocate SAP resources per ASAP methodology; however, it provides a high-level overview of the types of skillsets that are typically required during a full-lifecycle implementation.)

> **SAPanese — Technical vs. functional skillsets**
>
> For those outside of the SAP world, SAP is technical. This perspective believes that regardless of the skillset, *everything* is technical. Although this perspective might hold true to the layman, for those within the SAP world, it isn't true.

From an SAP insider's perspective, the truly technical SAP skillsets are either developers, programmers, administrators, architects, or managers responsible for those areas. These skillsets work in tandem with the SAP functional resources; however, they typically are "heads-down" and take direction from the functional skillsets.

Conversely, SAP functional skillsets are those who deal with business processes, interact with the customer business community (perhaps business analysts), and configure SAP from a functional perspective to behave the way the business desires.

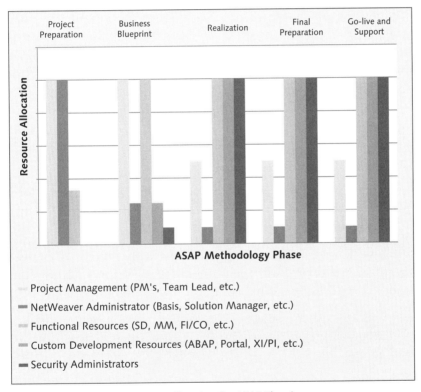

Figure 4.3 Typical SAP Resource Allocation (by ASAP Phase)

As you can see, SAP looks to provide more project management in the earlier ASAP phases and then tries to lower resource allocation after the business blueprint phase, to part-time involvement throughout the rest of the phases. Conversely, ASAP recommends a "heads-down" configuration with functional consultants (FI/CO, SD, MM, etc.) as needed for the project and technical consultants (ABAP developers, security administrators, etc.) during the heart of the implementation ramping up to full capacity during the realization phase. Although this project team construct and corresponding resource allocation is not a "one-size-fits-all" approach, the overall approach holds true: project management set in place during the early ASAP phases transitioning over to those responsible for its implementation.

4.3.2 Run SAP

Operations-centric With the onslaught of production support and more operationally focused productive clients, SAP has recently begun to promote a more focused operations-based methodology known as Run SAP (*www. sap.com/ecosystem/partners/partnerwithsap/services/run-sap/index.epx*). This operations-centric approach provides a structured roadmap on when and how to maximize your organization's productive environment, focusing on the SAP application management, its respective business process operations, and the administration of SAP's NetWeaver infrastructure platform.

For organizations interested in learning how Run SAP can better optimize their productive environment and ongoing SAP solutions, a Run SAP operations assessment is available.

Next, we'll discuss SAP's Run SAP solutions operations assessment approach; however, other operation assessments are available from other leading consulting partners:

Run SAP solutions operations assessment As a consulting service offering, SAP offers assessment services focused on assisting clients with how and when to implement their Run SAP methodology. Per SAP:

> *"The first step in the Run SAP methodology is the SAP solution operations assessment. The assessment is applicable when you want to optimize the implementation and ongoing management of end-to-end solution operation processes in your IT landscape and support organization."*

This service assists clients in better understanding how Run SAP methodology benefits their productive SAP environment as well as defining the appropriate steps, roadmap, and respective timing. This assessment covers the following: learning about the Run SAP methodology and its respective road map; providing direction for which SAP operations standards and processes of value to implement; identifying the missing skills to operate your specific IT environment; internal, client-focused education; developing an end-to-end road map with an action plan and high-level time schedule; and aligning the constructed action plan, if necessary, to planned or in-process implementation projects.

From a timing perspective, Run SAP methodology provides a framework for when the appropriate resources should be deployed, specific to your unique environment. When dealing with parallel SAP organizations (such as the project implementation team *and* the production support team) within the same organization, Run SAP recommends that your production support resources are phased in towards the end of the implementation. In essence, managing SAP outsourcing timing and the key driving factors such as operational scope, corresponding staffing needs, coverage, SLA's, and the like, is a project within itself. Thus, the planning for this transition must occur well in advance of the actual handover.

4.4 Managing Change

Establishing the correct infrastructure, mobilizing the appropriate resources, and bringing it all together at the "right" time are all key pieces in developing an effective post-production support mechanism. However, regardless of your team's exceptional skillsets and impeccable timing, an inability to effectively manage change can be paralyzing. Two key factors ensure that your post-production support resources are best equipped to deal with modifications to your production environment:

▶ Change management tools
▶ Change management processes/procedures

Figure 4.4 shows a standard change management workflow.

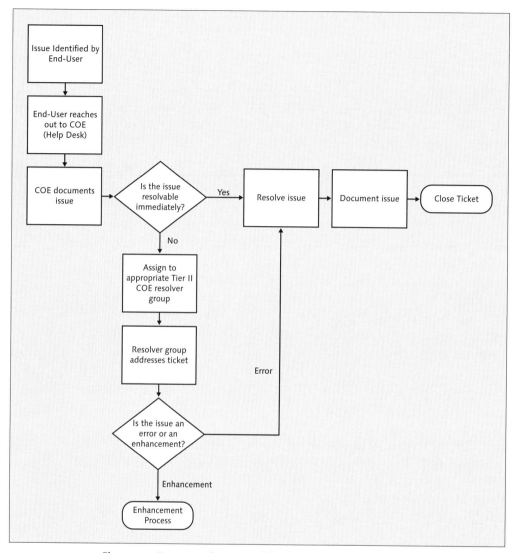

Figure 4.4 Managing Change Workflow

Choosing the tool   Using the proper change management tools can assist greatly in effectively managing change within a production environment. Numerous change ticket tracking tools exist within the market as stand-alone packages. Tools such as Remedy, Peregrine, and Track IT (among others) are effective ways of capturing change requests and following them through the modification process.

Issue tracking systems: Which one should we use?

There are literally thousands of issue tracking systems available today both for purchase and as freeware. Depending on your needs and budget, any number of these tools could suffice. However, to choose the optimal error resolution solution for your environment and evaluate a range of important features, you should address the following factors:

▶ **Workflow**
Does the ticketing system have the ability to assign responsibility to different resolver groups and then automatically inform newly assigned resolvers that the issue is now their responsibility?

▶ **SAP integration**
What — if any — SAP integration exists? Is it possible to interface data from SAP (perhaps SU53 authorization screenshots or transactional business data?)

▶ **Cost**
Enough said.

▶ **Email integration**
Does the error resolution system have the ability to send email notifications from the tool? Furthermore, can the tool *receive* email notifications (such as *helpdesk@yourcompany.com*)?

▶ **Customization**
Is it important that your organization has the ability to customize the tool to meet corporate needs?

▶ **Ticketing tool**
Choosing the proper ticketing tool can not only make your organization's life easier but resolve issues more quickly and effectively!

Regardless of the specific software you use, the purpose of all of these products is to easily document and track change requests from the end-user community. Typically, organizations provide a help desk or help desk hotline to which users can reach out when they identify potential errors within the system. All issues are initially documented within the tracking tool, describing the perceived problem. If the issue is either an end-user misunderstanding or easily resolvable, the help desk agent informs the end user, documents the resolution, and closes the ticket. If, however, the issue is not easily resolvable and requires additional research, the ticket is assigned to the proper "resolver group," which will follow up to resolve the issue.

Post-production support team members are assigned to respective "resolver groups" based on skillset. In the event that the issue spans across multiple resolver groups, the various resolver groups work together to address the given issue.

SAP Service Desk As part of Solution Manager's newest functionality, SAP offers a limited but practical ticketing-type functionality that is fully integrated with core SAP business applications (e.g., SAP ERP 6.0 Financials, SD, etc.). It is called Service Desk.

SAP's Service Desk product is a fully-integrated issue reporting, tracking and resolution system that also allows direct integration into SAP's support portal. Whether your IT group is supporting implementation testing or a post go-live situation, SAP Service Desk allows SAP end users to report issues or warnings directly from the SAP GUI and then centrally store them within Solution Manager.

SAP Service Marketplace integration Another great feature of SAP Solution Manager is that as of Solution Manager 7.0, SAP Service Desk can link directly into the Service Marketplace, simplifying issue reporting into SAP's support organization.

Here are several of SAP Service Desk's key features:

▶ Users can create support messages directly from any transaction.

▶ Automatic capture of environmental data such as system, patch levels, transaction, and screen number; however, business data is *not* captured for specific transactions.

▶ Central processing of messages from SAP Solution Manager:

  ▸ Rules-based processing (assign processors based on type)

  ▸ Turning support messages into knowledge base documents

  ▸ Email notifications

▶ Associating SAP Notes to specific messages.

▶ Forwarding issues on to SAP without logging into Service Marketplace and getting updates from SAP in the tool.

▶ SAP-provided APIs to interface with third-party tools such as the ticketing error resolution systems described earlier.

One of the compelling advantages of utilizing SAP Service Desk vs. other non-SAP ticketing solutions is its true integration with core SAP functionality. If users run into any issues, SAP Service Desk allows them to simply click on the SAP logo on their screen and a ticket is created, along with background information.

Tightly integrated into applications

Figure 4.5 show an example of how SAP Service Desk works.

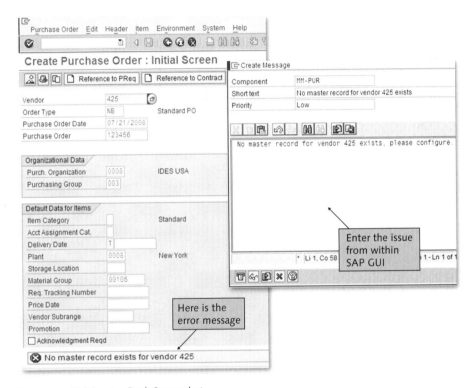

Figure 4.5 SAP Service Desk Screenshot

4.5   Control Advisory Board

Although day-to-day end-user errors should be addressed by your post-production support resources directly via help desk and tracking tools, major modifications to the system and enhancements should be addressed via a different mechanism. This mechanism (described earlier) is known as the control advisory board (CAB). Comprised of all of

Beyond the day-to-day issues

the necessary stakeholders and subject matter experts, the CAB is led by the integration manager. The CAB's role is to address any enhancements, major modifications, or significant change requests to the productive environment. Depending on the role of the COE, this may even include additional projects (both small and large) to your SAP system.

Typically, the CAB meets frequently (daily, weekly, or bi-weekly) to hear and discuss proposed changes. During this standing meeting, representatives from the COE team and other vested individuals (e.g., external project team members, etc.) present requested changes to the CAB. During the requestor's presentation, the CAB is able to ask questions to fully understand the scope and rationale for the requested change. In a sense, the CAB sits as a court to hear, interpret, analyze, and judge requests. After hearing all of the requests in a given session, the CAB approves or rejects the proposals. Approved proposals are assigned a priority together with any existing change requests and are subsequently worked on by the appropriate team members.

Man's yesterday may never be like his morrow;
Nought may endure but Mutability.
— Percy Bysshe Shelley

Section 2: Application — The Final "W" — How

This section moves us from the strategic perspective and the thought processes behind whether to choose outsourcing (as well as the strategic perspective's various decision-making components) to the tactical perspective. This less theoretical and equally as important perspective focuses on the processes, methodologies, and applications involved in employing an outsourcing model. In a nut shell: the "how." Although this section will also be relevant to those targeted in Section 1 (decision makers and executives), this section will be more focused on a target audience of those responsible for implementing the chosen strategy (production support managers, global delivery management, service leads, etc.). As you will see, the process of how to best maximize SAP consultants is more of an art than a science.

"Quality is never an accident; it is always the result of high intention, sincere effort, intelligent direction, and skillful execution; it represents the wise choice of many alternatives."
— William A. Foster

5   Implementations and Upgrades

Although not previously used a great deal for true implementation purposes, leveraging BPO for project work is becoming more and more common, and with organizations looking at cost-cutting measures, this delivery alternative is now coming front and center. Typically, however, higher risks are associated and experienced when implementation work is not performed by a completely onsite project team. This section will discuss how SAP outsourcing can be best utilized for implementation purposes — its challenges, benefits, and so on. This section will also highlight several client examples where this approach was taken.

5.1   ASAP (Focus) Methodology

SAP has its own implementation methodology, which was developed specifically for successfully and efficiently delivering SAP projects, similar to other leading project management methodologies such as:

▸ IBM's "Fastlane" project methodology

▸ Deloitte's "Project Management Methodology (PMM4)"

▸ Accenture's "Method One"

▸ Capgemini's "Software Development Methodology (SDM/SDM2)"

▸ Project Management Institute's "Project Framework(s)"

SAP's methodology is Accelerated SAP (ASAP). SAP also recently added a newer ASAP methodology variant known as ASAP Focus. This project methodology — originating with the release of SAP's R/3 version in the late 1990s — focuses on a structured five-phase development roadmap (see Figure 5.1).

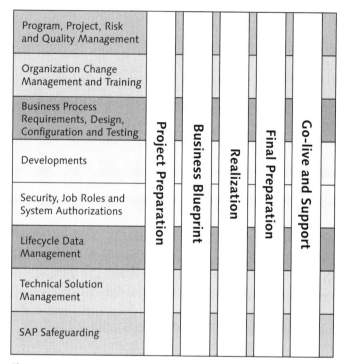

Figure 5.1 SAP's Project Roadmap: ASAP

The following is a high-level breakdown of each of the five roadmap phases (along with ongoing continuous improvement), along with their respective purposes.

1. **Project Preparation**

   In the project preparation phase, the SAP project is initiated and planning is started in earnest. Key implementation team members are included in this process to devise an action plan and identify proper resourcing needs. Although the project team at this point is small, key personnel such as the project manager are included.

2. **Business Blueprint**

   Moving from planning to the beginning of execution, the analysis activities are performed in the business blueprint phase, paving a clear path toward implementation. As the name of the phase suggests, blueprinting is performed to lay the foundation of what core project activities must be executed, including configuration, development, migration, integration, decommissioning/retirement of systems, and training. The final deliverable of this phase is a contract (or blueprint) with the business and key stakeholders clearly defining what the SAP envrionment will ultimately look like and its functionality.

3. **Realization**
   During the realization phase, the blueprint is brought to fruition. All of the necessary execution is performed based on the requirements defined within the blueprint. This is typically the longest stage, including development (and functional configuration), and rigorous stages of testing (i.e., unit testing, string testing, integration testing, regression testing, user acceptance testing, etc.). All hands are on-deck and the activities are typically performed by "heads-down" developers, testers, and configuration specialists.

4. **Final Preparation**
   A check list of the final activites prior to go-live is performed. Within a comprehensive cut-over plan, critical technical and business activities are executed in the proper order. End-user readiness is assessed (including any additional training and end-user testing) and the final "go/no-go decision" is made.

5. **Go-Live and Support**
   In this stage, the official transition from implementation to post-production has been made and the project team begins to transfer oversight responsibility to some form of a post-production support team or COE (even if the project team itself takes over this role).

6. **Continuous Improvement**
   Although not an official stage within ASAP methodology, this should definitely (and hopefully) be the *longest* stage in any SAP environment. As a diamond grows more brilliant with polishing, so too should your SAP environment with continued "care and feeding" (in this case, via error resolution and enhancement). Additional enhancements and refinement of existing functionality are part of this ongoing phase. In many cases, this stage is supported by a dedicated post-production support mechanism.

One key difference between some of the purely theoretically methodologies and ASAP is that SAP's implementation approach also incorporates SAP tools such as SAP Solution Composer, roadmaps, and SAP Solution Manager.

▶ **SAP Solution Composer**
This tool is typically leveraged at the beginning of an implementation to build a client's business requirements based on SAP solutions.

▶ **SAP Roadmaps**
Another SAP attempt to provide a predefined set of roadmaps specific to given implementations. These roadmaps span across different SAP technologies.

▶ **SAP Solution Manager**
Solution Manager is a multi-functional tool that can facilitate implementations in a variety of ways, including project documentation, configuration, and testing. (Solution Manager's project administration tool will be discussed in greater detail a little later.)

One key advantage in leveraging SAP's integrated suite of tools (such as those described) during an implementation is accelerated delivery. Because SAP outsourcing projects generally follow the same high-level activities (i.e., define SAP business process scope, identify needed SAP custom development objects, define integrated and dependent processes, etc.) for driving implementations, there is no need to reinvent the wheel. These tools provide the framework for repeatable activities. Furthermore, working with these tools allows customers to leverage countless hours of SAP innovation for maximizing project efficiencies.

Also, when working with an SAP outsourcing provider, using standard SAP delivery products during your project provides multiple additional advantages. Key advantages are "common language" and "common process." Due to the fact that SAP as a product can be implemented in multiple ways, using these tools with your outsourced SAP provider lets you establish the proper construct and shared approach. Of course, interpretation and varied approaches can still exist; however, leveraging these tools allows for at least a strong foundation.

5.2 Outsourcing by ASAP Phase

Digging deeper within each respective phase, there are unique SAP outsourcing requirements that may be engaged. For example, typically more "soldier" type resources are needed during the development and testing phases than earlier during high level project planning. Therefore, the composition of your SAP outsourcing needs — and, in turn, their respective SAP consulting skill sets — will typically vary from phase to phase. What follows is a breakdown by ASAP phase and the typical respective SAP outsourcing resource requirements.

5.2.1 Project Preparation

During this initial ASAP methodology phase, senior level resources are engaged. Prior to the deep-dive analysis and subsequent development activities within the blueprinting and realization phases, strategy and overall project roadmapping must be put into place. Key senior leadership and functional expertise are represented to identify the proper planning and resource needs for the duration of the implementation.

The following are several of the key resources that should be engaged during this phase and the corresponding value they bring:

Key resources during project preparation

▶ **SAP project manager**
Due to the SAP project manager's overarching responsibility, his involvement in this stage is obvious. Regardless of project size, every ASAP-driven SAP project must include this role, whether it is a dedicated individual for larger initiatives/organizations or a shared role in smaller, more limited bandwidth/resources/budget environments.

▶ **SAP technical infrastructure lead/manager**
Depending on the size of the given initiative, this role (and several others, as follows) is included in this phase as the representative responsible for all of the deliverables and resources responsible for the underlying SAP environment (which often goes unappreciated and is taken for granted). This lead covers the NetWeaver stack and its related technologies and skill sets (i.e., NetWeaver Basis, Solution Manager, security, business intelligence, networking, database, operating system, storage, etc). During this phase, this representative

begins planning for the proper resource pool responsible for supporting the implementation (via system installation and optimization, system migration, legacy system retirement, day-to-day project needs such as SAP transports, etc.) as well as cursory non-SAP infrastructure activities (whether directly or indirectly part of the role's responsibility).

▶ **SAP offsite global delivery manager**
If an organization plans to leverage an offsite delivery mechanism in some capacity (ranging from a smaller targeted resource pool to complete offsite delivery), the SAP offsite global delivery manager needs to be involved in this phase. Responsible for allocating the proper resources corresponding to the respective project phase, this position ensures that there is an agreed-on understanding of offsite required support and plans accordingly. Also, if there are any project-specific requirements for delivering a project remotely from a logistical and/or administrative perspective (such as telecommunications, video conferencing, time zone challenges, client expectations, etc.), the offsite global delivery manager plans and prepares accordingly.

▶ **SAP custom development lead/manager**
Depending on the number of SAP customer development objects and the size of the implementation team, this role is included in the SAP project management team to champion, oversee, and deliver all SAP custom development objects. SAP custom developments can include all new SAP developed programming and/or technical configuration for interfaces, data conversion, reports, enhancements (e.g., new module pool creation, user-exits, etc.), Smartforms and SAP script, Java/portal, XI/PI, and MDM. If the implementation chooses to leverage an offsite delivery mechanism, the custom development manager and the offsite global delivery manager will spend a lot of time together!

▶ **SAP functional configuration lead(s)/manager(s)**
Because most SAP implementations are business process-driven (of course, there are also technical implementations focused on purely technical upgrades and the like but in the end, all projects are meant to support the business lines), key knowledge on how to implement SAP's functional configuration is paramount. The SAP functional con-

figuration lead(s) are responsible for identifying specific areas of concern in the upcoming project and plan accordingly. Similar to the custom development lead, if much of the functional configuration is to be performed offsite, this manager will work with the global delivery team to ensure that the proper resources are selected and correctly allocated.

▶ **Key functional configuration specialists**
Finally, specific functional configuration "gurus" might be needed in the planning stages if their area is complex or mission-critical. For instance, if the given SAP project is an upgrade to SAP ERP with the new G/L, a financials configuration new G/L specialist might want/ need to be engaged in this initial phase to support the project managers in high-level resource planning. Key functional configuration specialists do not necessarily need to be involved in the entire project preparation stage; their involvement only needs to be enough to provide valuable subject matter expertise not possessed by project management.

5.2.2 Blueprinting

Within the ASAP methodology, the "devil" lies in the blueprinting phase. After building the proper roadmap consisting of a timeline, activities, and resources during the project preparation phase, pen is put to paper and hardcore analysis begins. It is also during this timeframe that any new analysis gathered that impacts the original project plan is raised and the plan is modified accordingly (if justified). The key resources we'll describe in this section focus on this very important stage and are responsible for raising any red-flags.

Senior level planners and project managers fade slightly into the background at this point, making room for those responsible for executing the plan. Business analysts, functional configuration specialists, technical architects, and the like all descend on the project to perform as much analysis as possible.

The following are several of the key resources that should be engaged during this phase and the corresponding value they bring. The outsourcing component and team composition depends a lot on some of the key

Key resources during blueprinting

SAP initiative factors described previously in the book; however, key factors that influence the make up of the outsourcing team include the complexity of the SAP initiative, the extent of the business process/functional requirements, and (of course) cost.

▸ **Senior project management**
Although the majority of the efforts during this ASAP phase is performed by more of the "soldiers" than of the "generals," senior project management is still involved to ensure that the project remains on course. Key project management identified during the project preparation phase such as the senior project manager, senior functional configuration manager, and the senior technical manager all remain involved, managing the project closely to both budget and timeline.

▸ **Technical architect(s)**
Deep technical analytical firepower is typically required during this stage to both clearly understand the existing technical landscape (*as-is*) and the ultimate future state (*to-be*). During the blueprinting phase, these technical experts such as NetWeaver Basis architects, XI/PI architects, and EAI architects (including EDI, middleware, interfacing and data conversion, and transformation gurus) all investigate what activities need to be performed to get the organization into the proper new environment. These resources might investigate hosting possibilities, migration scenarios, and so on.

▸ **Lead developer(s)**
These individuals work primarily with their SAP functional counterparts to define — at a very granular level — what SAP development activities must be performed. These ABAP, Java/portal, workflow, and programming specialists create technical specifications, clearly articulating what new custom SAP programs and enhancements will be delivered as part of the final product. Lead by the senior technical manager, this group of "heads-down" programmers will ensure that the business process-desired functionality is possible both from a timeframe and SAP programmatic capability perspective.

▸ **Lead configuration specialist(s)**
Responsible for understanding and, in turn, defining the organization's ultimate business processes, this role (or group, depending on

project scope) works to bring the organization into the desired future state. If the project scope is also focused around business process reengineering, these lead SAP configuration specialists understand the existing business processes and also determine whether industry best practices as delivered by SAP's standard functionality are the right client fit. Responsible for all SAP functional specifications, this group works with their SAP programming counterparts to define what is possible with SAP and if desired, how to get there.

▶ **Business analysts**
Implementing SAP software without intimate client organization knowledge is futile. Every business has specific organizational processes (whether best practice/ideal or not) that make their environment unique. It is organizational business analysts who hold this knowledge. As part of the blueprinting phase, business analysts (per given relevant project functional area) act as the champions, oracles, and protectors of their business area. This group (almost always client representatives) work with the SAP functional configuration team to define the as-is state and what is their ideal to-be state. No one understands the organization's business better than this team; therefore, they play a crucial role in the design of the project blueprint.

5.2.3 Realization

This stage is where the rubber meets the road and where heroes are made. Although this statement is a bit (though only slightly) dramatic, the project team executes what has been defined within the blueprint (constructed in the previous phase). If every implementation followed what was directed in blueprinting, all projects would run successfully and SAP projects could run on auto-pilot. Unfortunately, this is never the case. Thus, the role of the project team during the realization phase is to react appropriately to bring the project back on course.

It is during this phase that most of the "heads-down" outsourced SAP resources are engaged, which typically work offsite. During realization, due to the nature of delivery, SAP outsourced resources are focused on execution; therefore, their involvement — although great — can be delivered remotely.

Key resources during realization

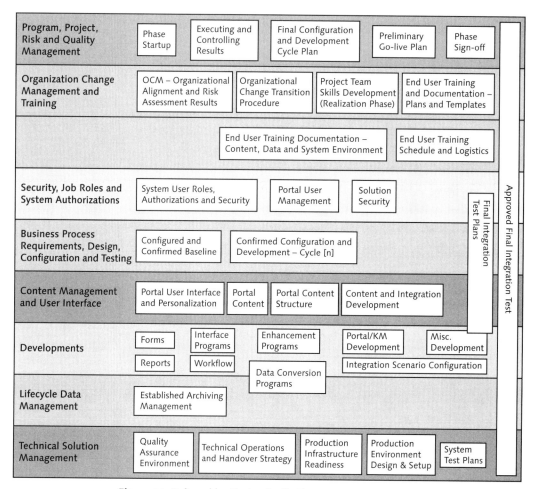

Figure 5.2 Deliverables During Realization

The major exception to this statement exists during the testing phases of realization. During this critical delivery stage, outsourced resources if offsite, should ideally be deployed onsite. The testing procedures and activities performed during realization cannot be only tedious but also challenging (as the point of testing is to detect errors). Therefore, during realization, these outsourced SAP resources should ideally be physically located with their customer business process counterparts to expedite this critical stage.

The following are several of the key resources that should be engaged during this phase and the corresponding value they bring:

▶ **Project management**

Similar to the earlier ASAP phases, project management is involved in this phase to oversee overall implementation progress. However, because the realization phase tends to be both the longest and the largest in manpower, project management must be heavily involved in all components ("moving parts") during this critical timeframe. Scope creep, failure to meet timelines, resource issues, and other typical project challenges all must be addressed quickly and resolved decisively.

▶ **Training manager/coordinator**

During the realization phase, new types of resources are brought into the project team, focusing on cursory but important activities. One such resource type relates to training. During the very beginning of this phase, the training manager/coordinator is responsible for developing a training curriculum for a multitude of users. These user groups may include project team members, super users, and end users. Moving from setting the curriculum to delivery, the training manager works with trainers to develop specific courses and to ultimately present the given material. All of these activities are performed together with the business to ensure that their perspective is properly represented.

▶ **Testing manager/coordinator**

The testing manager/coordinator has the thankless but critical role of ensuring that all of the proper testing is defined, performed, evaluated, and documented. With multiple testing phases (integration, end-user, user acceptance, regression, to name but a few) intended for different purposes and user communities, this pivotal position works long hours ensuring that everyone responsible for resolving issues follows through. Similar to the training manager, the testing manager's focus shifts from definition during the early stages of the realization phase to execution (and reporting) toward the end of this stage.

▶ **Quality assurance/testers**

These outsourced resources are crucial to the realization phase. Because testing must be part of any successful SAP initiative, these skill sets and corresponding resources provide all of the necessary testing support services. In some cases, the testing activities — although extremely important — are mundane and repetitive. Therefore, these types of realization responsibilities are ideal for your outsourcing provider: common activities of low complexity.

▶ **Change management**
A successfully implemented new SAP system is worthless without end-user acceptance and adoption; thus, this is where change management comes into play. This team is responsible for working with the training and testing teams, as well as with internal marketing, to promote the new SAP functionality and ensure that the organization is properly positioned to embrace the end product. Change management activities such as training and testing coordination begin at the early stages of the realization phase and continue through this phase via communication sessions with the end-user community (and executive management). Communication could include "lunch and learns," executive management embracement sessions, "all hands on deck" informative meetings, and so on.

▶ **Developers/configurators/business analysts**
Continuing their efforts from the blueprinting stage, all of the SAP developers, technical analysts, SAP functional configuration consultants, business analysts, and so on, now focus on translating the blueprint requirements into reality. This group is always the largest workforce within the realization phase and is the group that shoulders the most responsibility. This group also is the most visible throughout all of the phases across all ASAP project team members.

▶ **Global delivery/application management systems services**
If your implementation is leveraging offsite delivery, then this group of developers, configuration specialists, and administrators need to be heavily involved in the realization phase. Working in tandem with their onsite counterparts, this team performs the execution activities with direction from the offsite global delivery manager described previously.

▶ **End users**
Although not an outsourced SAP group, an organization's end users are a key project team population that provides tremendous value

and input during the realization phase. Specifically, this group participates extensively within the testing and training components of the realization phase. Playing both a more active participant role (during the testing phases), and a more passive observer role (during training), end users are integrated into the realization phase toward the later stages of the phase.

▸ **Integration manager**
One position that is widely overlooked and misunderstood is the integration manager. (This role is so important that an entire chapter — Chapter 13 — is dedicated to this topic.) Although not truly a role within the ASAP methodology, or a function within full-lifecycle implementations, the integration manager should be included in the realization phase because ultimately, the responsibility of supporting the system will fall into his domain. Every organization must grapple with how to support its productive SAP environment and one of the most effective first steps is involving the integration manager during the project build.

5.2.4 Final Preparation

Ready. Set. Wait!

At this point within the ASAP methodology lifecycle, the productive environment is poised for "prime-time," and the new SAP functionality is close to be becoming a reality. As the phase indicates, final preparations are made to ensure that go-live is as painless as possible. Rigorous cutover activities are performed, the "war room" is assembled, and late night pizza is ordered.

> **Stories from the Trenches: ASAP final preparation and the "war room"**
>
> During the final preparation phase just prior to go-live, projects bear down and prepare for the worst but hope for the best. An SAP time-honored tradition known as the "war room" is created at this time. It acts as the central headquarters and "nerve center" for all post-go live issues. Depending on the scope and breadth of the project, this command center is open 24 hours a day, seven days a week to support those now productive in the SAP environment.

Key project team members across the implementation — including business process functional configuration experts, super users, business analysts, and so on — are part of this task force meant to resolve issues during an agreed on "limited warranty" timeframe.

On a personal anecdotal note: While working in Brussels on a global SAP template implementation in the late 1990s, our international team was comprised of nationalities from around the globe. Because the project was based in Europe, many of the project team members were European. As go-live approached and the war room was to be assembled, the project management team comprised of Germans, English, Americans, Italians, French, Belgians, and so on, felt uncomfortable calling the war room the war room. After much discussion, our production support center was instead named "go-live headquarters."

Key resources during final preparation

The following are several of the key resources that should be engaged during this phase and the corresponding value they bring:

▶ **Cutover manager**

All eyes and ears remain fixated on this very crucial SAP position. During the project preparation phase, perhaps no other position holds as much clout and pressure as the cutover manager (except for maybe the project's champion[s]). During final preparation, the cutover manager is responsible for documenting all of the key cutover steps that must be taken during go-live; ensure that all of the resources are available and able to deliver; work together with the production support team to devise roles and responsibilities; and still maintain patience, control, and coordination. In smaller project teams, this role is sometimes performed by another team member such as the project manager, integration manager, technical manager, or strong key resource.

▶ **Project manager**

Almost out of the woods, so to speak, the project manager still remains ultimately responsible for the successful delivery of the implementation. Although the cutover manager alleviates some of the pressure, it's still the project manager's head if things turn bad.

▶ **SAP NetWeaver Basis administration**

Many technical activities around the NetWeaver stack are of high criticality (and visibility) during cutover. During this phase, key NetWeaver Basis administrators need to be heavily involved in critical activities such as SAP transports, SAP "box" optimization, and printer configuration and troubleshooting.

▶ **Production support/COE manager**

Depending on the long-term production support model chosen, key production support representatives should be included in the final preparation process and most organizations choose to hold the project team responsible for a specified "warranty period" after go-live. Integrating those responsible for maintaining the system during this phase (or, ideally, even earlier) assists in a smoother transition and more effective long-term support. At a minimum, the production support/COE manager should be included at this time to understand certain intimate details of the project, areas of potential challenge, and build relationships with key business analysts as well as project team members.

▶ **Integration manager**

Similar to the production support manager's role, the integration manager should be involved in the project to post-production transition. His role during this phase is mostly that of an observer attempting to gain as much knowledge and insight into what was implemented, via active observation and information absorption.

5.2.5 Go-Live and Support

Everything has now come to this point: go-live. The success or failure of the project up until now will be judged based on how smoothly go-live goes. Therefore, the team assembled for go-live support is crucial to organizational acceptance. Even issues arise, if they are resolved quickly and competently, the perception of success is saved. On the other hand, even if there are only a handful of issues but they are not resolved sufficiently enough per organizational opinion, the perception of success could be hindered

From an SAP outsourcing perspective, this might actually be the phase or hand-off that incorporates the most outsourcing. In many cases, customers view outsourcing as production support. Although this is not accurate, in some customer situations, it might be the case.

Even if the initial production support is being handled by your implementation team (which could still be comprised of some outsourcing resources), this might still present an excellent opportunity to engage an outsourcing provider for your production support services (see Chapter 6).

Key resources during go-live and support

The following are several of the key resources that should be engaged during this phase and the corresponding value they bring:

▶ **Security administrators**
Those who have participated in an SAP implementation and post-production support mechanism understand the amount of effort spent on SAP security. Most initial post go-live production issues are security-related, involving lack of proper SAP authorizations for end users. Therefore, having SAP security administrators available to troubleshoot and resolve end-user authorization issues is crucial to timely and effective post-production issue resolution. This role (or roles) works with business analysts to identify what additional SAP authorization is required while at the same time limiting unnecessary access.

▶ **Integration manager**
After go-live, responsibilities for the integration manager should increase dramatically. Activities previously performed by the project team leads and project manager now become the responsibility of the integration manager. There is much more to come on the subject this position and its corresponding duties, in Chapter 13.

▶ **Project manager**
Performing all of the necessary activities involved in project closure and transitioning responsibility to the appointed production support mechanism, the project manager then moves on to yet another high-paced, high-intensity implementation.

▶ **Production support resources**
A topic for a dedicated chapter, the production support resources (whether internal or external) now are responsible for "keeping the lights on," so to speak. Ranging from break/fix issues all the way up to

new initiatives (potentially including project-related initiatives), this long-term support mechanism takes over and continues to improve on what has been originally implemented during the project. If your organization chooses to leverage an SAP outsourcing provider for these support services, their involvement both strategically and tactically is mandatory.

5.3 Using SAP Solution Manager during Implementations

With SAP's strong promotion of SAP Solution Manager as both a robust tool with a wide rage of uses and a (from now on) mandatory component for all SAP platforms, it is no wonder that Solution Manager is now also promoted as a value-added *implementation tool*. Three specific Solution Manager features — one directly and two indirectly promoted by SAP — are excellent tools that can greatly assist productivity and long-term success during projects. All of these features — Project Administration/Work Centers, Maintenance Optimizer, and Service Desk, will be discussed in this section.

Touched upon earlier in the book, the use of SAP standard implementation tools such as those in Solution Manager is an excellent way to maximize your organization's interaction with your outsourcing provider. Regardless of whether you are the customer or the vendor, all organizations have different methods of how to drive an SAP implementation. Even though ASAP methodology is pervasive, its execution can vary from client to client. Therefore, the use of a common and widely accepted SAP project management tool is an excellent way to maximize your outsourcing relationship (and related end product).

Figure 5.3 shows a very high-level value Solution Manager proposition, including some of the functionality described in the features that follow.

Figure 5.3 SAP Solution Manager Value Proposition

5.3.1   Maintenance Optimizer

Mandatory tool

Of all of the Solution Manager features, Maintenance Optimizer is the least glamorous. However, due to SAP's following mandate, it is without question the most widely utilized. Per the announcement on SAP Service Marketplace:

> *"All corrective software packages, including support packages (stacks) for SAP NetWeaver 2004s and subsequent versions, as well as all applications that are based on this software, will be available exclusively through the Maintenance Optimizer in SAP Solution Manager as of April 2, 2007."*

Thus, moving forward, for all implementation-related work (as well as ongoing SAP operations); Maintenance Optimizer will be the "modus operandi" for keeping your SAP software platform running smoothly (pun intended.) Furthermore, any corrective SAP-created software (whether recommended configuration or core ABAP/Java code correction) will now only be available via Maintenance Optimizer (via SAP Service Marketplace).

(For those interested in navigating to Maintenance Optimizer, follow this path: TRANSACTION SPRO • SAP REFERENCE IMG • SAP SOLUTION MANAGER IMPLEMENTATION GUIDE • SAP SOLUTION MANAGER • BASIC SETTINGS • MAINTENANCE OPTIMIZER• SET UP WORK CENTER FOR CHANGE REQUEST MANAGEMENT — see also Figure 5.4.)

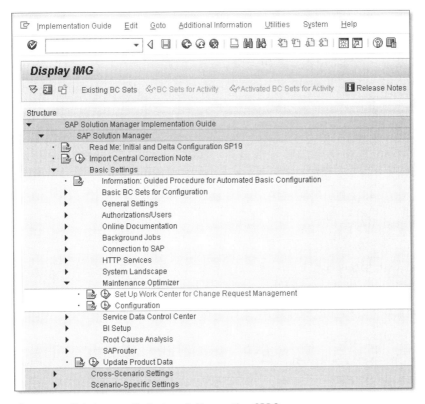

Figure 5.4 Maintenance Optimizer via Transaction SPRO

For those who take all of the background SAP NetWeaver activities for granted, this will be transparent. However, Basis administrators who keep SAP environments running smoothly will either already be intimately aware of Maintenance Optimizer or will be learning/using it in the very near future.

Maintenance Optimizer and its benefits can be used for all SAP applications, including earlier versions of core SAP such as SAP ERP 2004 and SAP R/3 Enterprise. However, if SAP support packages, patches, hot packs, and so on, for industry solutions are based on later SAP versions, they must now be downloaded through the Maintenance Optimizer.

SAP applications that require Maintenance Optimizer are as follows:

▶ SAP Business Suite 7.0

▶ SAP CRM 2005 and CRM 2007

▶ SAP ERP (5.0 and 6.0)

▶ SAP SCM 2005 and SCM 2007

▶ SAP SRM 2005 and SRM 2007

▶ SAP NetWeaver 2004s

▶ SAP Solution Manager 4.0 and 7.p

SAP applications that do not require Maintenance Optimizer are as follows:

▶ SAP APO 3.1

▶ SAP BW 3.0B

▶ SAP BW 3.1 Content

▶ SAP CRM 3.0

▶ SAP CRM 3.1

▶ SAP CRM 4.0

▶ SAP ERP 2004

▶ SAP NetWeaver'04

▶ SAP R/3 4.6C

▶ SAP R/3 4.6C (HR)

▶ SAP R/3 4.7x110

▶ SAP R/3 4.7x110 (HR)

▶ SAP R/3 4.7x200

▶ SAP R/3 4.7x200 (HR)

▶ SAP SCM 4.0

- SAP SCM 4.1
- SAP Solution Manager 3.2
- SAP SRM 2.0
- SAP SRM 3.0
- SAP SRM 4.0

5.3.2   Project Administration/Work Centers

SAP Solution Manager provides the tools and content needed to implement SAP solutions efficiently from both a technical and a functional perspective. All of this is integrated into SAP's ASAP project methodology. To fully support an organization's SAP implementations, Solution Manager provides implementation roadmaps via its Project Administration/Work Center feature.

Very few project management tools can better facilitate driving SAP projects with outsourcing providers than SAP Solution Manager's Project Administration (PA) component. This standard and common ASAP-integrated approach provides an excellent framework for managing SAP projects with your outsourcing partner.

PA is used most heavily during the business blueprinting and realization phases. Depending on whether you are performing analysis and data gathering activities or executing and developing functionality, different PA functionality is used differently.

For example during blueprinting, PA's business process repository functionality is used to capture your organization's business process requirements, documentation, and scoping documents. (Think of it as SAP's own business process document management repository.) This enables you to create your blueprint.

Business process repository

However, during realization, the use of PA is slightly different; in this phase, it can be used to capture configuration guides for standard business scenarios, project-specific implementation documentation, customized project-specific development, and so on. It can also be used for project-related testing services.

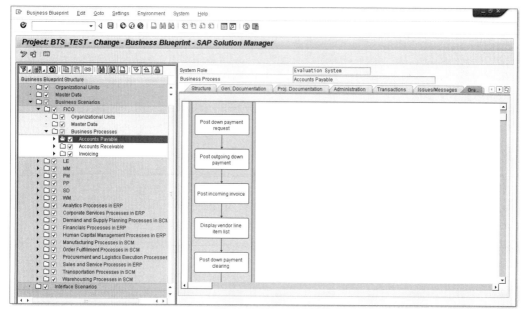

Figure 5.5 Example of Standard SAP Business Processes

Furthermore, one of the added benefits of working with PA is its tight integration with the SAP implementation guide (IMG) for the creation of SAP customization and configuration. By configuring a given business process within Solution Manager, you are able to directly link back to your core SAP environment for easy project-specific configuration.

Documentation value

Finally, most projects suffer from poor project documentation and even worse, poor relevant, ongoing operational documentation. By using PA as a project documentation tool (as well as for continued operations), your organization will be much better positioned. The bottom line is that SAP Solution Manager PA provides long-term value. Furthermore, making this step mandatory when utilizing an SAP outsourcing provider ensures that your organization is presented with the proper documentation as part of the overall outsourcing delivered package.

Testing

Another potential use of SAP Solution Manager during implementations is via the testing functionality within Work Centers (see Figure 5.6). This integrated, SAP-provided testing suite enables your organization to integrate testing into your implementation in relation to the work centers created within PA. Again, if utilized, this tight integration of business process and testing functionality enables your organization to leverage Solution Manager for multiple critical steps within the lifecycle in one integrated tool.

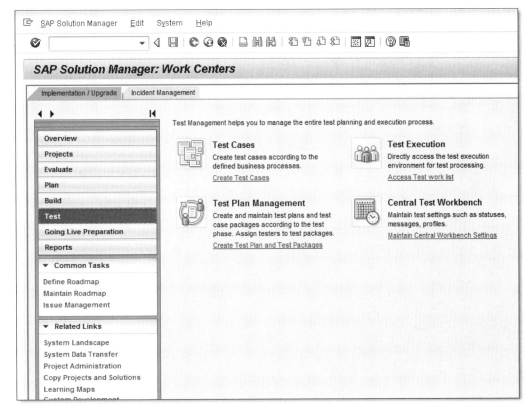

Figure 5.6 Work Center Testing Functionality

5.3.3 Service Desk

Although Service Desk was discussed briefly in Section 5.4 (related to post-production ongoing change management), it should also be mentioned when discussing implementations. Geared more toward ongoing post-production support, Service Desk can also be used as a valuable tool during project work to capture and track issues during system build (see Figure 5.7).

Figure 5.7 Service Desk Screenshot

Benefits during realization

During the realization phase — specifically regarding the construction and subsequent testing phases (regardless of whether you are using SAP testing functionality) — Service Desk can be used by the following project team members:

▸ **Developers**
SAP programmers can define the test plans and test scripts required per their respective developments areas. Also during unit, string, and integration testing, SAP developers can capture any bugs and related fixes either identified within their own code or within standard SAP code.

▸ **Functional configuration resources**
Similar to the development testing activities described, SAP functional configuration resources can define, document, and capture all testing phases specific to their given functional area.

▸ **Testing resources**
If an organization designates a specific testing team responsible for checking all project-related developments, this team can either work

with project team members to define the testing scenarios and then perform the testing or simply perform the testing after test scripts have been provided.

▶ **User-acceptance testing resources**
Leveraging Solution Manager's Work Center testing during user-related testing is also a beneficial scenario. This is a very important testing process both from a results and end-user "buy-in" perspective. Using Solution Manager testing functionality prepares the end user for SAP usage and builds the foundation for greater adoption and, in turn, acceptance (embracement).

5.3.4 Upgrades

Due to the number of organizations that will need to migrate from an older SAP platform to a more recent version, SAP Solution Manager provides multiple tools meant to ease the upgrade process. Specifically, Solution Manager provides what are called "upgrade roadmaps" — focused by SAP product — to speed up the migration process and lessen the pain.

Accelerators

SAPanese — Upgrade versus reimplementation

In the most technical sense, an upgrade within the SAP world denotes an actual SAP product versioning installation to a more recent release. Common examples include upgrading SAP's core ERP product from an earlier release such an SAP R/3 version to SAP ERP 6.0 or an SAP BW 3.5 release to SAP NetWeaver BW 7.0.

However, in some cases, organizations looking to get to SAP's "latest and greatest," perform a reimplementation instead, for various reasons (new start, highly customized legacy SAP environment, etc.). This reimplementation activity can be confusing for multiple reasons. Because organizations already have a productive SAP environment, a true upgrade approach seems to be the obvious approach. However, as mentioned, this might not always be true. Therefore, when dealing with a potential upgrade, be very clear as to what is going to be performed technically; it might not always be what you think.

Figure 5.8 shows the upgrade roadmap from within Solution Manager.

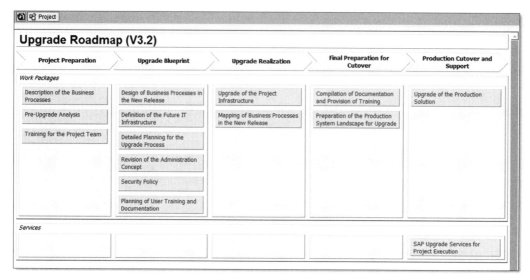

Figure 5.8 Upgrade Roadmap within SAP Solution Manager

Within each of these roadmaps are "accelerators" specific to the given upgrade product that support a more detailed business process. These accelerators cover over 90% of all defined application processes and 36% of all industry scenarios in 18 industry segments! For example, within the SAP ERP 6.0 roadmap, common business processes including financials, logistics, manufacturing, and so on are captured via designated accelerators. Table 5.1 shows some of the many valuable accelerators by source and target release. These types of upgrade "plug and plays" not only allow your organization to more rapidly upgrade your SAP environment, they also allow you greater visibility and autonomy with your SAP outsourcing provider.

Source — Release	Target — Release	Accelerators
SAP R/3 3.1i — SAP ERP 5.0	SAP ERP 6.0	110 (21 unique)
SAP Learning Solution 2.0 and 3.0	SAP Learning Solution 6.0	42 (15 unique)
SAP SEM 3.0 — 4.0	SAP SEM 6.0	49 (13 unique)
FSCM 2.0 and 3.0	FSCM 6.0	44 (16 unique)

Table 5.1 Upgrade Accelerators

Source — Release	Target — Release	Accelerators
SAP E-Recruiting 2.0 and 3.0	SAP E-Recruiting 6.0	45 (16 unique)
SAP cProjects 2.0 — 3.1	SAP cProjects 4.0	51 (41 unique)
ISA WAC 4.0	XECO 5.0	43 (16 unique)
SAP XXS 5.0	SAP XXS 6.0	39 (14 unique)

Table 5.1 Upgrade Accelerators (cont.)

The Solution Manager roadmap assists in facilitating the upgrade process through the entire lifecycle. Various components are available during each of the phases. For example, during project preparation, the project administration functionality is highlighted, enabling your organization to create the new upgrade project easily, including business-rich accelerators. During realization, instead of having to evaluate all of the needed upgrade delta configuration steps, Solution Manager's upgrade roadmap provides recommended upgrade and IMG configuration specific to your environment.

Another feature within the upgrade roadmap relates to project team training. Often underestimated and/or neglected, training the end-user community is typically either left to the last minute or left to any remaining budget.

Project team training

Leveraging Solution Manager's Learning Map Builder, you are able to create training material based on your upgrade materials created during blueprinting. This relatively intuitive functionality allows your organization to create role-specific learning maps. This upgrade feature can come in handy if you are low on additional funding for formalized training.

Real-life question: Can I leverage SAP Solution Manager's upgrade functionality without Solution Manager?

For organizations that do not currently leverage Solution Manager, other options exist. The Upgrade Roadmap is available as a standalone HTML version so that anyone can use it, even without SAP Solution Manager. Although not as powerful as a standalone (i.e., without true SAP integration), it nonetheless provides the SAP ASAP methodology, including all of the steps in an upgrade project.

However, according to Doreen Baseler of SAP AG in her article "How Solution Manager Can Smooth Your Next Upgrade Project," automation is one of Solution Manager's key value propositions. She explains that "it won't offer the automated access to content and tools such as upgrade and implementation content for new solutions, or system landscape analysis linked to your road-map as project accelerators that you'll find in conjunction with SAP Solution Manager." She recommends that to truly maximize Solution Manager's potential, one should install SAP Solution Manager along with the Upgrade Roadmap, especially because both are included with standard SAP maintenance costs.

SAP Solution Manager Roadmap packages multiple SAP products and functionality into a single tool. Those embarking on an upgrade, whether technical or functional, should definitely look into leveraging this no-cost SAP-supplied package.

Again, when specifically dealing with SAP outsourcing, Solution Manager can act as the central hub for collaboration between your organization, your SAP outsourcing provider, and SAP. Because SAP stresses this tool and its functionality so strongly, it is now no longer a nice-to-have when working with partners but rather a required component. Whether leveraging Solution Manager PA as a central repository for both clients and customers for all upgrade activities or other valuable steps, Solution Manager should be part of your SAP outsourcing strategy.

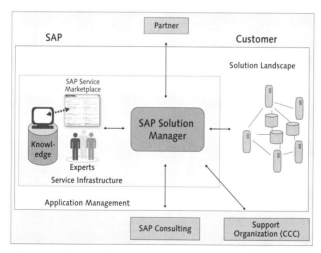

Figure 5.9 The Solution Manager Epicenter

5.4 Using the Custom Development Management Cockpit (CDMC) for Upgrade Preparation

Another useful tool outside of Solution Manager for upgrade initiatives is SAP's Custom Development Management Cockpit (CDMC). When working with your SAP outsourcing provider focused on an upgrade initiative, there is tremendous value in leveraging such a standard, SAP-provided accelerator. First, it ensures that your provider does not "reinvent the wheel," and second, it provides a high level of visibility of their actual activity. This SAP-provided tool provides great value for projects attempting to better understand what potential issues might exist within custom development in their SAP landscape.

Because most SAP installations make modifications to their SAP environment in some form or another, it is important to understand very well the potential impact when migrating from an earlier SAP release to another. Although some customers limit their modifications to organizational custom reports, others perform extensive custom developments, including — in some cases — making core SAP program modifications. (The latter practice is highly discouraged for a plethora of reasons!) Although custom SAP development provides clients with solutions tailored specific to their needs, this functionality can cause challenges in long-term maintenance and — for the purposes of this discussion — upgrades.

Impact of custom development

Because all organizations have some form of custom development, this can lead to an increase in your total cost of ownership (TCO). TCO is increased because custom development requires additional maintenance. Furthermore, during upgrades, it can be difficult to identify the need for some developments, in turn requiring unneeded analysis and resulting in wasted resource time.

The manual activities involved and corresponding work effort can be tremendous. For example, having to upgrade to a higher SAP release or applying support packages requires the labor-intensive exercise of research, testing, and analysis. This process represents a considerable amount of effort.

To address this issue, SAP provides its CDMC tool.

CDMC Features CDMC addresses the previously mentioned issues by providing a tool focused on the task of handling ABAP custom development objects in SAP environments. SAP's CDMC can:

▸ Analyze custom developments in your SAP system and identify obsolete developments (clearing analysis)

▸ Identify the potential consequences of an upgrade on custom developments (upgrade/change impact analysis)

Clearing analysis Two components of CDMC are focused on analysis activities. The first is known as *clearing analysis*. This feature enables you to analyze all of the custom objects and modifications made to SAP standard objects. This analysis allows you to clearly identify used and unused custom objects and modifications that might need to be upgraded as part of the migration. Furthermore, it allows you to delete custom objects and modifications no longer needed in the system. The clearing analysis process is referred to as the *clearing process*.

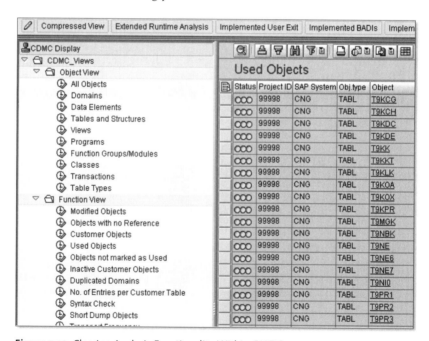

Figure 5.10 Clearing Analysis Functionality Within CMDC

The second CDMC component is known as upgrade/change impact analysis. It assists in the identification of potential impact areas a support package or upgrade might run into on any custom developments in the system. This component focuses on non-SAP program provided custom developments.

Upgrade/change impact analysis

The CDMC utility — which is delivered at no additional cost to customers — provides a comprehensive canned analysis feature. This allows organizations to see development impacts on both sides of the fence: core SAP-modified developments and non-SAP delivered custom developments.

Although it is not a silver bullet to fix all of the potential issues identified from the analysis, it does provide a good baseline and easy method of providing the information necessary for customer action. Both components include intuitive reporting features that provide detailed analysis ready for action.

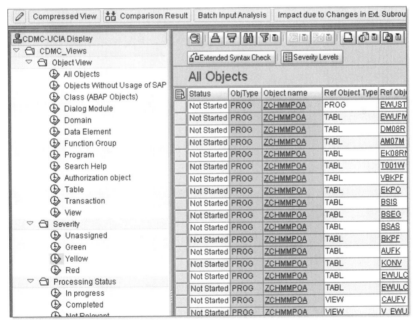

Figure 5.11 Upgrade/Change Impact Analysis Functionality Within CMDC

The search for static security — in the law and elsewhere — is misguided. The fact is, security can only be achieved through constant change, adapting old ideas that have outlived their usefulness to current facts.
— William O. Douglas

6 Production Support

When one thinks of SAP outsourcing, production support almost inevitably comes to mind; one might even go as far as saying that the terms have become synonymous. This now ubiquitous form of BPO has historically been associated with maintaining the ongoing operations of an SAP environment. This model typically exists as a break/fix mechanism — one focused on "keeping the lights on."

In this section, we will explore this type of SAP outsourcing and its various aspects including:

▶ Several of the most common production support models/options in the marketplace

▶ SAP's operations-focused methodology Run SAP and its advantages

▶ SAP's enterprise support and what it means for your production support environment

▶ SAP's business processes and technical areas that lend themselves well to the production support model

▶ Solution Manager tools focused on optimizing operations (Central System Administration and Central System Monitoring)

6.1 SAP Production Support Models

There are a myriad of SAP production support models; however, two are primary models: the first — break/fix — focuses on the bare minimum, while the other — production support plus — expands slightly beyond basic operational support to include enhancement development, not just support (see Figure 6.1). Although several of the main decision-making factors for which model to employ have been discussed at length earlier, just to reiterate, the primary factors are bandwidth and cost.

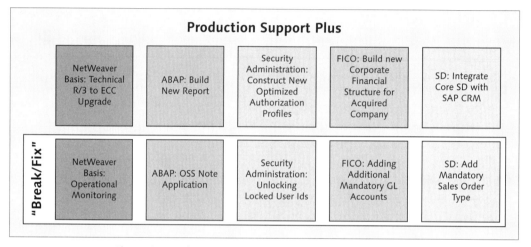

Figure 6.1 Production Support Plus' Expansion of Break/Fix

Let's dig deeper into these two models and how your organization can tactically leverage each alternative.

6.1.1 Break/Fix Model

Some organizations choose to only provide the bare minimum support for their SAP production environment. As described briefly in Section 4.2.6, this is known as the break/fix model. Companies who leverage this model can choose to utilize SAP break/fix outsourced mechanisms for a wide range of SAP areas, technologies, and functions.

As the name suggests, modifications to the productive environment are limited to changes that "fix" a business deficiency. *No enhancements are included in this model! Regardless of how small the new functionality may be, it cannot be done.*

Outsourcing these types of functions — that is, routine, non-strategic, "robotic," and so on — to an SAP-centric outsourced provider enables your organization to focus on higher priorities. Many organizations across the spectrum have found this support alternative to be a cost-effective and optimal method of keeping their SAP environment stable and running.

Focus on higher priorities

Multiple SAP areas lend themselves well to this model. Here are several examples:

▶ **Vanilla SAP installations**
As with many SAP installations, organizations look to implement SAP ERP with minimal customizations. These types of organizations make great candidates for the break/fix model. Because little additional enhancements were included in the original implementation, the production support lends itself well to this outsourcing alternative. Furthermore, if an organization was successful in limiting any client modifications during the initial project, there is a high probability that no further modifications will be necessary.

▶ **Upper midmarket space**
If your organization sits squarely within the yearly revenue band between $300 million and $1 billion, it is a likely candidate for leveraging the break/fix model. Most organizations within this space do not have the appropriate resources or desire to internally build a comprehensive support mechanism. Even if an organization wishes to internally support a subset of the areas, this does not preclude the offloading of another area. For example, perhaps your organization wishes to support level 2 and above areas, while offloading level 1 services to free up time and money.

▶ **Leveraging an SAP hosting provider**
If your organization is already working with an external SAP hosting provider for your NetWeaver operations and maintenance, moving up the food chain, so to speak, should not be a major transition and it might even be the next logical choice. Because your organization is already comfortable with leveraging SAP outsourcing for some of your NetWeaver Basis needs, broadening the outsourcing scope to other technical components such as ABAP and Security Administration should not be that challenging.

▸ **Upgrading to ERP in the "near future"**

If your organization's platform sits on an earlier version of SAP, including a version of R/3 (R/3 3.1H, R/3 4.x, or ERP 5.0) and you plan to upgrade to SAP ERP 6.0 within the next several years, the break/fix model might be the answer. With the upgrade looming on the horizon, there is little need to either modify your existing SAP functionality and/or make any investment into a soon-to-be-outdated version. Instead of spending the money, limit your modifications by enforcing a break/fix strategy. This approach positions your organization well for the upgrade ahead of you.

▸ **Acquisition mode**

Although an organization should not necessarily limit its activity based on an uncertain future, some organizations strategically position themselves as acquisition targets. (Some organizations even implement SAP to make themselves appear more attractive to potential suitors!) Thus, if an organization is positioning itself for a buy-out, additional SAP customization is not the easiest sell for IT integration. Minimizing SAP code change is the answer in this situation. The break/fix model provides clear, corporate vision and evidence to those looking for quick SAP system integration.

> **Case Study: Tuthill Corporation's NetWeaver operational (break/fix) model**
>
> Having implemented SAP ERP 5.0 in 2006, Tuthill Corporation — a diversified global manufacturing company developing and supplying industrial products in over 150 markets — had initially chosen to support their NetWeaver operational activities. However, shortly thereafter, they decided to leverage an outsourced partner focused on these more technical activities. Dan Amend, Tuthill's SAP director, remembers making the switch and never looking back. "Our move to NetWeaver outsourcing enabled our SAP production support team to focus on level 2 and above issues. Although we still do maintain some SAP technical resource skill sets internally (such as ABAP and security), Basis is out." This mostly operational NetWeaver support model provides Tuthill with an expert partner committed to a wide range of Basis activities such as transport windows, system performance tuning, system monitoring, system copy maintenance schedules, and other break/fix activities. Furthermore, agreed on service levels, metric reporting, and resolution agreements provide the proper teaming framework. Amend believes that for his situation, operational SAP services can be better served by outside services.

He writes: "We felt that the more commoditized type break/fix SAP Basis services were better suited to external partners. Our approach has allowed us to keep our eye on the ball."

6.1.2 Production Support Plus

If your organization needs more than just operational support and password resets, your solution is production support plus. As Figure 6.1 above shows, production support plus is simply the natural extension of break/fix, expanding support coverage from operations through production support enhancements. Coverage stops when true project work is required and either a different model or a different team (i.e., global delivery, implementation team, upgrade team, and so on) must be engaged.

> **SAPanese: What constitutes a "project" per the production support plus model definition?**
>
> Although the definition for what constitutes a "project" is subjective per organization, traditionally, the metric used is approximately 80 hours. That is, if a given development or customization requires approximately two weeks worth of dedicated resources, most organizations would consider this a project and in turn, the project would either be covered via the "plus" component within production support plus or handled via another team.
>
> However, the 80 hour threshold needs to be known upfront. This caveat provides the framework for defining an initiative as a project, that is, the amount of effort is known *prior* to embarking on the project. Of course, some development efforts are thought to be small amounts of effort at first and then balloon to well above the time frame initially anticipated. In these situations, there is nothing one can do (except do a better job next time in estimating new work).

In the production support plus model, SAP outsourcing still remains focused within the operations space; however, as part of normal day-to-day operational support, organizations sometimes still require enhancement efforts. Let's take a look at several examples on where this model and additional effort can be utilized:

Enhancements included

▶ **Routine new functionality**
  If an organization performs routine activities based on their business

model (e.g., adding new companies to their business requiring new SAP company code construction and supporting financial structures, or developing new projects requiring setup within project systems) it makes a lot of sense to have your production support plus mechanism handle these types of tasks. In these types of scenarios, your outsourcing mechanism can construct a checklist and then easily execute tasks on an as needed basis.

▶ **Low hanging fruit**
Inevitably, in every implementation, decisions are made limiting delivered functionality. Whether the decision is made to use ABAP-related custom developments such as customized client reports instead of standard (and limited) SAP reports or to use manual workarounds for relatively easy automated interfacing (think daily exchange rate table maintenance), the business always wants more. The production support plus outsourcing delivery model can provide low cost and low complexity developments (also called "low hanging fruit") with little investment and larger business return.

▶ **Midmarket**
For many smaller organizations, building a comprehensive SAP production support mechanism is not feasible, optimal, or desired. Furthermore, for those who work with SAP intimately, enhancements rarely — if ever — stop. Therefore, many midmarket organizations have found that working with outsourcing providers specialized in SAP production support plus is a far more optimal arrangement. With the myriad of production support models available from SAP outsourcing providers (including fixed-fee, monthly minimum, and "pay-as-you-go" models), cost effective alternatives have proven to be a large seller to this segment of the market. (Furthermore, with SAP focused on growing this market segment aggressively in the near future, this post-production support strategy and engagement model will continue to mature, commoditize, and decrease in cost.)

6.2 SAP's Run SAP Methodology and its Advantages

Focused on providing a complimentary, operations-focused methodology to its existing implementation methodology (ASAP), SAP created

Run SAP. This end-to-end continuing production support and ongoing improvement model focuses on five key areas:

▶ **SAP standards for solution operations**
Ensures that a given organization is working with operational best practices, including tools and standards.

▶ **Roadmap and Best Practices documents**
Establishes a framework beyond pure operational activity for new implementation work.

▶ **Training and certification**
Educates organizations on the latest and greatest SAP functionality via training and, in turn, certifies that the organization is prepared to work with the functionality.

▶ **Services**
Provides SAP consulting professional services as a delivery vehicle, if desired.

▶ **SAP Solution Manager**
SAP's highly effective tool can be leveraged in a wide variety of process improvement areas.

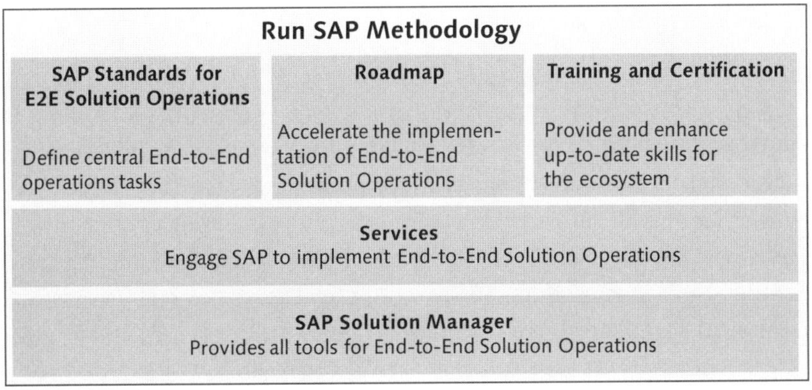

Run SAP Methodology		
SAP Standards for E2E Solution Operations	**Roadmap**	**Training and Certification**
Define central End-to-End operations tasks	Accelerate the implementation of End-to-End Solution Operations	Provide and enhance up-to-date skills for the ecosystem
Services Engage SAP to implement End-to-End Solution Operations		
SAP Solution Manager Provides all tools for End-to-End Solution Operations		

Figure 6.2 SAP's Run SAP Value Map

6.2.1 Why is Run SAP Important for Organizations?

For organizations exploring the possibility of leveraging an SAP outsourcing partner, Run SAP should come into play. At the time of this writing, Run SAP as a codified SAP methodology has only been recently introduced to the marketplace. Therefore, most organizations and partners have not had the opportunity to become certified. Nonetheless, just as ASAP methodology has become the standard (and requirement) for SAP implementations, so too will Run SAP become an operational mandate. Therefore, when choosing with whom to partner, certified Run SAP outsourcing organizations should be considered. Although not necessarily the "end all, be all," this should be a determining factor in how your organization approaches SAP operational support (whether break/ fix, production support plus, or other).

Likewise, if your organization is looking to supplement its production support or COE with external production support resources, Run SAP certification and/or experience working within a Run SAP operational environment might be additional criteria.

6.2.2 Run SAP Advantages for your Production Support Environment

Beyond adopting SAP's Best Practices for operational environments, adhering to Run SAP provides your organization several advantages. We'll explore them next.

Run SAP certification — SAP assurance

First off, if your organization has chosen to leverage an SAP outsourcing provider for any number of production support services, SAP's blessing is paramount. SAP's Run SAP certification provides this assurance. (SAP's current Run SAP certification program consists of two levels: global services and local services. If global support is important, be sure to look for a global services certified partner.) Although the Run SAP certification (nor any certification, for that matter) does not necessarily ensure that your production support partner will never make any mistakes, it does provide an additional level of credibility and added comfort level. Certification ensures that your provider has been trained on the phased methodology based on SAP best practice procedures, content, services, training, and tools for end-to-end solution operations. Working with a Run SAP certified organization gives your organization the opportunity to leverage proven operational procedures and supporting tools, ensuring that your environment is running optimally.

Figure 6.3 shows SAP's Run SAP ecosystem interplay (SAP, Partner, and customer). As you can see, SAP strongly promotes the use of third-party outsourcers (denoted as "AMS Provider" — Application Management Services — within the diagram) who have this accreditation. Within the context of the figure, you are able to see what target offerings and tools are integrated into this methodology.

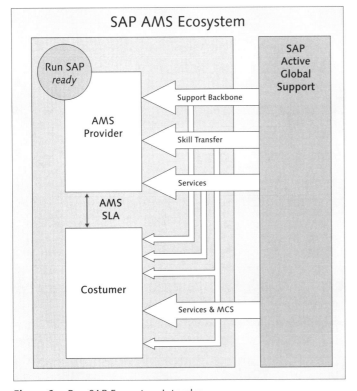

Figure 6.3 Run SAP Ecosystem Interplay

Per SAP's own value proposition declaration for Run SAP, the following four key offering are provided as part of this model:

Run SAP as part of SAP Enterprise Support

▶ Tools and Global Support Backbone integration

   ▹ SAP Solution Manager Service Desk

   ▹ Provider integration into SAP Global Support Backbone

   ▹ Access to preview/test new SAP solutions

- ▶ Skill transfer and enablement
  - ▷ IT-SAM and Best Practices
  - ▷ E2E standards and methodology
  - ▷ IT-governance model
  - ▷ Partner enablement services
  - ▷ Training and certification
- ▶ Services
  - ▷ Technical quality management and onsite engagement
  - ▷ SAP empowering and solution optimization
  - ▷ SAP safeguarding
  - ▷ Component integration
  - ▷ Balance investment protection
  - ▷ TCO reduction
- ▶ Mission-Critical Support (MCS)
  - ▷ Integrated escalation and exception handling
  - ▷ SAP ecosystem access and integration

As you know, Run SAP is heavily integrated with SAP Enterprise Support. This also exists as another advantage of working with a Run SAP-certified production support provider. SAP's new mandate for end customers to use SAP Enterprise Support as part of the relatively new licensing agreements has shifted how customers leverage SAP for software issues (i.e., software bugs/Notes via Service Marketplace). SAP Enterprise Support will be discussed in greater detail later; however, the point is that SAP's new SAP Enterprise Support model leans heavy on Run SAP. This, in turn, further substantiates why working with Run SAP trained outsourcers is very important.

6.3   SAP Enterprise Support

SAP's latest operations support service, which comes as part of an organization's software licensing costs, is known as SAP Enterprise Support. This support model can range from standard customer support to SAP software maintenance support all the way up to comprehensive SAP production support services — utilizing SAP Global Support for your company's production support needs (if you were not aware, SAP offers its own SAP outsourcing services).

Shown in Figure 6.4, the SAP Enterprise Support service offering is delivered via three key SAP methods: Run SAP (SAP's proprietary operations best practice methodology), Mission-critical Support (SAP's most responsive operations consulting services offering), and Global Support Backbone (SAP's standard support tools and services such as marketplace). These three primary and complementary delivery alternatives provide organizations with the value propositions necessary for maximizing your organizations SAP investment.

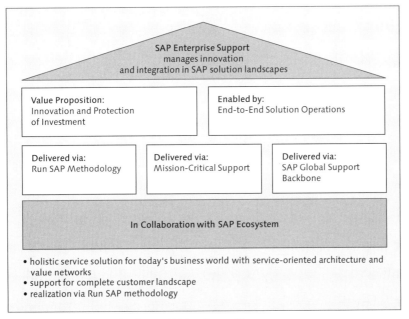

Figure 6.4 SAP Enterprise Support Value Proposition

Assuming that your organization is not using SAP Global Support and is instead using third-party production support services, the question that comes to mind is: *"Why is SAP Enterprise Support important?"* We'll look at this next.

SAP Enterprise Support provides your organization with a specific level of client support. As mentioned earlier, this level includes base soft-

Benefits

ware-focused issue resolution rather than configuration or implementation of specific code. Therefore, when working with an SAP outsourcer, it is imperative that clear support roles and responsibilities are defined and understood. Because multiple support mechanisms could be engaged at a single client (including client production support resources), it is crucial that all parties are aware of which production support responsibilities will be handled by their own organization and which by their respective partners. In some areas, undefined lines between support groups could cause confusion.

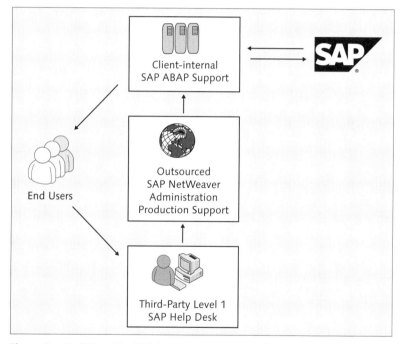

Figure 6.5 Multi-Provider SAP Support Integration with SAP Enterprise Support

Example process   Let's look at a production support model that includes SAP Enterprise Support:

1. As with 95 % of production support issues, an end user begins the support process by identifying an issue, in this case, within an SAP-provided report: A calculation in the SAP report is not accurate.

2. In this organization, a third-party SAP help desk is leveraged primarily for SAP security password resets and simple SAP navigation ques-

tions. Because the issue identified by the end user needs to be handled by level 2 resources, the help desk assigns the ticket to a different outsourced provider for NetWeaver administration production support.

3. After brief investigation, the outsourced Basis production support provider identifies that the issue is an ABAP-related issue and reassigns the resolver group to the ABAP production support team, a customer-internal mechanism.

4. The client's ABAP support team (which now owns the issue) digs into the SAP code (whether SAP delivered or client custom development) to address the issue. After some investigation, standard SAP code is identified as the source of the problem and that resolution will require SAP Enterprise Support. The ABAP team then creates a Service Marketplace ticket (OSS Note).

5. Via SAP Enterprise Support, SAP confirms that the issue is an SAP base-code issue, creates a fix for the issue, and sends the Note (including the issue resolution details) back to the ABAP team for customer environment application.

6. After applying the code, testing its effectiveness, and confirming that it resolved the issue, the ABAP team notifies the end user that the issue has been resolved and that it can be closed.

As you can see, a simple issue such as this requires multiple resolution parties, *including* Enterprise Support. It is therefore imperative that third-party SAP application management services support mechanisms understand who needs to contact SAP Enterprise Support under various scenarios. Depending on the situation, different parties might contact SAP Enterprise Support.

6.4 SAP Business Processes and Technical Areas that Work Well for Outsourced Production Support

Certain SAP business functions and technical areas are better suited for an outsourced production support model than others. Although the decision-making factors are numerous (not even speaking to the non-SAP related factors described earlier such as corporate culture, perception, etc.), the following are several best practices that could be followed:

▶ **SAP hosting**

Outsourcing an organization's SAP infrastructure from a hardware, software, and supporting services perspective can be an easy cost savings proposition. With numerous proven SAP hosting providers as well as flexible packages based on a laundry list of choices (database, operating system, availability, number of users, etc.) available, SAP hosting has become a popular production support option. (This holds especially true within the midmarket space, to be discussed later.)

Scope of hosting services

One note regarding external SAP hosting services: most SAP hosting providers provide the infrastructure administration (such as database and operating system) and NetWeaver operational support services; however, they do *not* provide anything beyond these services. If your organization is looking to outsource SAP application-level functions (such as ABAP, security, functional configuration, etc.), these need to be provided by another SAP provider.

▶ **SAP NetWeaver operations**

SAP infrastructure is typically another "easy sell" for SAP outsourcing. As opposed to having your internal resources spend energy on carrying out daily, mundane Basis activities such as checking background jobs, reviewing system logs, and so on, their valuable energy can be spent on other — perhaps more strategic — responsibilities. Using certain Solution Manager accountability and visibility tools such as Central System Administration and Central System Monitoring (discussed in Sections 6.5.1 and 6.5.2), can make working with outsourced NetWeaver partners much easier.

▶ **Level 1 and 2 support**

Using SAP outsourcing for lower levels of SAP production support is another common customer practice. Whether the services provided are more technical in nature (such as the resetting and unlocking of SAP userid accounts, NetWeaver transports, systems performance oversight, etc.) or functional (end-user basic SAP navigation, unlocking of financial posting periods, maintenance of master data, etc.), outsourcing more routine activities provides your organization with the freedom to focus on more strategic and business-focused areas.

▶ **Custom development**

Without question, this area (and skill set) is the most readily available in the marketplace. In fact, SAP custom development was the first outsourced SAP offering. This commoditized delivery option behaves very much like a factory and fine-oiled machine. Custom development objects such as ABAP WRICEFP and Java/portal objects are particularly easy ways to leverage SAP BPO. With such an array of choices and availability of skilled SAP development centers at your disposal, sending this type of SAP work to an outsourced provider could be a cost-effective way to reduce development expenditures.

6.5 Tools to Optimize your Production Support Center

Regardless of whether your organization chooses to work with an SAP outsourcing provider for production support services, many powerful SAP tools exist that can assist in optimizing your operational services. (Even better, because they are part of Solution Manager and thus your existing SAP licensing agreement, the software is free!) Several of these tools such as Solution Manager Project Administration and Service Desk have been covered earlier but should still be considered valuable tools in this discussion!

If your organization is interested in engaging with an SAP AMS provider, several of the tools we will discuss in this section are invaluable. Leveraging tools such as Solution Manager's Central System Administration and Central System Monitoring can prove to provide excellent oversight and management functions. Because the functions of these tools assist in providing an operational administration framework and standards, their use can give you great insight and reporting into the activities that your SAP production support partner is performing (or conversely, not performing).

SAPanese — SAP Solution Manager's evolution

SAP's Solution Manager product suite (we'll call it a product suite due to its wide range of functionality and breadth of capabilities) has evolved greatly since the release 2.1 days of 2002 (refer to Figure 6.6 for a high-level diagram of its evolution). Since these early days, Solution Manager has developed from a NetWeaver- and technical team-focused SAP services optimization tool into a pivotal component within SAP's strategic toolkit.

The suite of Solution Manager tools is now the epicenter for most SAP initiatives, methodologies, and processes. Whether for its function as the foundation for all SAP Service Marketplace system downloads via Maintenance Optimizer; for its use for SAP implementations via PA; as Run SAP's primary tool for optimizing SAP operational processes; or for its many additional features described in this section for managing SAP outsourcing partners, Solution Manager is here to stay.

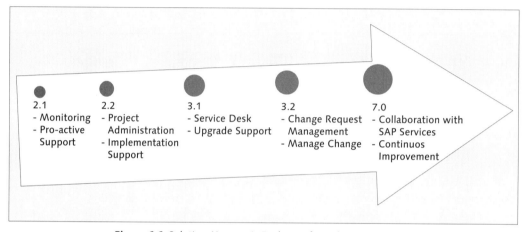

Figure 6.6 Solution Manager's Evolution from the 2.1 Days to Today

6.5.1 Central System Administration

In short, Central System Administration (CSA) is a central repository for all NetWeaver administration activities. This Solution Manager tool documents and provides visibility into all of the tasks your NetWeaver team should be performing on a regular basis (hourly, daily, weekly, etc.). Furthermore, it lets you see whether the activities have been performed, when they were executed (date/time), and allows for administrator notes and other handy features. *The bottom line is this: If you are leveraging a third party to support your NetWeaver platform, you must implement CSA!*

NetWeaver administration operational Best Practices

Another great feature of CSA is all of SAP's recommended best practice tasks. Out-of-the-box CSA provides hundreds of suggested component-specific administrative tasks (both ABAP and/or Java), based on the system that is assigned to a solution landscape. Using the graphical inter-

face, you can easily see what uncompleted tasks exist and receive alerts
for these open items (see Figure 6.7).

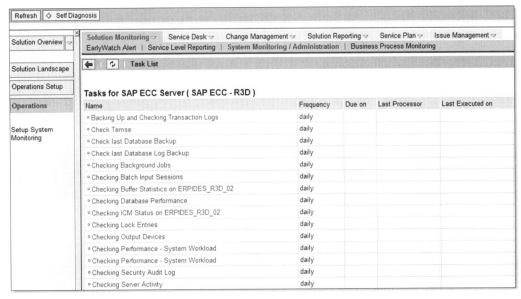

Figure 6.7 CSA Task List Including Customized Client-Specific Tasks

This depth of visibility and transparency provides an invaluable tool for
gaining insight into the activities performed by your outsourced
NetWeaver partner. No longer are activities hidden and uncertainties no
longer exist as to what your offsite partner is actually doing. Using CSA
allows your organization to easily understand what you are paying for
and, in turn, modify priorities, activities, and even providers if necessary.

As part of CSA, your organization can take advantage of SAP's recommended activities but can also add customized client-specific tasks. For
example, if your organization has created custom interfaces, you can
capture tasks associated with it. Such task might include checking that a
given background job executing the interface program performed properly; that you received an acknowledgement from the receiver; and that
the transmission report was delivered to the appropriate business user.
Previously, all of these activities would have been captured via an Excel
spreadsheet or sticky notes. Now, the tasks are documented centrally,

capturing all records automatically as to what was completed, by which user, and the activity date and time. Knowledge is now available to the team and is no longer available to only a select few. This empowers the organization and safeguards against loss of information during attrition.

Standardization of tasks

As with everything in SAP systems, there are a million ways to perform a single task. With CSA, however, you can standardize activities. If, as an organization, you believe that there are specific methods for performing a given task, CSA allows you to capture this process and make that process the standard. Not only does this allow your overall NetWeaver operations environment the ability to standardize system maintenance but it also facilitates knowledge transfer. As part of "out-of-the-box" CSA functionality, all tasks contain standard SAP documentation. Even better, CSA allows you to include your own company-specific documentation! This feature standardizes tasks completed by technical resources, whether they are part of your internal NetWeaver administration resource pool or whether you are working with an outsourced partner.

CSA canned reporting

Enhanced oversight is not as powerful without the ability to report on it. As part of standard, "out-of-the-box" CSA functionality, this Solution Manager tool provides multiple methods of reporting. From within Solution Manager, CSA allows you to easily create reports in either Word or HTML format. Both versions provide easy-to-use, easy-to-understand, comprehensive reporting details. Figure 6.8 shows an example of the HTML version.

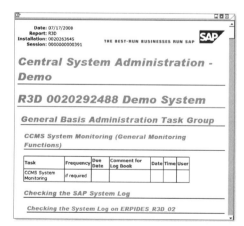

Figure 6.8 Example CSA Canned Report

CSA provides real-life solutions to day-to-day issues. Table 6.1 is a snap-shot of some of the challenges that can be tackled via CSA.

Example
CSA scenarios

Challenge	CSA Solution
Ensuring that your SAP hosting provider is performing all required activities.	With CSA, you are able to easily report on open tasks and how completed tasks were performed.
Verifying that systems are not only functional but are also being maintained properly.	By documenting all of the necessary tasks within CSA, beyond the functional, you are able to see what outstanding items remain.
Capturing what activities are being performed by the internal Basis team today.	You can leverage CSA as a repository for the tasks performed by your existing staff; and know what they do and when. After standard and custom tasks are configured, the transition to an offsite team becomes more fluid.
Sharing Basis activity workload and reduce impact when someone leaves the organization or goes on vacation.	You can pull back the curtain on tasks performed by all of your system administrators; ensure that your outsourced providers assign tasks to their backup resource during vacation or sick days; and activate email alerts.
Standardizing the team's NetWeaver administration tasks so that everyone (including outsourced resources) performs the given tasks using the same method.	You can easily upload your organization's best practice documentation for any task. Make this method the single method of execution.
Providing long-term support for activities, including the maintenance of customized objects.	You can add a custom task to CSA that covers the custom interface end-to-end, including items both inside and outside of the SAP system. This will allow your outsourced provider to easily support the development.

Table 6.1 Challenges and Respective CSA Solutions

6.5.2 Central System Monitoring

Another Solution Manager tool that can empower your organization is Central System Monitoring (CSM). Regardless of whether your organization uses an outsourced provider, CSM provides robust operational system information crucial to the effectiveness of your overall SAP production environment. Furthermore, if your organization uses an SAP AMS, this information is invaluable.

Although capturing and acting on this type of information is possible without implementing CSM, the effort involved would be tremendous. By utilizing CSM, all of the monitoring, and corresponding configuration and setup is easily controlled via a central location.

Let's first learn what CSM does and then why it can be a great safeguarding management oversight tool.

CSM features   CSM is a holistic Computing Center Management System (CCMS). As opposed to performing CCMS activities on each of your organization's respective environments (by landscape: DEV, QA, PROD; or by product: ERP, CRM, XI/PI, etc.), CSM acts as the central hub with visibility to all SAP CCMS activities. For NetWeaver administrators, this all makes sense. For the layman, here is the basic purpose: CSM provides your NetWeaver team valuable connectivity/availability (are all SAP and non-SAP systems up and running) and quality (are users able to access these systems) metrics. Based on how you choose to configure CSM, you are able to leverage a range of alerting mechanisms for proactive information gathering and resolution. Figure 6.9 is a pictorial representation of CSM and its alerting and reporting features.

Leveraging CSM with Offshore Providers   Due to CSM's strong reporting and proactive alert monitoring features, organizations working with third-party NetWeaver operation providers now have the ability to both clearly understand and monitor what their provider is doing (and how they are performing). Similar to CSA, CSM empowers your organization to understand the up-to-the-second health of your SAP landscape; therefore, if issues exist and your provider is not resolving or worse, not acting on them, you now are in the know.

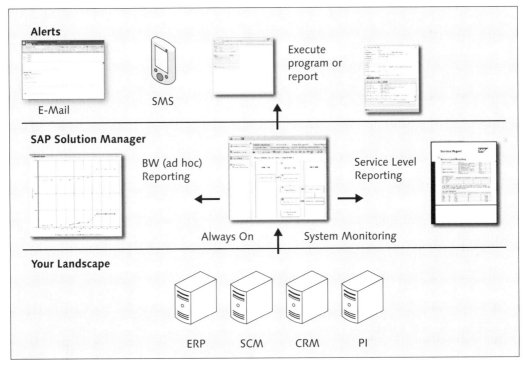

Figure 6.9 CSM Alerting and Reporting Features

CSM can communicate with all of the systems any SAP environment might touch. Of course, CSM can speak with SAP environments; however, only with SAP releases later than or equal to R/3. Likewise, CSM can also communicate with non-SAP components, regardless of whether they are Java-based. Because Solution Manager can work with the dual ABAP and Java stacks, communicating to multiple environments is seamless.

Based on the alert settings configured, your organization can see vital statistics about your landscape. Examples include the following:

Benefits of alert settings

▶ **Security oversight**
  With CSM, you can use CCMS agents to monitor cross-application system logs focused on security events. If a user account gets locked, an entry is written to the system log (Transaction SM21). A monitoring agent for the system log can pick up all activity in real time, which

can trigger an email alert. This is an excellent proactive tool to monitor potential system attacks if several user accounts get locked at the same time.

▶ **Disk space**
Disk space is precious, especially when speaking about SAP system transaction logs because overloaded transaction logs can cause critical issues. If a transaction log logical disk fills up, transactions within the SAP system will come to a grinding halt, which will, in turn, slow down your business. By proactively configuring trigger alerts focused on monitoring disk space and based on your organization's customized thresholds, you can automatically trigger notifications.

▶ **J2EE components**
Standard with CSM are several canned CCMS agents. One such agent is SAPCCMSR, which monitors J2EE components. Using the SAPCCMSR agent, the system is able to monitor web services on SAP and non-SAP landscapes (it's more of an "are you there?" monitoring/listening agent). Whether employing real-time or batch interface programs, it is important to know if the sending and receiving systems are both available. Many organizations have sophisticated customer and vendor web-based applications that are critical to running their business. Failure to have any part of the interface work properly could not only cause critical business delay but even worse, result in loss of revenue.

Having the ability to understand your SAP landscape's health status at any moment in time in real-time empowers your internal NetWeaver/infrastructure management team and ensures that your business continues to run smoothly. Furthermore, this vital information enables visibility into your outsourcing provider's activities and holds them to the highest performance standards. (Not that you need to be suspicious but having them know that you are watching doesn't hurt.)

6.5.3 SAP Solution Manager and SAP NetWeaver BW Integrated Reporting

Another valuable reporting technique you can use to optimizing your production support center is leveraging both SAP Solution Manager and

SAP NetWeaver BW in tandem. "Out of the box" standard Solution Manager and SAP NetWeaver BW enable you to run a range of valuable reports that can provide important metrics/statistics related to your out-sourced SAP provider.

Some of the reports include important information such as system avail-ability, Service Desk messages or change request management across your SAP landscape. (Although this reporting functionality is available as part of standard SAP systems, there is still some development effort and configuration required as part of setup.)

Let's assume that your organization is working with an SAP outsourcing provider to support a given business process level 2 SAP functionality such as SAP ERP 6.0 Financials configuration break/fix. From within SAP NetWeaver BW, your managers could review the history and trend-ing involved in the level of service and corresponding SLAs.

Another valuable Solution Manager and SAP NetWeaver BW reporting mechanism you can leverage for measuring your SAP outsourcer's per-formance is Central Performance History (CPH, see Figure 6.10).

Central Perfor-mance History (CPH)

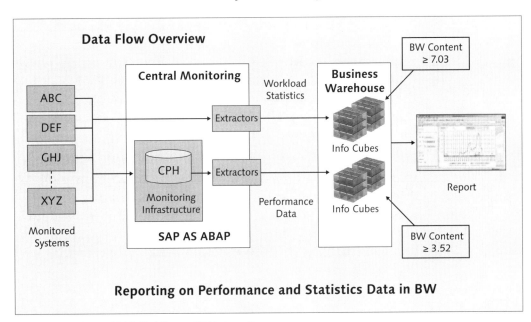

Figure 6.10 CPH and SAP NetWeaver BW Integration

As you can see in the figure, Solution Manager's CPH allows you to centrally monitor all of your SAP (and non-SAP) landscapes via real-time monitoring of technical SAP components and business processes. This should reduce the entire NetWeaver administration effort. By leveraging this Solution Manager feature, all of your monitored systems (as depicted by the "Monitored Systems" on the left side of the figure) provide valuable data to CPH. Utilizing standard SAP provided extractors, SAP NetWeaver BW can provide performance reporting and statistics. This is all out of the box!

This feature provides two benefits:

1. **Recognize areas of opportunity**
   Regardless of whether you are working with an SAP outsourcing provider, CPH reporting provides your technical NetWeaver manager or internal Basis team with visibility into SAP landscape issues. And regardless of whether you have defined specific SLA's, this reporting ability enables your organization to pinpoint SAP system problems and then act on them, if desired.

2. **Partner effectiveness**
   When dealing with SAP outsourcing providers, a common challenge and issue cited by clients is measuring partner effectiveness. With CPH, your organization can accurately measure operational effectiveness against SLAs. If your agreed on SLA with your SAP hosting provider requires a specified metric such as system availability for your production landscape, hard and cold statistics can easily, quickly, and accurately answer that question.

CPH can be used as an effective and meaningful method to identify how your overall SAP environment is performing via SAP NetWeaver BW. This is especially valuable for organizations that are utilizing an SAP outsourcing provider to support their SAP infrastructure operational activities. This centralized collection and long-term reporting capability for your SAP landscape can provide an effective tool for optimizing your SAP operations.

6.6 Managing Work Effort

To ensure that production support needs are properly addressed, an organization should employ some method to manage and track effort. This philosophy holds true regardless of whether an organization is working with an outside SAP outsourcing provider or handling all of the work effort internally. This effort is handled via two components: process and tools.

6.6.1 Managing the Work Effort Process

Philosophically, when dealing with any SAP effort (project, upgrade, production support, etc.) that is being delivered by multiple resources and potentially across multiple decentralized locations, a work effort process is imperative. The rationale for this is multi-fold. Here are several of the primary reasons that a formalized process is required:

▶ **Human nature**
Although every manager would like to believe that his employees are working to task, unfortunately this is not always the case. Being on top of this is even more important when working with distributed organizations where virtual management takes place.

▶ **Productivity**
Even if employees are working hard — as is most often the case — productivity is sometimes still not at the needed level or falls short of requirements and we all understand that there is a distinct difference between working hard and working smart. Therefore, work effort, although tremendously important, is not the only factor involved in production. Without a formalized work management process, opportunities for improvement could not as easily be recognized.

▶ **Normal tracking**
Tracking work effort should be a common practice as a base standard for any SAP initiative. Understanding where your team is against what is/was planned is the only way to deliver your SAP project on time and within budget.

6.6.2 Formalized Proven SAP Work Effort Processes

The method used for managing efforts within SAP outsourcing initiatives comes down to each project and program management style. There are a plethora of options and this section does not pretend to be comprehensive. However, there are many more commonly utilized approaches that have proven to be very successful within SAP initiatives. One such formalized approach is the formal standing meeting. This work effort management meeting can manifest in multiple ways, as we will discuss.

"The 9:00am daily" The early morning, every day meeting provides a quick forum for SAP project management to highlight key activities and goals for the day. It also allows for project team members — whether onsite or offsite — to identify key issues and updates. The purpose of this meeting is to provide management-level direction in a concise manner. It is not meant to be an all-hands meeting with detailed, long-winded discussion.

"The round robin" Meant to serve a different purpose, the "round robin" meeting framework is meant for a broader audience than the "9:00am daily." Typically, this meeting is held at the team level, where each team member briefly describes his work activities to his fellow team members. The sharing of information assists the entire team in reaffirming their understanding of the dependencies and knowing where team members should focus their efforts. If working with an outsourcing partner, this can be performed via many teleconferencing techniques including web conferencing, telephone, or video telecommunications. From a managerial perspective, this also provides management with a daily update as to activities going on.

Weekly planning Normally held early on in the workweek (such as on Monday mornings), team planning sessions provide the proper framework for what activities must be performed in the near term, that is, the upcoming week. This detailed planning session consisting of team members and their manager provides the opportunity to document and commit to the work effort that will be acted on. Typically, when utilizing this management model, very detailed activities are captured down to the half hour level. The execution logistics — such as those described in the round robin section — are equally as effective with this method. Also, various tracking tools exist that help facilitate such a detailed tracking process. This will be discussed next.

6.6.3 Tracking Tools

Beyond tracking management philosophy lays execution. The methods and first steps are important; however, without a formal tool to document and track progress, commitment and onus is next to impossible to enforce. The specific tools available in the market place are exhaustive; however, we will discuss several main and/or leading categories that have proven to be very effective when managing SAP outsourcing operations.

The defacto project management tool — right, wrong, or indifferent — is Microsoft Project (see Figure 6.11). This ubiquitous project management tool has been around for quite some time and has proven to be an effective method of documenting work tasks, their dependencies, associated team member responsibility, and planned deliverable due dates. Most everyone working in the industry is familiar with this tool.

Microsoft Project

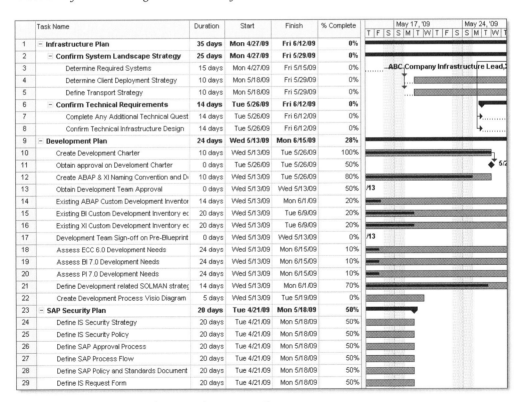

	Task Name	Duration	Start	Finish	% Complete
1	− Infrastructure Plan	35 days	Mon 4/27/09	Fri 6/12/09	0%
2	− Confirm System Landscape Strategy	25 days	Mon 4/27/09	Fri 5/29/09	0%
3	Determine Required Systems	15 days	Mon 4/27/09	Fri 5/15/09	0%
4	Determine Client Deployment Strategy	10 days	Mon 5/18/09	Fri 5/29/09	0%
5	Define Transport Strategy	10 days	Mon 5/18/09	Fri 5/29/09	0%
6	− Confirm Technical Requirements	14 days	Tue 5/26/09	Fri 6/12/09	0%
7	Complete Any Additional Technical Quest	14 days	Tue 5/26/09	Fri 6/12/09	0%
8	Confirm Technical Infrastructure Design	14 days	Tue 5/26/09	Fri 6/12/09	0%
9	− Development Plan	24 days	Wed 5/13/09	Mon 6/15/09	28%
10	Create Development Charter	10 days	Wed 5/13/09	Tue 5/26/09	100%
11	Obtain approval on Develoment Charter	0 days	Tue 5/26/09	Tue 5/26/09	50%
12	Create ABAP & XI Naming Convention and Dr	10 days	Wed 5/13/09	Tue 5/26/09	80%
13	Obtain Development Team Approval	0 days	Wed 5/13/09	Wed 5/13/09	50%
14	Existing ABAP Custom Development Inventor	14 days	Wed 5/13/09	Mon 6/1/09	20%
15	Existing BI Custom Development Inventory ec	20 days	Wed 5/13/09	Tue 6/9/09	20%
16	Existing XI Custom Development Inventory ec	20 days	Wed 5/13/09	Tue 6/9/09	20%
17	Development Team Sign-off on Pre-Blueprint	0 days	Wed 5/13/09	Wed 5/13/09	0%
18	Assess ECC 6.0 Development Needs	24 days	Wed 5/13/09	Mon 6/15/09	10%
19	Assess BI 7.0 Development Needs	24 days	Wed 5/13/09	Mon 6/15/09	10%
20	Assess PI 7.0 Development Needs	24 days	Wed 5/13/09	Mon 6/15/09	10%
21	Define Development related SOLMAN strateg	14 days	Wed 5/13/09	Mon 6/1/09	70%
22	Create Development Process Visio Diagram	5 days	Wed 5/13/09	Tue 5/19/09	0%
23	− SAP Security Plan	20 days	Tue 4/21/09	Mon 5/18/09	50%
24	Define IS Security Strategy	20 days	Tue 4/21/09	Mon 5/18/09	50%
25	Define IS Security Policy	20 days	Tue 4/21/09	Mon 5/18/09	50%
26	Define SAP Approval Process	20 days	Tue 4/21/09	Mon 5/18/09	50%
27	Define SAP Process Flow	20 days	Tue 4/21/09	Mon 5/18/09	50%
28	Define SAP Policy and Standards Document	20 days	Tue 4/21/09	Mon 5/18/09	50%
29	Define IS Request Form	20 days	Tue 4/21/09	Mon 5/18/09	50%

Figure 6.11 Example Microsoft SAP Implementation Plan

The beauty of Microsoft Project is its industry acceptance and ease of use. Almost every SAP project manager is familiar with Microsoft Project and its ability to let you plan easily, including dependencies, upper management acceptance, and SAP integration. (In fact, Solution Manager PA allows you to download the business blueprint activities from within Solution Manager into Microsoft Project!)

Solution Manager PA
Another potential use of Solution Manager is its project management tracking capabilities. Within Solution Manager's PA component, basic project tracking and analysis functionality exists. (These comments are based on Solution Manager's 7.0 enhancement package 1 version.)

Although a bit crude, there is a nicely woven integration between the business blueprint activities and this feature. PA's tracking features allows management to assign team member responsibility, actual and planned delivery dates — all specific to a given project administration node. Furthermore, via Transaction SOLAR_EVAL, basic tracking reporting is available.

Development implementation plan
Especially useful for development management, the development implementation plan (DIP) is a powerful tool that can be utilized to define, track, manage, and report against all SAP (and even non-SAP) developments.

This Microsoft Excel spreadsheet tool provides a clean and centralized tracking method for capturing all development activity requests during the course of a project or focused SAP initiative.

So how does the DIP work? During blueprinting activities, the business process teams define all potential developments within their respective areas. This will include any of the standard type of SAP custom development objects such as reports, enhancements, interfaces, conversions, forms (Smartforms and SAP Script), portal iViews, workflows, and so on.

Case Study: The hip DIP in action with Josh Baillon

While working on multiple implementations as a Custom Development Delivery Manager, Josh Baillon, a veteran Senior SAP consultant of over 15 years, has found the DIP to be a very valuable and powerful tool, affectionately coining it the "hip DIP."

Using it on every project for which he has held managerial responsibility, Baillon attributes delivery success to "its comprehensive and robust tracking capabilities." Baillon has driven complex and large SAP development efforts via the DIP (among other tools) to enable a clear understanding of the work effort at hand between the technical team and business process. "The DIP essentially provides a contract of sorts between the development team and our respective counterparts. With clear published and agreed on delivery dates along with business process responsibility, we are able to accurately and easily track progress. The excuse of 'I didn't know' is no longer a valid excuse." Baillon's hip DIP has been a constant stable within his repertoire, one he is unwilling to let go.

Depending on how a project team wishes to utilize the DIP, non-SAP development activities may be included as well as developments that touch and/or impact the SAP initiative. Examples might include legacy system re-writes for interfaces or elimination of functionality, third-party integration activities, internal website modifications, and so on.

Figure 6.12 The All-Powerful DIP

As the SAP implementation progresses, the DIP can be updated with responsible delivery team members including technical (programmers, IT analysts, architects, etc.), business process (functional configuration consultants, business analysts, business process owners), and testing resources. Furthermore, if a development is no longer needed, it can still remain on the DIP (as opposed to being deleted) to provide a history or inventory of all original development requests. (These eliminated requests can then potentially be transitioned over to a "wish-list" to be tackled at a later time).

> **Note**
>
> The DIP is not meant to act as an ongoing repository for *all* SAP development activity after go-live. There are other, more effective tracking tools for such work efforts.

Off-the-shelf, detailed work effort tools

If you are looking for more of a third-party, off-the-shelf work effort tracking tool, an entire market space is devoted to this. These work tracking tools provide a software product designed exclusively to document, track, assign, and report against.

The value of a formalized tool is that it clearly assists in enforcing the formalized process. Such a tool also enables the team to truly understand to which work activity they are assigned and what effort remains. When working with such a tool, the work effort "chunks," "stories," or tasks should be broken down into detailed work activities associated with an actual estimated work effort.

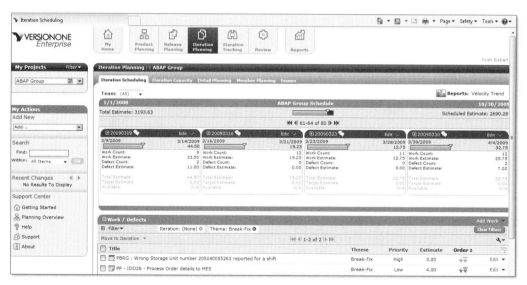

Figure 6.13 Example Off-The-Shelf Tracking Tool

The work effort breakdown thresholds are entirely dependent on the organization's desire; however, the point of leveraging a formalized work effort tracking tool is two-fold: to clearly define work to be performed and then accurately capture *actual* work effort. Therefore, creating a work effort of 40 hours does not clearly identify what activities comprise the work effort. In some cases, organizations choose task activities to be detailed to the half hour level. Thus, work effort by task is assigned to the responsible team member at a granular level.

There are multiple methods of utilizing the tool but typically, the work assignment effort is either handled by the manager independently (the manager assigns work effort to his respective team members) or collectively (the team sits together and each team member defines what work activity he will perform in the coming week, with management buy-in; this process is often handled in the weekly planning meeting described earlier).

Although utilizing such a tool can often benefit organizations, as with anything, potential drawbacks exist. Here are several of the main potential challenges that could actually hinder work effort progress:

Drawbacks

- ▶ **Another tool**
  Using another software product specifically for tracking work effort might be viewed as needless. Use another tool for this purpose? Why not just use Excel?

- ▶ **Additional maintenance**
  Along the same train of thought, using another tool requires additional training, maintenance, and support.

- ▶ **Decrease in productivity**
  Although this argument might be more difficult to prove, there could be a decrease in overall productivity if too much time is spent working with/on this tool as opposed to the actual work. If too much planning is spent on defining work effort and activity, coupled with extensive maintenance, the tool itself could contradict its very purpose.

Therefore, an organization must explore whether these types of tools ultimately improve overall productivity or, conversely, hinder it. For structured organizations that require high visibility and metrics for resource productivity, such a tool might be of great value. However, for organizations that operate more effectively in a less formal environment, these types of tools might backfire. As with much of this overall outsourcing discussion, the decision to leverage this tool and methodology should be addressed on a case-by-case basis.

Change is the essence of life. Be willing to surrender what you are for what you could become.
— Anonymous

7   Global Delivery

Global delivery has emerged as a relatively new, widely accepted SAP outsourcing mechanism previously unexplored. Depending on who is providing the definition, however, the services involved can vary significantly. For some, global delivery equates directly to standard SAP production support while to others, it is far more robust.

In this chapter, we will discuss the various aspects and key value propositions surrounding global delivery, including:

- ▶ A basic definition, including advantages and disadvantages of partnership
- ▶ Center of Excellence (COE)
- ▶ Customer Competence Center (CCC)

Again, for some, these are all nuances and marketing. However, it is important to be familiar with the different terms to be able to speak the appropriate language and ultimately define what your organization requires.

7.1   The Basics

In its most boiled down definition, global delivery is a combination of both ongoing operational SAP support *and* as needed implementation services. The extent of what specifically is covered within either of the services is completely dependent on the customer, the respective needs/ initiatives, and the construct agreed on by both parties.

Operational support and implementation services

Regardless of the extent of SAP outsourcing services, the fundamental point is that the service offering spans both some form of implementation *and* production support delivery services. Failing to incorporate both of these primary pieces results in an SAP outsourcing model other than global delivery.

7.1.1 Advantages of Global Delivery

One partner   The primary advantage of global delivery is the ability to work with a single SAP outsourcing partner for multiple and parallel services. This "one stop shop" is one of the most recognized (if not *the* most cited) value proposition.

Engaging a single outsourcing provider allows the selected SAP outsourcing provider to become truly intimate with your organization on a range of levels. The following are several of the main advantages:

▸ **Ramp-up time**
If you engage a single global delivery partner for all of your SAP needs, the "ramp-up" time is eliminated after the very first "ramp-up" period. This overreaching advantage enables much quicker execution throughout the relationship. Imagine how much energy and effort is spent each and every time a new partner is brought into your organization as part of an SAP initiative. This is eliminated with the "one-stop shop" approach.

▸ **Business processes**
Understanding an organization's specific business processes and special areas that set them apart from the competition not only takes time but potentially might include dealing with sensitive corporate information. Working with a single organization for both your SAP projects as well as production support enables your outsourcing provider the ability to leverage gained knowledge and continue delivery momentum.

▸ **Corporate culture**
Much focus is spent on the SAP-specific components of partnered outsourcing. Conversely, not enough focus is placed on the non-technical SAP aspects. One important facet that impacts productivity is corporate culture. Every organization has a unique corporate "way of

life," which in some cases takes time and energy to understand. Learning an organization's culture provides credibility and employee acceptance. Regardless of SAP technical knowledge, failing to "click" bi-directionally (organization to partner and partner to organization) could be debilitating to outsourcing success.

▶ **Administration/logistics**
It is not uncommon within larger organizations for partners not to receive SAP logins, networking authorization, and other taken-for-granted due-diligence access until more than two weeks *after* a partner has been brought on board. Furthermore, if your organization is working with an outsourcing provider in areas some distance away, setting up networking channels and taking the proper security measures could take even longer. You can mitigate this challenge by working with a single SAP outsourcing provider.

▶ **Single point of responsibility**
Working with one global delivery organization consolidates the number of partners an organization works with and thus, all responsibility lies with a single SAP outsourcing group. Conversely, when dealing with multiple (and competing) SAP outsourcing providers, lines of responsibility typically become a bit blurred regardless of how hard a client tries. When issues arise (and they always do, even in the best of cases/relationships), finger pointing runs rampant. With one outsourcing provider, responsibility is clear and understood.

7.1.2 Disadvantages

No model in SAP outsourcing is without its disadvantages and global delivery is no different. One might even make the argument that choosing a single provider for all SAP outsourcing services could be wrought with risk and even dangerous. Here are several of the primary arguments against global delivery:

Again: one partner

▶ **Best of breed**
Working with a single SAP outsourcing provider for all of your delivery needs might not provide your organization with the best services available within a given area. Depending on how robust your needs are, your chosen SAP outsourcing provider might not be the strongest

delivery partner across all of the services provided. This holds especially true when dealing with specialized and hard to find SAP services. For example, if your organization is looking for Business Planning and Consolidation (BPC) implementation services along with SAP-IS Professional Services production support, you might be hard pressed to find a single provider who excels (i.e., is the best of breed) in both areas.

▶ **Too much risk**

Another common argument against a single outsourcing provider is risk because working with a single provider places all of your risk *and* trust in a single resource. Of course, every organization has a different risk tolerance and for some organizations, this is not an issue. For others, it is too much of a potential bomb waiting to explode. A recent high-profile SAP outsourcing provider situation highlights the potential issues that can exist even with some of the most-respected organizations in the industry (see the Satyam case study in the box).

Case Study: Satyam and the risk of putting all of your eggs in one basket

In January 2009, the outsourcing world was in a buzz over the fourth largest global outsourcing provider, Satyam Computer Services. Satyam, one of the strongest players within the outsourcing space, including SAP Global Delivery services, had revealed that its chairman had systematically falsified accounts and revenue reporting. Setting the industry into turmoil, this powerhouse serving over a third of the Fortune 500 companies across the globe forced clients to quickly reevaluate their outsourcing partnerships and even switch from Satyam to its competition.

As recent as December 2007, Forrester Research touted Satyam as "a leader in SAP implementation services" (December 28, 2007; The Forrester Wave™ Vendor Summary, Q4 2007). "Satyam has a strong overall value proposition in addition to a long track record with SAP. Its client satisfaction scores are high, its pricing is reasonable, and a large number of clients were willing to attest to its value. Satyam's SAP capability put it at the top of the Forrester offshore SAP services Wave evaluation conducted in 2005."

Working with Satyam for SAP Global Delivery services caused some organizations to reconsider their SAP outsourcing approach philosophically. Obviously, this scenario does not hold true for all or even a majority of the SAP outsourcing providers.

This situation was truly a surprise to almost everyone. Nonetheless, when exploring SAP outsourcing, organizations must enter into this space with their eyes wide open because working with SAP outsourcing providers is wrought with risk even when dealing with some of the seemingly most reputable providers in the world.

7.2   Center of Excellence (COE)

The concept of a COE has been around for quite some time within the SAP world. Organizations either wishing to build internal core SAP competencies or to work with external SAP providers have leaned on these models for years for comprehensive production support and ongoing SAP initiatives and enhancements. The COE model is perhaps one of the most recognized forms of SAP Global Delivery.

The almost ubiquitous term of COE has flooded the SAP world. However, depending on the individual and their respective experience and perspective, the definition provided might differ either slightly or greatly from another's.

SAPanese: COE

The term COE has a very specific meaning within the SAP world. Although COE means center of excellence to most organizations, COE as defined by SAP designates "center of expertise." The center of expertise concept is actually a specific, two-level SAP accreditation program that designates an organization's capabilities as a center of excellence.

There are two levels of SAP Center of Expertise certification. The first level — known as the primary certification level — designates that an organization has the basic infrastructure and fundamental elements of a basic COE (expertise) organization. The advanced certification focuses on the additional integrated quality management functions, including SAP's Run SAP methodology.

In the past, COEs traditionally have been focused on acting as the primary support mechanism for SAP production support. However, due to their success and growing popularity, COEs have expanded their coverage to include more than "keeping the lights on" and COEs have grown to include additional enhancement activities.

Production support

The extent of how much additional coverage is included with the COE model depends completely on the client's wishes, outsourcing tolerance, and SAP outsourcing partner's capabilities. Also, as with any of the outsourcing models, a COE can manifest in any number of ways.

Focused excellence   To specialize and differentiate themselves from the competition, some SAP outsourcing providers focus on a specific subset within the greater SAP space. Here are several of the different categories in which SAP outsourcing providers have specialized:

- **Product**
  Some SAP outsourcing providers have specialized to focus on a specific SAP product (such as NetWeaver Basis) or module (such as SAP ERP Financials) while others have focused on a more robust suite of interrelated SAP products (such as *all* of ERP 6.0, including NetWeaver and technical services).

- **Industry**
  Certain organizations desire their SAP outsourcing COE providers to understand the specific nuances within their industry. To meet the customer demand, SAP outsourcing providers have arisen specializing within SAP's IS functions. This requirement was primarily driven by the unique business functions specific to a given IS product. For example, Oil & Gas's Joint Venture Account and Production & Revenue Accounting are unique features and configurations within SAP's IS-O&G. Due to the specific IS functionality within these given business functions, some SAP outsourcing COEs have specialized to serve this market need.

- **Market size**
  Another common COE differentiation relates to market size. This is most apparent within the midmarket space. For a number of reasons (described previously), the midmarket space has found it cost prohibitive to build a comprehensive internal SAP COE. As such, the SAP outsourcing world has responded with a market-focused approach of providing comprehensive SAP Global Delivery capabilities to this market. Large enterprise organizations also leverage COEs; however, due to their expanded set of options, these Fortune 500 organizations tend to outsource a bit differently and rarely outsource their entire SAP COE responsibilities.

▶ **Service level**

Sometimes, COEs are designed based on service level requirement. If an organization wishes to carve out a component within their overall SAP outsourcing pie by level of resolution complexity, the service level-based COE is their model. For example, an organization may wish to outsource all of their level 1 (Service Desk activities such as basic navigation and password resetting) and level 2 activities (more complex SAP resolution such as SAP master data creation) but leave the most complicated level 3 activities to their internal SAP COE, or vice versa. Regardless of how an organization slices and dices their COE responsibilities to their SAP Global Delivery partners, the service level-driven COE is driven by resolution complexity and thresholds.

Although not tremendously common, some global delivery COEs have been born out of an organization's internal SAP IT department. For a myriad of reasons (corporate contraction, tough economic times, entrepreneurial aspirations, etc.), these previously internal SAP COE support mechanisms have morphed from full-time employees to SAP Global Delivery COEs almost overnight.

COEs arising from internal IT departments

From the customer's perspective, the beauty of this model is twofold:

▶ From an organizational perspective, no knowledge is lost

▶ The cost is moved from an operating expense to a discretionary expense

If your organization switches to this model (and assuming that all of the employees remain with the COE), your organization loses nothing from a knowledge and experience perspective. This fact is amazing. It provides your organization with the luxury of maintaining the same level of global delivery capabilities without missing a beat.

Experience

Case Study: Ouest Business Solutions

Ouest Business Solutions, an SAP consulting company providing practical business solutions to their clients, is based out of Vancouver, British Columbia, Canada. This global delivery organization originally was born out of the world's largest gold mining companies and their in-house SAP implementation and sustainment team. Tanya Peachey, Ouest CEO and co-founder, started this company in 2006 to support its previous employer and expand its services to other SAP clients.

Peachey believes that the value proposition that Ouest provides both its previous employer and current client is a true market differentiator. "Our understanding of our client's SAP environment holistically — both technically and from a business process perspective — is a distinct market differentiator. Because we were part of the original sustainment organization, we intimately understand the design and the initial thought process behind the design. This provides us deep insight and knowledge obtained after much involvement with the client. For us, it is inherently built into our model." Due to Ouest's genesis, their value proposition to their former employer is easily understood. While Ouest and the outsourcing model of being born out of an internal IT department is not very common, when it does occur, the win-win scenarios for both SAP outsourcing partner and client can be tremendous.

Cost The other advantage from a corporate perspective revolves around the discretionary shifting of cost. When previously utilizing internal SAP resources to provide COE SAP services, unless your corporation was willing to let go of employees, the employee cost was fixed and ongoing.

However, when shifting to this arrangement, your organization has much more flexibility around pricing and resource needs than before. For example, previously, your organization may have carried the cost for an entire 20 person SAP team regardless of utilization. Within this new SAP Global Delivery mechanism, this is no longer case.

Depending on how your arrangement is structured, the client is now able to design a delivery model that can be flexible and nimble. Perhaps a fixed monthly retainer construct is arranged or a "pay-as-you-go" model. Regardless of the specific model, the opportunity now exists for greater flexibility surrounding cost. Whether it is used is completely up to the partners involved.

7.3 The Rise of the Customer Competence Center and the Center of Expertise

With so many organizations either investing internally, with the construction of a COE, or leveraging third-party SAP COEs, CCCs or Centers of Expertise (SAP COEs) have quickly been becoming the next desirable accreditation and designation.

CCC's and SAP COE's are essentially COEs from an SAP perspective (see the "Real life question" box). SAP's CCC concept was created to address several key deficiencies within the SAP partner ecosystem. We will next discuss several of the primary reasons.

Any SAP organization with a call-in hot line and a warm body can call themselves a COE; however, their true capability to effectively meet the needs of their respective business lines is not guaranteed. With the creation of the SAP CCC model, organizations around the globe can now clearly articulate what exactly an SAP CCC consists of. This common language ensures that SAP CCCs in Australia provide the same levels of services as those in Minneapolis.

Creating a common language

The scope of services between CCCs may differ greatly from one SAP CCC to another; however, the baseline model and characteristics are now consistent from CCC to CCC. Via SAP's CCC certification process, the fundamental building blocks are mandatory for an official CCC designation. This accreditation allows SAP clients to now have the confidence that if blessed by SAP, the CCC organization has — at a minimum — the appropriate qualities worthy of an SAP CCC.

Creating a baseline model

The greater SAP outsourcing community has a unique perspective on what truly constitutes an SAP COE. This no longer holds true for an SAP CCC. Similar to the baseline model value proposition, the creation of the SAP CCC designation ensures that all vendors tow the line and agree to what is and is not a CCC. (This designation is becoming highly sought after by SAP outsourcing providers as the market demand increases.)

Elimination of SAP partner interpretation and misrepresentation

Finally, the key characteristics required for CCC designation have been established and provided to the SAP ecosystem. The four primary building blocks required for the establishment of a CCC include:

Defining the key CCC elements for any SAP COE

- ▶ Support desk
- ▶ Information management and internal marketing
- ▶ Development request coordination
- ▶ Contract management

These pillars provide the proper foundation for strong, comprehensive, and end-to-end SAP operational support.

The evolution of
the CCC: From the
tactical to
the strategic

Paul Kurchina has been an SAP customer since 1993 and has been involved in numerous SAP full-lifecycle implementations and many post-production support mechanisms. Through his extensive customer and SAP user group experiences, Kurchina has been involved with the design, construction, and operation of multiple SAP CCCs.

From his perspective, the standard functions of a SAP CCC began as focused break/fix reactionary vehicles geared toward keeping a system up and running. However, in his view, as the CCC model matured, CCCs have evolved from a focused, tactical, and operational SAP production support mechanism to more of a strategic corporate vehicle. This new approach has likewise created a new COE term, the Customer Center of Excellence (CCoE). According to Kurchina:

> *"With the evolution of SAP's product suite such as NetWeaver, a CCoE is now required to be much more strategic in nature. Now, a CCoE is also forced to look beyond just SAP needs. Based on the very nature of the SAP product integration with tools such as Enterprise Portal, Master Data Management (MDM), and the Process Integration (PI) Infrastructure, we are now required to interact with more non-SAP systems, keep our overall systems evolving, and deliver greater organizational business value."*

Although all of this information is well and good, the question remains why this is important when dealing with an SAP outsourcing firm? The reason is that if the organization is a CCC, then there is an extra level of credibility. Why? Read on!

Real life question: What is the difference between a COE, SAP COE, and CCC?

Depending on whom you ask, a great deal. With the onslaught of centers of excellence (with the term being used generically here) from both a client and SAP outsourcing providers perspective as well as with the wide range of definitions propagated throughout the SAP world, SAP as an organization has found it necessary to design a designated certification program for COEs. This certification designation is officially known as the "SAP Customer Competency Center" ("SAP CCC") or "SAP Center of Expertise" ("SAP COE").

Until recently, SAP's CCC designation was *the* sought-after SAP center of excellence (with the term again being used generically here) certification. However, very recently, SAP rebranded the SAP CCC designation to SAP Center of Expertise.

This evolution involved more robust requirements based on Solution Manager enhancements. (For more information see "FAQ — Customer Center of Expertise" on the SAP Service Marketplace at *https://websmp105.sap-ag.de/~sapidb/011000358700001464952008E.PDF* for more information.)

The structured certification process is divided into two distinct phases:

▶ Preparation phase

▶ Certification audit and service report

After a successful audit from SAP's auditors, an organization is officially blessed and deemed a certified COE for a period of two years. (Every two years, an organization must reapply for the COE designation.) Beyond the benefits of the official certification and the corresponding SAP recognition, the certification process itself provides the customer with a tremendous amount of experience and knowledge gained. Focusing on process improvement and end-to-end SAP support services enables CCCs to better streamline their SAP operational capabilities and, in turn, better support the business. For more information regarding CCCs, refer to *Implementing SAP Customer Competence Center*, by Boris Otto and Jörg Wolter (SAP PRESS 2009).

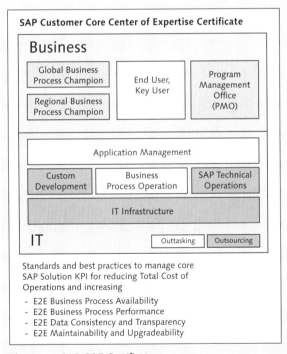

Figure 7.1 SAP COE Certificate

7.4 Summary

Global delivery is another effective SAP outsourcing delivery mechanism that provides comprehensive implementation *plus* production support capabilities. Whether the model is designated Center of Excellence, Center of Expertise, or Customer Competency Center, all three provide clients with the ability to lean on their SAP outsourcing partner for more than simply operational SAP support.

Depending on the needs of your organization, partnering with an SAP accredited COE or CCC vendor might provide your company with the level of services you demand. Regardless of certification, it is imperative that the proper due diligence is performed to ensure that the right fit is made.

Understanding your SAP outsourcing needs is the first step and if your organization requires a single partner to perform multiple SAP initiatives concurrently, then global delivery might be the proper path.

Peak performers see the ability to manage change as a necessity in fulfilling their missions.
— *Charles A. Garfield*

8 Engagement Construct

Just as the outsourcing models are infinite, so too is how an organization can engage with their outsourcing mechanism. The goal is to build the proper model or mechanism to maximize engagement. Engagement models run the gamut, including offshore/never seen but heard of models on one extreme, to onsite presence on the other extreme, to everything in between. Furthermore, organizations are now exploring how to maximize their BPO model, including the use of integration management.

SAPanese: Engagement model

The term engagement model is defined as how an organization partners with an outsourced delivery mechanism. The physical presence is relevant, meaning that the outsourced delivery resources could range from a single resource onsite on one end of the spectrum to a 100 % outsourced offsite team. As part of the engagement model, various aspects must be defined such as how teams interact, resolve issues, communicate, track progress, and so on.

Although every organization has specific, unique characteristics and needs which might lend themselves to a specialized engagement model, a standard set of widely utilized engagement constructs exist.

In this section, we will discuss several of the key aspects involved in the engagement construct:

▸ Primary models for an SAP organization

▸ Methods to maximize engagement

▸ Challenges sometimes associated with engagement constructs

- The role of key management (integration manager and offsite support manager)
- Communication

8.1 Primary Models

Organizations leveraging SAP — whether Midmarket or Fortune 500, National or International, small SAP footprint or enterprise-wide, or other — all have an infinite set of choices on how to effectively engage with their offsite model. However, regardless of your organization's nuances, a standard set of proven models exist. In the text that follows, we will discuss some of these common models and why a company would choose to leverage one over the other.

8.1.1 Offsite: "Three Wise Monkeys"

Completely offsite

This commonly utilized engagement method leverages a completely off-site SAP delivery mechanism with no outsourcing partner onsite presence. Taking its name from the proverbial Japanese maxim of the three wise monkeys of "see no evil, speak no evil, hear no evil," the offsite partner and end-client interaction is kept to a minimum. All interaction and engagement is typically performed via ticket tracking systems. Of course, the "three wise monkeys" name is an over-exaggeration; however, the intent behind the title is actually not that far off. This model is specifically designed to keep the offsite presence remote and the interaction limited.

Reasons for the decision

The rationale for this can be for many reasons, including the following:

- **Organizational sensitivity**
  An organization does not wish to broadcast its use of offsite resources.
- **Remarketed services**
  Remember that SAP consulting organizations partner with SAP BPO to deliver on sold services. SAP outsourcing is not just leveraged by end-clients.

▶ **Communication**
An organization wishes to shield the internal organization from potential communication limitations. (Note that this is not meant to insinuate that all offsite SAP delivery has poor communication; however, to be fair, while some offsite SAP BPO partners excel technically, they do not excel in communication.)

Furthermore, this engagement model lends itself better and is more effective in some SAP technologies and services than others. Due to its intentional design, communication and interaction is extremely limited. It might not even be that uncommon for the onsite delivery mechanism to not even know their offsite counterparts! Therefore, SAP areas requiring little to no interfacing are ideal for this engagement model. Example areas such as technical and operational areas are better suited for the "three wise monkeys" model than more business process-heavy services.

What SAP areas work best

For example, this engagement construct works well with the following:

▶ NetWeaver offsite operational activities such as system monitoring and performance tuning

▶ Security administration password resets

▶ Job scheduling oversight

▶ Offsite global SAP call centers

▶ ABAP break/fix activities

As you can see, all of these activities are SAP technical skill sets and areas requiring little end-user and business process input. On the other hand, highly complex SAP functionality and initiatives would not work well within this model.

As mentioned, by definition, interaction between the offsite delivery mechanism and the onsite team is kept to a minimum within the "three wise monkeys" engagement construct. However, offsite delivery and development activities cannot be performed in a vacuum. Therefore, activity direction and ongoing status must be carefully maintained.

How it works

Within this model, all activity is typically handled via a specified activity tracking tool. Although the tool can differ, the primary purpose of this application is to:

▶ Clearly track outstanding activity

▶ Allow for issue maintenance

▶ Provide easy reporting to gauge performance

This central activity application exists as the "bible" and connection between the onsite ongoing support and/or development team to the offsite SAP team. Although direct communication can be (and sometimes is) employed, due to the nature of the activities, it is not necessary. (Think about this: If your offsite delivery team is responsible for monitoring batch jobs and restarting incomplete reporting programs, what need is there to speak with the onsite team? Most likely, there isn't one.)

8.1.2 Manager to Manager Integration Model

Integration manager

Much has been discussed already regarding the integration manager and his very strategic role within the organization, especially when leveraging an offsite delivery mechanism. (Chapter 14 is entirely devoted to this role/position.) Nonetheless, another major integration model revolves around this position. This model focuses again on minimizing direct end-client and end-user interaction with the offsite delivery mechanism. However, instead of eliminating communication completely (clearly not an ideal situation and also impossible), the end-user and client communication is driven through a single onsite resource, the integration manager. In turn, the integration manager communicates with the offsite production support manager responsible for driving offsite delivery.

Alternative to the monkeys

This model could be chosen as an alternative to the "three wise monkeys" model for the following reasons:

▶ **Mandatory onsite presence**
If the client requires onsite presence to assist in pushing resolution both on the offsite delivery side as well as for the onsite team, an onsite integration manager solves this challenge. Justifiably so, some customers are not comfortable with 100% offsite delivery. Again, a dedicated integration manager sitting side-by-side with your team provides this much needed comfort.

▶ **Challenge/hot spot**

Some organizations implement complicated and high profile functionality requiring extra attention (e.g., complex sales custom pricing procedures). Most frequently, these types of hot spots fall within the business process areas and not the underlying SAP technologies (XI/PI, ABAP, portal, etc.). If this is the case, providing an onsite resource skilled in this area is an excellent way to kill two birds with one stone (metaphorically). By providing a single resource onsite to act as both integration manager and functional specialist, your organization has the luxury of immediate onsite issue resolution along with an overall issue resolution manager.

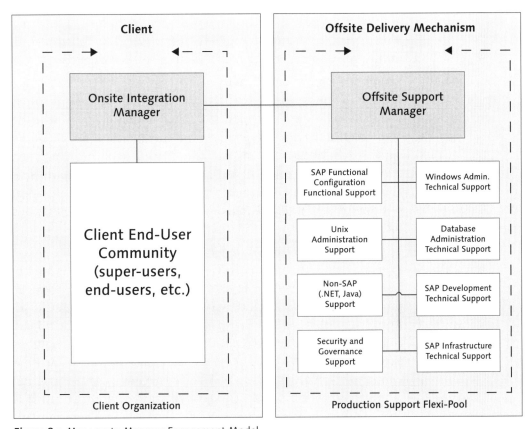

Figure 8.1 Manager to Manager Engagement Model

Many SAP areas work well within this model. The primary difference between the areas that work well in this "manager to manager" engagement construct versus other models revolves around offsite delivery presence. With this model, there is greater onsite presence while still keeping this presence to a minimum, that is, to one key resource.

Here are several areas that lend themselves well to this offsite delivery engagement model:

▶ **Medium complexity SAP landscapes**
Typically, higher complexity SAP landscapes — whether functionally or technically complex — require more end-user/COE to offsite production support communication. If this is the case, then this model (which minimizes contact) is not ideal. However, if the SAP environment is low to medium in complexity, this model works well, especially if the onsite integration manager has hot spot expertise.

▶ **Strong SAP operational activity**
SAP environments that perform routine procedures such as frequent and standard SAP processes are well-suited for this model. Due to the SAP system's repeatability and predictability, much, if not all, of the support can "easily" be maintained offsite. The onsite integration manager simply exists as an added bonus and/or challenge area specialist. Environments that are constantly in flux or require a great deal of attention are most likely not the right type of environment for this model.

▶ **Mini-project/enhancement environment**
Another great SAP area that fits very nicely into this model is the frequently enhanced environment. If your organization has a stable SAP productive environment and is frequently adding minor functionality, this model is perfect. Example enhancements include additional ABAP custom developments such as reports, or functional additions such as adding new company codes mirroring similar or identical existing business processes. By leveraging your onsite integration manager as the enhancement project manager, your organization is able to take advantage of a proven manager who is deeply and intimately familiar with your environment. This deep understanding helps mitigate any potential mini-project issues. Please note that the "level" of enhancements do not include *major* SAP initiatives such as

upgrades (R/3 to SAP ERP, BW 3.5 to BW 7.0, etc.) or complex implementations (installing the components Governance, Risk, and Compliance [GRC] or Environmental, Health, and Safety [EHS]).

Case Study: Manager to manager engagement model

One organization that has seen benefits from this model is Houston-based Scorpion Offshore Ltd. Leveraging an experienced onsite integration manager — Sumit Manocha — Scorpion has been able to take advantage of an onsite senior resource able to drive day-to-day SAP production operational activity as well as manage mini-enhancement projects as needed. "Our engagement management construct has enabled us to be able to maximize our offsite delivery production support resources for both 'keeping the lights on' *and* project work when required" reflects Manocha. "Our offsite delivery resources are able to quickly address and deliver new client initiatives *because* they are already deeply aware of Scorpion's environment." All of this is facilitated by Manocha as the organization's onsite enhancement project manager working hand-in-hand with his offsite production support counterpart. "Based on the low complexity of the enhancements, onsite resource delivery deployment would be overkill and unneeded cost for the client." Both Manocha and Scorpion feel that this model works best for their environment based on their unique needs.

Within this model, development and delivery activities are driven via the two managerial touch points. In essence, all delivery activity is funneled through these two very important resources.

How it works

From an onsite perspective, all activity and direction is provided to the onsite integration manager. It is the onsite integration manager's responsibility to work with the onsite team to understand the requirements and their priorities, capture the detailed requirements as best as possible, and act as an escalation point for the onsite site team.

From an offsite perspective, the offsite delivery support manager drives delivery efforts for his team of resources. Prioritization, development activity, issue escalation, onsite requirements support, and so on, are all the responsibility of the offsite support manager. He acts as *the* central point of communication and works closely with the offsite resource pool to ensure that all delivery activities meet the required deadlines and timelines.

Of course, development is not performed in silos and therefore a dedicated communication channel must exist. This is where the two managers come in. Acting as *the* bridge between the two resource pools, the two managers work together, representing their respective camps. It is via this primary communication channel that direction and feedback is both given and received.

In this engagement model, the onsite team is meant to communicate almost exclusively with the onsite integration manager. Nonetheless, this does not preclude the onsite resources to communicate directly with their offsite delivery counterparts. Although this model is specifically designed to reduce this type of communication, some direct communication might be necessary and that is understood. In the event that onsite resources require reaching out to offsite resources, this request must still be coordinated with the two pivotal managers. Based on necessity, the offsite production support manager and the onsite integration manager will mobilize the proper resources and coordinate appropriately.

8.1.3   Hybrid

Increased onsite interaction

Moving across the spectrum and, in turn, shifting from a heavy offsite to heavier onsite team construct sits the hybrid engagement model. Unlike the two previously discussed engagement constructs, this delivery strategy provides a stronger client-facing presence. Heavier onsite interaction is purposely achieved, relying more on the physical onsite presence than with the previous described models.

Reasons for the decision

This engagement construct is utilized for multiple reasons. Here are several primary examples:

▸ **Higher complexity business processes and customized development**
More complex SAP-implemented functionality requires greater discussion and interaction. Whether implementing core R/3 or ERP functionality such as complicated tax configuration, or customized organizational enhancements such as building a new suite of screens (ABAP module pools), face-to-face interaction typically helps facilitate clearer communication and less confusion.

▶ **Bleeding-edge SAP products**

With SAP's ever-changing and evolving product suite, both clients and consultants understandably struggle to remain on top of SAP's "latest and greatest" offerings. Products such as GRC or SAP Manufacturing Integration and Intelligence (SAP MII) are challenging to implement onsite, let alone from a distance.

▶ **SAP IS**

As the name infers, SAP IS provide specific functionality unique to a given market vertical. Unique Oil & Gas Joint Venture Accounting (JVA) or Production Revenue Accounting (PRA) are business-specific SAP functionality designed exclusively for handling oil and gas industry drilling. Similar to the point made earlier regarding bleeding-edge SAP products, implementing this functionality is more effectively achieved when onsite.

▶ **Security**

Perhaps your given environment works within a highly regulated, federated, or sensitive environment. This example especially holds true within the federal government space. Based on the sensitivity of government projects and their confidentiality (perhaps specific levels of government clearance are even required), outsourcing some of the aspects to either offshore or even onsite personnel might not be legally permitted. If this is the case, then some aspects of the implementation must be performed by full-time employees.

> **Case Study: An insider's perspective from high security environments**
>
> Vlad Eydelman of Reditech Incorporated has been involved in multiple SAP implementations involving high security clearance environments. From his inside perspective and extensive experience, these types of SAP projects not only require additional upfront logistical and administrative procedures but also present ongoing challenges throughout the project.
>
> For these types of engagements, all projects require a myriad of security checks verifying a multitude of background screens. Several of the primary background checks include: proof of U.S. citizenship (dual citizenship is not allowed) and a background check covering criminal, financial, and personal references going back seven years.

On average, these clearances can take two to three months to process. In the interim, the consultant is not allowed to work on any of the SAP systems or have access to any documentation at all! This even holds true within an organization's development environment, without exception. This is serious business held to the letter of the law.

Eydelman remembers vividly the extent to which the regulations were held. "During one of my projects, I was escorted to the restroom and was forced to call to be able to walk from the lobby to my desk."

As one can understand, the additional costs to clients under this set of regulations can increase cost on many other levels. Logistics in itself can increase cost. Furthermore, under this model, ramp-up time can be long while consultants learn the new environment. SAP projects under this scrutiny must include a buffer to account for such inefficiencies and when planning project deliverables.

Another security hurdle in some SAP environments such as the U.S. Department of Defense is the common access (CAC) card. The security clearance process requires consultants to first receive clearance and then receive a CAC card, which is needed to log into any SAP environment or document repository. One benefit of the CAC card is its ability to allow for secure remote access for remote connections.

One additional security measure that might not be intuitive for those unaffiliated revolves around production. For access to an SAP production environment, greater safety measures are mandatory. This includes "hardened" computers, which are provided by the organization to ensure greater safety. These systems are always accounted for and tracked.

"Overall, the system does work and enables the consultant to do his job." comments Eydelman. "It is a small price to pay for the safety of highly critical information."

How it works When working with this SAP outsourcing engagement model, an organization must be cognizant of several key factors. Perhaps the most important factor revolves around resource skill set; both from a project-specific perspective and an ideal (mandatory) deployment perspective. When using this engagement model, an organization must first understand what skill sets are required for the outsourcing piece. For example, does your project truly require six onsite SAP Logistics functional configuration consultants or will two suffice? After identifying what resources are actually needed (and budgeted and approved), the next step within the hybrid model is determining what resources *must* be deployed onsite.

Although ideal, not all resources are actually needed onsite. (Onsite resources almost always equate to higher cost.) Therefore, an exercise must be performed to determine which of the outsourced resources need to be deployed onsite either due to the complexity of area, security concerns, or other issues justifying the onsite presence.

Although it has certain advantages, the hybrid model is not without its challenges. Because the team is distributed across multiple locations and potentially even time zones, strong organizational and implementation frameworks must be put in place. As discussed in Section 7.6.3, there are a variety of SAP project management tools (e.g., Solution Manager PA, third-party work effort tool such as Version One, etc.) and methodologies (e.g., ASAP, Run SAP, etc.) that can assist in delivery and mitigate risk.

Challenges

8.1.4 Dynamic Resourcing

Leveraging hybrid outsourcing in a given method does not preclude them from modifying the model as needed. This scalable and flexible resourcing mechanism provides dynamic modeling or dynamic resourcing. Based on a multitude of factors, this SAP offshoring model enables your organization a scalable and flexible resource pool to shift up and down as need.

Flexibility

This resourcing hybrid model is becoming more and more common within SAP implementations as organizations are thinking more creatively about how to properly deliver more with less.

A perfect example of how an organization would use this revolves around the project lifecycle. Traditionally, organizations have deployed SAP resources onsite throughout the duration of the project regardless of project needs. With the use of dynamic resourcing, not only are resources load-balanced to specifically match the project's requirements (see Figure 8.3), they are also only deployed onsite for mandatory and crucial project timeframes.

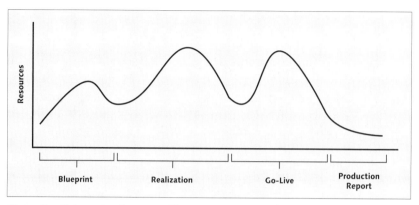

Figure 8.2 Outsourcing Resources Fluctuate per Project Phase

How it works   To make this engagement construct clearer, let's use the example of an organization that is leveraging an offshore partner for supplemental project support. As opposed to deploying an army of resources for the blueprinting phase (a costly proposal), your organization could instead deploy resources on a couple of key resources for business requirements gathering. This does not mean that offsite resources could not still support the business process analysis work; however, it would be performed offsite at a much lower cost. This model of deploying resources onsite for certain phases and then having them return offsite keeps cost low while maintaining the needed high SAP project standards.

Challenges   Leveraging this model requires strong project management and perhaps more important, strong project planning. Because this engagement construct utilizes a flexible resourcing model, organizations must have the proper planning capabilities to ensure that the correct resources are available at the right time within the project time frame.

8.1.5   Pure Onsite

At the far end of the engagement construct spectrum sits the pure onsite model. In this model, all outsourced resources perform all of their activities directly at the client site. This resourcing model at one time was *the* SAP engagement construct; leveraging offsite resources was not explored, let alone leveraged. This engagement model is therefore the easiest to grasp.

With pure onsite resourcing, distinct advantages exist, including the   Advantages
clearest communication, elimination of time zone issues, quicker delivery, and less potential for recycling.

This engagement construct is used for several reasons, as follows:

▶ **Highest complexity**
If your SAP initiative is implementing the most challenging components within the SAP product landscape, onsite delivery is the most
effective engagement strategy. Furthermore, onsite face-to-face delivery is the strongest implementation method, regardless of SAP initiative. This argument becomes even stronger when complexity
increases.

▶ **Lack of alternatives**
Another common reason for pure onsite outsourcing delivery is lack
of client understanding. When organizations engage outsourcing
partners, options, strategy, alternatives, and use of "best practices"
are limited to the breadth and depth of what the partner will and can
share. If a given partner is not able or unwilling to support a client
remotely, the organization is typically not familiar with all of the
alternatives. Although not necessarily meant as a deceptive tactic, not
presenting any of the engagement construct options that utilize an
offsite component severely limits a client's choices.

▶ **Critical timelines**
Rarely does an SAP implementation have padded delivery timelines
or room for fudge factors. However, if your given SAP initiative is
more aggressive than normal, onsite delivery is the best alternative.
Most SAP implementations are driven by business process requirements, demanding that certain SAP functionality is delivered specifically for a mandatory or desired business activity before a mandatory
go-live timeframe (year end, end of quarter, start of new tax legisla-
tion, etc.). Having immediate access to onsite SAP expertise expedites
solution delivery and minimizes the possibility of missing a critical
business deadline.

> **Case Study: Pure onsite delivery**
>
> After an initial implementation of a comprehensive SAP product landscape including ERP 5.0, BW 3.5, XI 3.0, and SCM 4.0 in 2005, one of the nation's leading independent manufacturers of residential and commercial roofing products, waterproofing, composite decking and railing systems, and cements and coatings — decided to upgrade their SAP systems to the latest releases to maximize functionality. "Our focus was efficiency and accuracy" reflected the CIO. "We felt that the upgrade effort would be best served with experienced internal resources supplemented by onsite consultants. Onsite consulting was the only viable solution for our rapid and aggressive schedule." Based on the organization's need to upgrade its existing SAP suite while simultaneously implementing newly available SAP products, the executive team decided to employ the pure onsite engagement construct. After analyzing multiple engagement strategies, the perceived advantages outweighed any potential disadvantages. Although still in implementation mode during the writing of this case study, the company has been pleased with their engagement construct approach thus far. The CIO cites accelerated execution, the ability to identify issues more rapidly, tighter alignment with business processes, and increased consultant delivery visibility as key benefits. "Our implementation has been smooth. Onsite consultant presence is one of the contributing factors."

8.2   The Role of Key Management

One of the primary success factors involved in any engagement construct is the role of key management positions. Although each of the main engagement constructs use different SAP lead roles, several key positions are crucial to success with any SAP engagement model. Each of these roles is pivotal in the overall SAP implementation puzzle. In this section, we will discuss several of the key resources, their respective responsibilities, and the function(s) they serve.

8.2.1   Integration Manager (Internal or Outsourced Resource)

Much has been said about this position already and the entire Chapter 14 will be devoted to this crucial role. In essence, the integration manager acts as the human interface between the onsite and offsite delivery mechanism. This role is also very much needed if the model does not leverage offsite delivery. In that scenario, the integration manager exclusively coordinates and facilitates delivery activities among the onsite delivery team (which is no small task).

8.2.2 Offsite Delivery Manager (Outsourced Resource)

For any delivery that utilizes any offsite mechanism, this role is mandatory. Acting as *the* primary contact, escalation point, and offsite representative, this crucial position provides all of the direction to the delivery pool across all SAP (and possibly non-SAP) resources. Regardless of whether the offsite activities are technical (NetWeaver administration, custom ABAP development, security administration, BW reporting) or functional (SD configuration, financials G/L configuration, production planning) in nature, the offsite delivery manager provides the leadership to drive all activity. Furthermore, different service levels and responsibilities exist, depending on the type of activity (i.e., production support, global delivery, or project). The offsite delivery manager must understand the different needs, act appropriately, and juggle multiple initiatives at the same time.

Mandatory leadership role

8.2.3 Technical Architect (Typically Internal Resource)

This important role is responsible for providing the SAP infrastructure vision as well as direction for the overall SAP landscape. Connectivity, efficiency, latency, availability, and other key infrastructure details are driven by the technical architect. It is his responsibility and *raison d'etre* to design the most optimal SAP structural design. If issues arise involving the landscape, the technical architect is responsible for identifying the root cause of the issue, providing direction for resolution, and seeing resolution through to completion.

It is understood that not all organizations can staff such a dedicated position. If that is the case, this responsibility must be handled by another resource. Typically, if an organization does not have this role, another technical resource such as a senior NetWeaver administrator, network administrator, or other experienced team member will serve this function.

8.2.4 SAP NetWeaver Administrator (Internal or Outsourced Resource)

Whereas the technical architect is the "brains," the SAP NetWeaver administrator acts as the "brawn." All execution designed by the technical architect will be performed by this role or team. In essence, NetWeaver administrators turn the vision of the technical architect into reality. After the system landscape has been designed, this team carries out the activities that are necessary to implement it, including SAP system installation, fine-tuning, system patching and upgrades, connectivity, system optimization, and other key technical actions.

This role is fundamental to ensuring that the proper SAP environments are available for the offsite delivery team. Failing to provide a sufficient SAP workspace could not only cause an SAP initiative to stall, it could ultimately lead to SAP program failure. This (often) thankless job, if performed properly, usually receives little credit and is typically taken for granted.

8.2.5 Business Process Leadership (Internal Resources)

Almost every SAP initiative (if not all of them) is ultimately driven by the business. Even seemingly non-business initiated, "pure" technical upgrades are still meant to serve business needs. Therefore, business process involvement is imperative in any SAP project.

Ensuring that the business is directly involved in your engagement not only provides your overall SAP program with valuable business-related insight (e.g., direct SAP functional configuration, business process design, etc.) but also ensures that the issues and concerns of the business are heard and addressed (a "political" issue).

The SAP initiative "kiss of death" (i.e., recipe for failure) is failing to involve the business process or lack of business process leadership.

8.2.6 Executive Sponsor (Internal Resource)

Moving up the hierarchy you will find the executive sponsor. Although not typically intimately involved in the SAP initiative's details or design, the executive sponsor role is nonetheless important. This mandatory component within your organization's engagement construct is crucial to its viability, credibility, and long-term success. Driving any SAP initiative without senior level management support ultimately undermines the integrity of the project.

This is even truer when dealing with outsourcing. If there is no executive sponsorship or the team perceives that senior leadership does not believe in the engagement construct, those responsible for its implementation will lose faith in the goal. Just like soldiers need to be able to have faith in their general, members on SAP initiatives need to know that there is senior leadership buy-in for the project. (Although this may seem obvious, many SAP outsourcing projects fail due to lack of executive sponsorship buy-in.)

Crucial for outsourcing

8.2.7 Project Governance (Both Internal and Outsourced Resources)

Finally, in any SAP initiative, standardized project and production support policies and procedures must be established and followed. This is even more important when dealing with an offsite provider. Clear governance is essential in not only ensuring that your partner is performing at clearly agreed on and defined levels (i.e., response times, SLAs, and performance metrics) but also is using the proper protocols.

Based on your organization's given security and corporate policies, a distinct governance agreement must be established with your outsourcing provider. Whether administrative (i.e., using a specific remote logon software package such as Cisco AnyConnect VPN client) or process (i.e., providing definitive documentation per activity by, for example, using a certain technical specification template for all development objects) in nature, agreed on and followed rules of engagement must be upheld. It is the responsibility of this group to both define and oversee that all established governance procedures are followed properly.

This typical SAP program construct should be followed under normal circumstances; however, with a "perfect storm" consisting of an offsite delivery mechanism coupled with a non-client partner, the importance of this function is heightened and requires additional attention.

Key Engagement Roles	Primary Role	Engagement Construct Value
Integration manager	Human interface between the two delivery mechanisms	Ensures on-time delivery; facilitates resolution; onsite delivery owner; liaison between onsite team and offsite delivery
Offsite delivery manager	Responsible for all offsite delivery	Offsite delivery cannot be provided without oversight, management, and responsibility
Technical architect	Devises overall architecture plan to ensure environment is efficient and seamless	Without a technical architect, the SAP environment and remote connectivity would be impossible or inefficient
SAP NetWeaver administrator	Implements technical architect's infrastructure plan	Ensures that the SAP environment for all parties, including the offsite team, is operational and running smoothly
Business process leadership	Provides SAP business process direction	Business process is crucial to the success, adoption, and involvement of the organization; Without business process buy-in, SAP system installation would be fruitless
Executive sponsor	Validation, support, and executive involvement	Provides highest level of organizational support and leadership; without this role, the project team and organization potentially lose faith in offsite delivery
Project governance	Responsible for ensuring that proper processes, security, and procedures are followed	Sets up governance framework for all systems and processes; construct imperative especially when working with an offsite and non-client partner

Table 8.1 Key Engagement Roles and their Primary Tasks

8.3   Conclusion

Choosing the proper engagement construct with your outsourcing provider is not only a fundamental component in the success of your overall SAP initiative but can actually be a showstopper. Therefore, careful thought must be given and due diligence employed when choosing the proper engagement model. Together with its outsourcing partner, every organization must carefully explore what model works best for its specific SAP initiative. Although the decision-making process might be time-consuming for some organizations, the investment can yield high returns if the construct is chosen wisely.

We change, whether we like it or not.
— Ralph Waldo Emerson

9   Selecting a Partner

There is no silver bullet as to which partner is the best fit for a given organization. A multitude of factors exist that impact this important decision, based on your outsourcing requirements, your given industry, the size of your organization, budget, location, security, and so on. However, there are several universal factors related to how you select the outsourcing provider that can dramatically increase your chances for success.

Although many of these decision-making factors are logical, this section will highlight methods that can greatly assist in tackling this challenging task. Also, several alternative models will be discussed. The following are several of the main topics tackled in this section:

▶ Overview of various SAP partner types (strategic business consulting, "big 4", boutique, staffing) and the client value for each

▶ Comparing apples to apples (establishing baseline criteria)

▶ Structured processes such as request for information (RFI) and request for proposal (RFP) available for selection

▶ Alternative sourcing models such as contract-to-hire, buy-operate-transfer, vendor management systems, and acquisition strategies

▶ Real world SAP client examples regarding the thought process behind choosing a given partner

9.1   Understanding What You Need (not Want)

When approaching which partner type to work with, it is imperative that your organization clearly understands its needs. Building a mansion when your organization requires a hut is equally as ridiculous as engaging a full-service provider when all you need is a strategically placed single resource.

Requirements
inventory

Human nature sometimes pushes us in the wrong direction toward desire versus necessity. Therefore, a serious requirements inventory must be performed; otherwise, the wrong decision could prove to be costly. Knowing exactly what your SAP initiative demands is important. Examples include the following:

- End-to-end Order-to-Cash design through delivery
- A heads-down ABAP developer during realization
- On-going level 2 production support services
- Strategic SAP business process reengineering
- Quick hit architecture analysis

These provide the proper framework for employing the correct SAP resources. After defining your initiative's needs, the next step is understanding what type of outsourcing organization is the proper partner.

9.2   Overview of Various SAP Partner Types

As with any industry, the consulting and staffing industry offers a multitude of partnering choices. Ranging from "body shops" through full-service consulting companies, each partner type provides a different service offering tailored to different client needs. (It is actually quite common for an organization to work with different partner types simultaneously for different needs.)

We will discuss several of the primary SAP outsourcing partner types common in the marketplace, in no particular order. Although these are the main categories, hybrids exist that combine multiple partner types.

▶ **Strategic SAP business consulting**

Focused on providing in-depth business process and functional expertise, this category of SAP outsourcing partner offers an organization a strong understanding of both SAP and business process reengineering. Strategic SAP business consulting concentrates on business process reengineering, balancing SAP Best Practices, a client's unique business practice (perhaps a competitive edge), and industry leading processes. For example, if your organization is looking to redesign the entire financial close process, engaging such a partner might be the proper path.

▶ **Pure staffing**

This SAP outsourcing model supports a client by addressing lacking areas via contingent resourcing. This valuable service essentially connects the dots between supply (the SAP talent) and demand (the client). This type of partner's expertise lies in finding the right resources for an organization's needs rather than having an in-depth understanding of the specific SAP process or technology. If your organization is simply looking for a resource or team of resources to supplement your organization's SAP initiative *and* are not looking to the SAP partner for SAP expertise, engaging such a partner might be the right strategy.

▶ **"Big 4"**

This partner type originated with the leading accounting firms. Also called other nicknames such as the "big 5" or "big 6," this group originally grew out of the top-tier accounting firms choosing to diversify into the IT consulting space, has added and replaced "members," and over time has become synonymous with "tier-1" SAP consulting services. From an SAP outsourcing perspective, this group's value proposition is multi-fold:

▷ Large multi-national consulting companies able to support multi-national clients   Value proposition

▷ Well-trained consultants steeped in SAP methodology

▷ Thorough experience and access to subject matter expertise

Some clients even request existing or previous "big 4" experience for outsourcing requirements.

▸ **SAP boutique**

On the opposite end of the outsourcing spectrum you will find SAP boutique firms. This niche group (actually very large in numbers although small in individual size), as the name suggests, consists of much smaller SAP services providers. These types of organizations have fewer resources available to the end client. As a generalization, most SAP boutiques specialize in a given SAP discipline. This group's value proposition centers around client loyalty. Due to the size of the boutique SAP shop, every client holds tremendous importance. This is not to say that other types of partners do not value clients; however, compared to dealing with a much larger "big 4" firm, client organizations are less likely to be lost in the mix if they are serviced by a boutique SAP shop.

▸ **Service-specific**

Most SAP partners cannot be everything to everybody; therefore, specialization is quite common. Specialization within a given discipline allows these organizations to build a core competency in a unique SAP space and in turn, provide differentiation among the competition. Whether building an SAP practice around the less commoditized SAP technologies such as BPC or GRC; around unique SAP services such as SAP hosting; or around third-party products that integrate with SAP (e.g., printing solutions such as ESKER), working with an SAP outsourcer concentrating on a given SAP discipline could provide your organization with the most knowledgeable resources available.

As you can see, there are a myriad of partner types available for most every type of SAP partnering opportunity. Furthermore, although one SAP vendor might be a perfect fit for one of your successfully delivered SAP projects, they might actually be the entirely wrong match for another SAP opportunity. As with any of these important decisions, the pervasive theme of proper due diligence and careful assessment must be performed to ensure that your chosen partner meets your initiative needs.

9.3   Establishing Baseline Criteria

When deciding which SAP outsourcing partner to work with, it is imperative that baseline selection criteria are established. Selecting a partner based on immeasurable, subjective, or arbitrary standards not only is unadvised, it is downright dangerous!

To properly select your SAP outsourcing provider, definite, objective, and comparable criteria must be identified and followed. In essence, a "scorecard" must be created based on your specific needs, enabling you to compare vendor against vendor. This scorecarding process provides the necessary baseline against which all outsourcing partners will be judged.

Scorecard

9.3.1   Common Baseline Criteria

As part of the scorecarding process, different categories are established pertaining to the SAP outsourcing initiative on which your organization is embarking. Although unique SAP initiative criteria are important for definition and measurement, common scorecard criteria categories exist across all SAP delivery models. Examples include the following:

▶ **Client references**
  You must check your potential partner's references; ideally, more than one. Verifying the references is required as well. Finally, it is also recommended that you ask to speak with one client reference who is no longer working with the candidate.

▶ **Cost**
  Cost is king. This common and important measurement often receives the most visibility and scrutiny. Although definitely important, it should not be the only qualifying factor. Looking exclusively at cost at the expense of other equally as important factors could be catastrophic to the success of the SAP project.

▶ **Experience**
  Of course, having experience is very important; however, having the *right* experience is even more important. When selecting a partner, it is imperative that you select a consultant who has performed the *same exact* task multiple times. You are not paying for someone to learn on your dime.

207

▶ **Financial stability**

Another sometimes overlooked selection criteria is an organization's overall financial health. Checking into a potential candidate's fiscal health (requesting three years of financial statements or reports) is an important step of due diligence. It is your responsibility to ensure that you partner with a consultant who will be around for the initiative's entire project length.

▶ **Consultant resources**

Understanding who will actually be performing the given SAP outsourcing activity is very important to a client. Simply learning of your prospective partner's overall experience is not sufficient; a successful SAP initiative is only as strong as those who are actually assigned to it. Therefore, it is a common practice to request consultant resumes and/ or backgrounds for the resources assigned to the given SAP program. To be fair, however, your organization must understand that the presented resumes might only be representative of the skill set based on resource availability. However, the goal of this "exercise" is to assess consultant capabilities and avoid "the bait and switch" (presentation of a strong consultant and then intentionally replacing that person with a weaker resource).

Common language within the organization
By first tackling and identifying the common baseline selection criteria, your organization is able to effectively establish a common language that can be utilized both within the given SAP initiative as well as on other projects. This useful set of criteria can provide your company with key measuring metrics used and compared time and time again.

9.3.2 Baseline Criteria Unique per Initiative

Beyond the common measuring standards described, unique baseline criteria must also be established that provide an additional quantitative benchmark necessary for comparison purposes. Specific SAP implementation criteria for the given outsourcing technology (e.g., BusinessObject Xcelsius capabilities), geographic reach (e.g., local supporting offices located in the silicon valley), or market vertical (e.g., environmental health and safety industry expertise) all are examples of key SAP initiative measurements crucial to a consultant's ability to successfully deliver. The following are several key example categories that should be reviewed when constructing selection factors:

▶ **SAP technology**
A thorough understanding of the given SAP product or products is fundamental to successful project delivery. Because the SAP world is so incredibly broad, proven knowledge and proven experience is a mandatory prerequisite for partner selection. Therefore, specific SAP technology-related criteria must be included to verify a partner's true grasp of the product. Experience within SAP Logistics customer service functionality might not be enough if your organization is looking to implement CRM.

▶ **Business process**
Equally as important as a partner's grasp of the given SAP technology is business process expertise. Strong business process functional expertise unique to the given SAP program is required and therefore must be incorporated into the selection criteria. If your organization is looking to install Advanced Planning Optimizer (APO) Supply Chain Management (SCM) within a manufacturing environment, key experience and relevant questions must be incorporated to validate consultant competency.

▶ **Industry**
Not all industries are alike (e.g., telecommunications vs. healthcare), and even within industries, different subareas exist (e.g., oil and gas upstream vs. oil and gas downstream). Therefore, specific industry knowledge and knowledge of corresponding SAP product capabilities are crucial to success. SAP IS expertise (IS-Telecommunications, IS-Professional Services, etc.) are valuable benchmarks for your potential partners.

▶ **Initiative type**
Working with the strongest SAP specialized business process strategy and reengineering-specific partner might not be the best approach if you are looking exclusively at pure heads-down execution partners. Furthermore, the skill set needed for pure implementation work (e.g., ASAP methodology certified, onsite delivery capabilities, rapid deployment experience) is not the same skill set needed for 24x7 production support (SLAs, lower cost modeling, strong integration man-

agement methodologies). Therefore, identifying the unique initiative-specific selection criteria is a must.

▶ **Language requirements**
In this day and age of global business, a single SAP support language might simply not be possible. Perhaps your organization requires partner team delivery in the local language (e.g., English in the United Kingdom, Spanish in Argentina, and Russian in Russia) across multiple countries. If this is the case, these important and unique selection criteria must be included within the deciding factors.

▶ **Performance**
Sometimes specific, project-unique performance criteria exist as an important decision-making factor relevant to the given SAP outsourcing need. Examples include technical performance evaluation measurements such as hot backup capabilities and extensive disaster recovery capacities for your SAP hosting provider; SAP transport SLAs for your NetWeaver Basis group; or PI/XI message delivery commitments of 10,000 transactions a minute. In essence, if a performance criterion is unique and relevant to your initiative, you should include it.

▶ **Regulatory requirements**
Perhaps your organization resides within a given federally regulated, industry monitored, or security level environment. If this is the case, there is a high probability that given accreditations are not only highly valued but required. If so, it might be wise to partner with an SAP outsourcing organization that, at a minimum, has extensive experience with your given field or better yet, has a required "seal of approval." Accreditations within the financial services sector (US GAAP), pharmaceuticals (HIPPA), and manufacturing (good manufacturing principles [cGMP]), are all potentially important areas of consideration in selecting an SAP outsourcer.

▶ **Location**
Proximity to a partner's location might be an important factor when choosing with whom to partner. If your organization does not have enough office space to house your partner's resource but face-to-face delivery is required, SAP outsourcing partner location is relevant. If so, this factor must be added to the list.

Case Study: Kirk Schamel and the art of the RFP baseline (no more apples to oranges comparisons)
When Kirk Schamel, GAMBRO's director of business solutions, was presented with the daunting task of building an RFP for their upcoming major SAP implementation, he knew exactly what components needed to be included. The standard RFP SAP implementation staples of experience, methodology, pricing, proposed team, and references all were mandatory. However, Schamel understood that without some baseline scoring criteria, all of the vendor's responses would be of little use. "We knew from past SAP proposal experience that establishing some quantitative vendor response matrix was imperative. Failing to establish some 'apples-to-apples' criteria would compromise and challenge the decision-making process." Therefore, after much research and discussion among the team, Schamel constructed a weighted set of values and scoring factors to provide some objective ranking metrics. "In previous RFP's in past-lives, organizations failed to definitively delineate the criteria used in partner selection. One reviewer's perspective varied from another's due to uncertain measurement criteria. We did not want to allow for that possibility." Schamel's rigorous approach and upfront due diligence enabled GAMBO to select the proper SAP outsourcing partner based on clear measurement devices. No more "apples-to-oranges" comparisons.

9.3.3 Scoring Allocation

Designation of criteria is important. However, without objectively quantifying their respective meaning, they exist as hollow, immeasurable (and useless) nuggets of data. After defining all of the relevant and important baseline selection criteria for your organization's SAP initiative, an objective and quantitative weighting exercise must be performed. In essence, a ranking must be made and a respective value (typically either a percentage of worth across all factors or point allocation) is assigned. This quantitative scoring system then provides a level playing field according to which you can measure all criteria and corresponding consultant responses.

Making criteria measurable

For example, if your organization is planning on performing an SAP BW 3.5 to SAP NetWeaver BW 7.0 upgrade, your organization will define multiple selection criteria including common/generic factors, SAP NetWeaver BW upgrade-specific criterion, and perhaps other organizational and industry-specific decision-making factors. Working with all of the key stakeholders (e.g., procurement, technical, business process, and project management office, just to name a few), the group will collectively assign a given scoring metric, based on priority, to each of the given factors.

Subjectivity
within the
selection process
Of course, the scoring relevance assignment (e.g., 10 % vs. 60 %) is a subjective process, and unfortunately, the elimination of bias is not possible within a selection process. However, by assigning a respective ranking of each of the criteria at the beginning of the review process, an organization can define an objective benchmark.

Table 9.1 shows an actual evaluation criteria example used within the BW upgrade example.

Evaluation Criteria	Allocation
Vendor capability, financial stability, and demonstrated ability to meet commitment requested in RFP	20 %
Experience of the firm in general SAP consulting in public and private sectors	20 %
Experience with the firm's past performance	10 %
Qualifications of staff	10 %
References	10 %
SAP partner or SAP certified	10 %
Proposed cost	20 %
Total	**100 %**

Table 9.1 Real Life Scoring Example

Example
breakdown
As you can see from this table, the organization chose to quantify seven specific decision-making factors as part of their SAP outsourcing partner selection criteria. Ironically, the organization did not select any industry- or client-specific quantitative metric measurements. The only real client-specific factor revolved around what previous direct client experience the prospective partner has. Most of the factors selected were general factors applicable to any other SAP initiative.

An interesting factor to highlight relates to the partner's actual SAP ecosystem status. This organization found it not only relevant but tremendously important to work with a partner who has a specific SAP ecosystem accreditation of either "SAP partner" or "SAP certified." This was so important that 10 % of the overall score was based on this badge! Right, wrong, or indifferent, this example allows us to take a look into an organization's thought process and shows us how they not only chose to define their critical decision-making factors but also how these rank within their SAP initiative.

However, all of the discussion surrounding the scoring allocation does not answer how to actually design the weighting of the scoring criteria. Although you might easily identify the most important factors, defining their respective weighting percentages might be more challenging. Unfortunately, this section (and book) can provide neither a simple nor a direct answer.

Scoring criteria weighting

Similar to many of the complex decisions and discussions covered in this book, the answer to how to design the weighting of the scoring criteria is completely dependent on the key motivating factors that drive your organizational culture along with your respective SAP initiative.

However, a key recommendation for how to weight the process is to create a simply hierarchy. After you have determined what the key criteria are, rank them from highest to lowest on a scale of 1 to 10; then, assign a percentage to each of the criteria ensuring that the overall total adds up to 100. Although more of an art than a science, through experience, you will be able to define the appropriate weighting for your SAP initiative. In reality, the weight is not as relevant as the fact that a consistent set of scoring criteria has been created. This "apples to apples" scoring system will allow your organization to assess your prospective partners more objectively.

9.4   The Selection Process Lifecycle

The process for selecting a partner follows a structured lifecycle. Just as an SAP initiative adheres to a standard and repeatable process, so too does vendor selection. Beginning with an introductory meeting between the client and prospective partners, the process culminates with the selection of a partner or partner(s). Figure 9.1 shows the typical high-level selection process.

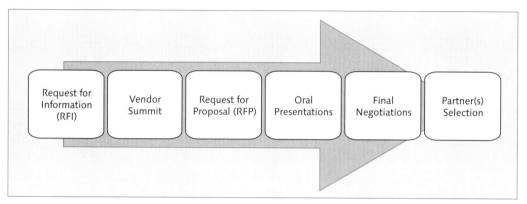

Figure 9.1 Selection Process Lifecycle

9.4.1 Request for Information (RFI)

At the very beginning of the structure selection process, an organization looking to partner with an SAP outsourcing consultant initiates the process via an RFI. This information gathering initial step sets the stage. Meant to better understand the group of potential suitors, in this first step, an organization invites all interested parties (sometimes subject to the organization's chosen greater vendor pool) to participate in a formal "interview" process.

The RFI document, its contents, and the information pertaining to partner selection are described in detail in Section 9.5.1.

9.4.2 Vendor Summit

After all of the prospective partners have received and reviewed the RFI, they can typically attend a vendor summit. This prospective vendor meeting provides SAP outsourcing firms the opportunity to ask specific questions directly of the organization responsible for creating the RFI. The actual format and location of the summit can take shape in a variety of ways. Whether in person at the client's location, at a conference center, or virtually via teleconference, the vendor summit can be an excellent opportunity for clarification from both camps. In many cases, vendor inquiries can even assist in clarifying the initiative's intent.

During the vendor summit, any questions asked are captured. If answers are provided during the summit, they should also be documented (see Figure 9.2). Questions that are deferred are taken by the organization and, based on an agreed on schedule, the organization responds later to all vendors with the respective answers. This information is also made available for prospective partners who were unable to attend the summit.

The vendor summit doesn't always take place, however. Sometimes, for various reasons, organizations decide not to hold this event. (This is highly discouraged!) If this is the case, the organization almost always allows vendors to submit questions to a designated client contact for clarification in some fashion (e.g., email, phone, mail, or a combination of these). Again, the questions and responses are provided to all vendors to maintain fairness and impartiality.

Win-win event

ANSWER TO QUESTION #2:

(1) Yes, provide the information as you have stated in the first paragraph. (2) A combination of both (managem technical consultants) are acceptable for all categories offered. The number of resumes submitted is up to th proposer. Yes.

➤ **QUESTION #3:**

Page 5 of 18 Pages, Section 6.2.4 of the RFP references Attachment C, and the "Proposer is to describ requirement point-by-point listed in Attachment C." Attachment C bullets 1-5 ask for specific information to w proposer can respond; however, bullets 6-8 appear to be statements. Please advise the type of response requires for the last three bullets in the first section of Attachment C.

ANSWER TO QUESTION #3:

The RFP is asking if you can meet these requirements and explain how they will used in your recruiting procedur

➤ **QUESTION #4:**

Page 5 of 18 Pages, Section 6.2.5 refers to background checks. To what extent does a background check ne complete prior to resume submission? Please specify at that time in the submittal/hiring process each check sh performed (please add or subtract those checks that are not listed or required, also specify the number of yea that they require for each check). Our concerns are cost and the time required for a background check, if requir

---

Figure 9.2 Vendor Summit Questions and Responses

Finally, the timing of this event varies based on whether the organization chose to begin the selection process with an RFI. If the organization bypassed the RFI step and began directly with an RFP (more on this in the next section), then the vendor summit would follow the release of the RFP. If both an RFI and RFP are implemented, it is likely that multi-

Timing

ple vendor summits would take place. These would follow the release of both requests after some time to allow prospective partners time to review and meditate on the documents, and generate any questions they might have.

9.4.3 Request for Proposal (RFP)

The RFP is a fundamental component in any partner selection process. Although there might not always be an RFI, if an organization is utilizing a selection process (vs. preselecting a partner for delivery, a common practice), then an RFP-type step is always taken. At its core, the RFP is meant to drastically narrow down the field of players to the chosen few who either are immediately selected or chosen to continue in the process.

The RFP document, its contents, and relevant information pertaining to partner selection are described in detail in Section 5.5.2.

9.4.4 Oral Presentations

From the lucky vendors who make it this far in the selection process, an organization wishing to further narrow down their final choice(s) will request a formal face-to-face presentation. During this stage, the client will invite the vendors still "in the race" to present their proposal in front of the organization's key stakeholders and decision makers.

During the presentation, the vendor typically provides an overview of their organization, SAP experience related to the given initiative, key team players potentially to be assigned to its delivery, delivery methodology, proposed pricing, and specific SAP-relevant details why they would be the best-suited organization for the initiative.

Oral presentations do not always take place, for example if the client is well acquainted with the prospective partner's capabilities and proposal, or if the client has already selected their partner. However, in cases where the initiative is very important, high-profile, expensive, a strategic corporate project, or high-risk, this process is typically performed.

9.4.5   SOW/Final Negotiations

Prior to selection, the final negotiation stage takes place. During this phase, an organization's legal and procurement department are typically engaged to ensure that all of the "i's are dotted and t's are crossed." This sometimes lengthy and laborious step rests mostly outside of the SAP world where lawyers and procurement experts lay down the specifics of the SOW and legally binding contractual agreements.

When specific SAP knowledge, understanding, or expertise is required, the SAP team is brought into the discussion for subject matter expertise. Examples would include scope clarification, timeline requirements, concise and thorough deliverable documentation, and the like. These are documented in the SOW, ensuring complete and accurate terms and conditions.

9.4.6   Partner(s) Selection

Finally, at the end of this sometimes lengthy selection process, a single partner or multiple partners are selected for project delivery. In some cases, multiple partners are chosen. This is typical for larger organizations with well established internal SAP practices and skill sets who are simply looking to augment their SAP needs on an as needed basis.

> **Thinking outside of the box — Insourcing (using your internal SAP IT organization as a potential partner)**
>
> Typically, when one thinks about partners, one thinks about *external* SAP outsourcing providers (as assumed, for example, as the foundation of this book). An alternative, however, is the utilization of *internal* SAP resources to address your SAP RFP requirements.
>
> For example, let's assume that your organization is currently leveraging an SAP outsourcing provider for technical SAP programming services (such as ABAP or Java) and is in the midst of revisiting your partner selection because the current contract timeframe is ending. (Perhaps the reason is to negotiate more competitive rates or improve the overall level of service.) Why not include as one of the potential alternatives your internal SAP development team (assuming that your organization has these skill sets)?
>
> Although your organization decided at one point to outsource these services, this does not mean that you cannot bring these SAP support services back internally if the business case is justified.

Outside of SAP context

Simply include this group as one of the alternatives and treat them as if they were another external SAP "outsourcing" provider. If the pricing and delivery capabilities are compelling, they just might be the right "partner."

9.5   The RFX — Structured Deliverables Used in the Selection of a Partner

The selection criteria definition and their corresponding weighting values would exist as an island if they were not brought together into a structured process. Enter the RFX!

Criteria for comparison

RFX documents are used for selecting a partner and provide the necessary construct to compare one potential partner to another. Within the SAP world, two RFX documents exist: the RFI and the RFP. Both of these selection-related documents serve different and distinct purposes; however, their intentions are focused on the same goal. Let's dig a bit deeper into the purpose of each of the documents.

9.5.1   The Request for Information (RFI)

The RFI is the first qualification- and selection-focused document used by organizations looking for prospective partners. As the name suggests, the primary goal of this process and corresponding partner inquiry revolves around information.

When an organization is exploring with whom to partner, it should first identify what potential *pool of partners* is best suited to be included as viable options. Some organization new to the SAP world might not be familiar with their choices and not all SAP outsourcing firms are created equal. The RFI assists organizations in paring down and weeding out unqualified suitors while identifying firms that are worthy of further consideration.

High-level RFI sample content

Because the RFI begins the partner search process, by design, the information sought is generic. Very high-level and general partner or SAP consulting firm organizational information is requested such as information about corporate history, corporate overview, financial viability, adherence to certain client-specific desired accreditations, reference checks, and the like. In addition, high-level questions regarding the given SAP initiative are also presented for response.

For example, if an organization is interested in acquiring external SAP consulting resources for internal client SAP training purposes, general SAP training-related questions would be asked. Specific questions focused on detailed SAP training material, course curriculum, training process flowcharts, and so on would not typically be asked.

Another section typically included in the RFI document centers around organizational policy adherence. Do you as a potential partner agree to x, y, and z? These policy and procedure measures are not meaningless formalities but iron-clad and non-negotiable prerequisites. Statements of confidentiality and intellectual property are often part of this due diligence area. Failure to agree to any of these terms can lead to immediate disqualification from further consideration. (Refer to Appendix A for an example of an RFI.)

Policy and procedure measures

Another section frequently included in an RFI revolves around government-driven legal considerations. Questions regarding "supplier diversity" and minority women business owned enterprises (MWBEs) are often included in RFI documents. These types of questions and the expected responses are usually not deal-breakers but do provide differentiation if the outsourcing firm does fall within this space.

Because certain SAP outsourcing firms excel in given SAP specializations and are well known for certain delivery capabilities, reputations precede these companies. Industry-specialized SAP firms or technology-focused outsourcing consultants obtain many an opportunity based on this invaluable market recognition. For example, SAP America — when consulted — sometimes points clients toward a given consulting partner direction based on their understanding (and experience) within the greater SAP partner ecosystem.

Although RFIs are common within the SAP world, not all organizations necessarily follow this step. Sometimes, the contrary is true, that is, that an RFI is considered a waste of time and effort. Some organizations — based on experience, reference, or market place knowledge — are well versed enough to already know and identify which SAP outsourcing

Not always necessary

firms should be included in the pool of prospective partners. If this is the case, an RFI is not needed and you could and should (and probably already do) skip this step. Simply put, in these cases, it is overkill.

9.5.2 The Request for Proposal (RFP)

Another common selection process utilized frequently within the SAP outsourcing space is the RFP. In some cases, the RFP follows the RFI. In these scenarios, only those selected — the subset of firms chosen from the original RFI submission pool — are invited to participate in responding to the RFP. Alternatively, some organizations skip or bypass the RFI process completely and go straight to the RFP.

Regardless of how the RFP arises (whether directly or subsequent to an RFI), the purpose of the RFP is to choose the partner or partners responsible for delivery (multiple SAP outsourcing providers can be chosen depending on the organization's intent and given SAP initiative). For focused SAP projects such as the implementation of a single SAP product such as Solution Manager or a service such as providing SAP project management, most frequently, a single SAP outsourcing provider is chosen.

Multiple partners

However, for larger, more comprehensive SAP initiatives — such as global SAP production support or a robust SAP upgrade involving multiple functional modules — it is not uncommon for an organization to work with multiple providers. Furthermore, very large organizations such as those in the Fortune 500 who utilize SAP outsourcing a great deal from both a consulting and staffing perspective almost always work with multiple partners. In fact, many of the large companies that require a constant stream of external SAP consultants often leverage a vendor management service or system. (This model will be discussed later in Section 9.8.3.)

High-Level Sample Content

There are similarities in content between an RFI and an RFP. For example, for organizations that do not go through the RFI process, some of the high-level outsourcing corporate overview material would instead be included in the RFP.

However, regardless of whether an organization bypasses the RFI, the RFP's purpose is to provide more detailed specifics regarding the prospective SAP outsourcer's proposed solution, proposed delivery model, and estimated cost. (Refer to Appendix B for an example RFP.) Specific SAP details pertaining to the organization's unique SAP request must be defined. Therefore, it is your responsibility to clearly define your needs within the RFP to receive responses that most accurately address your project. If the RFP is confusing or misleading, you can expect less than ideal and sometimes useless vendor responses.

Proposed solution, delivery model, and cost

Below are a few typical high-level SAP categories — beyond what has already been discussed in the earlier RFI section — that are frequently found in SAP RFPs:

▶ **SAP methodology**
As part of any true SAP initiative, a followed methodology should be employed. Regardless of the type of SAP program — whether project, production support, or other — a formal delivery approach must be chosen and maintained. As discussed previously, SAP has multiple SAP-specific and widely utilized methodologies such as ASAP and Run SAP. Additionally, a multitude of other project methodologies exist ranging from broadly leveraged strategies such as Six Sigma and AGILE to more vendor-specific intellectual property.

▶ **SAP-centric RFP-focused questions**
SAP-specific questions tailored directly to the given initiative must be included in the RFP. Questions regarding proven experience (and related background) identical to the company's task at hand; direct technical and architectural inquires relating to the proposed implementation strategy; SAP development capabilities involving client-specific needs around Java, ABAP, PI/XI, and portal; and other detailed questions are included to get an understanding of the prospective partner's grasp of the challenge.

▶ **Quality assurance**
What quality assurance mechanisms are practiced and included in the prospective SAP outsourcing partner's delivery model? Questions such as this one regarding quality assurance, along with quality management, are often requested as part of the RFP. Furthermore, the RFP often inquires whether the vendor has any ISO accreditations.

▶ **Cost matrix/rate card**

This component is always included in the RFP. Of course, price point plays a major role in the decision of which partner to work with. In many cases, the requesting organization wishes to see some form of rate card or pricing matrix by resource category (e.g., jr. ABAP developer, mid-level ABAP developer, sr. ABAP developer). Although this does not provide a definitive overall project cost or a cost written in stone (resource pricing can change both up and down during negotiation), it can provide an excellent comparative figure enabling an "apples-to-apples" vendor comparison.

SAP Resource Title	Category	Skill experience	Additional Skill Information	Max Bill Rate
R3, CRM, APO RICEF Analyst	SAP Development	2 to 4	R3, CRM, APO RICEF	$84.57
R3, CRM, APO RICEF Consultant	SAP Development	5 to 6	R3, CRM, APO RICEF	$104.41
R3, CRM, APO RICEF Lead Consultant	SAP Development	7 to 9	R3, CRM, APO RICEF	$124.89
R3, CRM, APO RICEF Manager	SAP Development	6+	R3, CRM, APO RICEF	$135.59
R3 Functional Modules, APO Analyst	SAP SCM Planning & Logistics	2 to 4	R3 Functional (SD, MM, FI, PP, PM, SM, HR, CRM, APO)	$83.52
R3 Functional Modules, APO Consultant	SAP SCM Planning & Logistics	5 to 6	R3 Functional (SD, MM, FI, PP, PM, SM, HR, CRM, APO)	$104.97
R3 Functional Modules, APO Lead Consultant	SAP SCM Planning & Logistics	7 to 9	R3 Functional (SD, MM, FI, PP, PM, SM, HR, CRM, APO)	$125.73
R3 Functional Modules, APO Manager	SAP SCM Planning & Logistics	6+	R3 Functional (SD, MM, FI, PP, PM, SM, HR, CRM, APO)	$136.99
BW Technical/Functional Analyst	SAP Business Intelligence	2 to 4	BW Technical/Functional	$87.78
BW Technical/Functional Consultant	SAP Business Intelligence	5 to 6	BW Technical/Functional	$108.29
BW Technical/Functional Lead Consultant	SAP Business Intelligence	7 to 9	BW Technical/Functional	$132.24
BW Technical/Functional Manager	SAP Business Intelligence	6+	BW Technical/Functional	$143.08
SRM Technical/Functional Analyst	SAP SRM & Procurement	0.5 to 1	SRM Technical/Functional	$90.06
SRM Technical/Functional Consultant	SAP SRM & Procurement	1 to 1.5	SRM Technical/Functional	$111.89
SRM Technical/Functional Lead Consultant	SAP SRM & Procurement	2+	SRM Technical/Functional	$131.35
SRM Technical/Functional Manager	SAP SRM & Procurement	2+	SRM Technical/Functional	$145.25
Basis Technology Analyst	SAP Technical Architecture	2 to 4	R3, BW, CRM, APO - Basis (Technology)	$86.94
Basis Technology Consultant	SAP Technical Architecture	5 to 6	R3, BW, CRM, APO - Basis (Technology)	$109.23
Basis Technology Lead Consultant	SAP Technical Architecture	7 to 9	R3, BW, CRM, APO - Basis (Technology)	$131.78
Basis Technology Manager	SAP Technical Architecture	6+	R3, BW, CRM, APO - Basis (Technology)	$140.06
Portal/XI/Netweaver/MDM Analyst	SAP Technical Architecture	0.5 to 1	Portal/XI/Netweaver/MDM	$93.07

Figure 9.3 Sample SAP Rate Card for an RFP

▶ **Project team**

Along with cost, organizations must understand who is ultimately delivering the project (or production support); therefore, within most RFP's, a project team construct (including resumes and organizational chart) is frequently requested. As mentioned in the RFI section earlier, to be fair, there is always the possibility that some members of the proposed project team might not be available at the time the project gets underway. (This depends heavily on how long your organization actually takes to kick-off the project. If internally, your organization takes a tremendous amount of time to select a partner, perform contractual negotiations, and finalize legalities, you can expect to lose some of the proposed resources).

▶ **Project plan**
Finally, a project plan is often requested as part of the RFP process. Usually presented in Microsoft Project, the responding vendor is asked to construct a proposed project plan capturing resources, dependencies, milestones, and overall timeline. This request is difficult and even potentially unfair to the vendor. However, the primary point of this request is not to hold the SAP outsourcing partner to the specific project plan provided but to see the thought process, experience, and overall grasp of the SAP initiative from the vendor's perspective. You can tell a great deal based on *how* the vendor responds regardless of *what* is actually presented. (The prospective vendors understand this as well. Everyone is playing the game and understands the rules.)

9.5.3   The Statement of Work (SOW)

After the rigorous process of choosing with whom to work, an SOW must be constructed. This contract between vendor and customer is intended to clearly identify what work product, timeline, and corresponding cost will be provided to the client by the vendor.

The SOW is usually created based on the chosen partner's presented proposal. The proposal provides the framework for what deliverables will be provided and how the SAP outsourcing partner is going to achieve the given initiatives' goals. In many cases, the evolution from proposal to SOW is the injection of "legalese," that is, contractually binding language holding both parties to specified agreements.

Based on proposal

However, the SOW is not a one-way agreement; it is very much bi-directional. Within the SOW, the selected partner must also document all of their requirements including what must be provided by the customer. Common generic requirements might include access to proper client facilities and equipment such as laptops, phones, and so on; client involvement including key resources; payment terms; and time and expense policies.

Bi-directional agreement

Beyond the generic requirements applicable to most SOWs, client initiative-specific requirements must also be defined. For example, if the given SAP project revolves around complicated new SAP functionality deeply rooted in complex industry practices or business processes (such as SAP Global Trade Services [SAP GTS] involving international customs and compliance management), client business process expertise must be heavily involved in the SAP GTS rollout. Although SAP GTS functional and technical experts are equipped to address how SAP functionality can be configured, *only* client representatives can define *how* the product should be designed and implemented.

In Appendix C, you will find example SOW categories (and corresponding examples) that are typically included in an SOW.

Although there is some standard content that is typically included in an SOW, there is a great deal of variety depending on a multitude of factors. The biggest factor is often how the organization views the document and its significance. If an organization tends to be more formal in nature, its SOW style would be drastically different than that of a more relaxed organization.

In some cases, an SOW might not consist of more than:

- Timeframe — for example, January 1, 2009 — December 31, 2009
- Assigned resource(s) — for example, Sally Smith and Rajeev Shah
- Billing rate — for example, $50/hour, not to exceed 40 hours per week per resource
- Responsibility — for example, support global ACME Co. SAP rollout with ABAP expertise

Regardless of its specific content, both parties must agree to the terms and conditions as documented in the SOW. For the duration of the SAP initiative (and in many cases longer, when extensions occur), this mutually agreed on contract sets clear expectations from the get-go, attempting to ensure that no disconnects exist between what is meant to be delivered versus what was interpreted.

9.5.4 Contract Negotiation

Although this book is clearly not intended as a how-to guide for negotiating SAP contracts or a lessons learned guide to be used in procuring SAP outsourcing services, it is important to highlight a few key points regarding the contractual components.

When dealing with SAP outsourcing providers regarding the duration terms, you should be careful committing to a long-term contract regardless of the potential pricing incentives.

Contract time

Depending on the specific initiative, the ideal contract time could be anywhere from several months (for a small SAP initiative with just a few consulting resources) to multiple years (this is typically in the best interest of both the client and the vendor for most robust SAP initiatives). The specific ideal duration depends greatly on the specific SAP project; however, Table 9.2 provides some baseline time lengths to be used for various SAP initiatives.

SAP initiative	Minimum recommended contract length	Maximum recommended contract length
Strategic consulting	1 hour	1 year
Small project (module)	Based on project plan	Based on project plan
Large project (SAP ERP)	Based on project plan	Based on project plan
SAP hosting	1 year	3 years
Global delivery	1 year	3 years
Production support	1 year	3 years

Table 9.2 Contract Length Examples

As you can see, for the larger, more comprehensive SAP initiatives, there is a careful balance between too short (less than a year) and too long (more than three years). This three year number is the traditional "rule-of-thumb" used by many organizations for major SAP initiatives. Most vendors will do their best to attempt to increase the contract duration to longer than three years; however, in most cases, the advantages provided do not warrant the additional contract length.

Conversely, a contract of less than three years — depending on the specific SAP initiative — can also prove to be counterproductive for both parties. In this case, the vendor might not feel the partner commitment, which could result in less than ideal attention, and so on.

9.6   SAP Accreditations

The SAP partner ecosystem is both broad and deep. To meet the needs of its ever-expanding (and justifiably demanding) customer base, SAP has been actively and strategically growing their partner network. To provide its customer base a more comprehensive, thorough, meaningful, and competitively priced delivery offering, SAP has been very aggressively working on expanding its overall consulting services capabilities, mainly through partnerships. In SAP's own words:

> *"At SAP, we recognize the vital role our partners play in our ecosystem —*
> *a community of organizations and individuals focused on a common goal*
> *— customer success. Our partner programs provide a strong foundation*
> *of support and collaboration that fosters unparalleled value and mutual*
> *business success for our customers, our partners, and SAP.... SAP offers*
> *global and local partnership categories for every strategic business area*
> *and customer need in all market segments."*

SAPanese: Ecosystem

SAP frequently uses the term "ecosystem." This ecosystem consists of a wide range of partners, SAP organizations, third-party integrated software providers, service providers, industry specialists, value added resellers, customers, and other important SAP contributors who all add to the greater SAP universe. SAP has done an excellent job to encourage and cultivate this ecosystem. Their philosophical approach has enriched the overall SAP community and created an environment fostering inclusion.

SAP's focus in consulting

SAP as a company has been slowly moving away from the professional services consulting space as an overall strategic path to focus more on the sales and cultivation of its product suite, and its professional services and delivery organization has been reduced dramatically in recent years. Although the overall SAP delivery mechanism has been decreased by significant numbers, SAP still maintains a powerful delivery ability focused on providing more platinum level consulting for the most challenging and senior positions.

As part of its robust partner ecosystem, SAP has designed and instituted a rigorous SAP partnership program with accreditations and distinctions. These partnership categories are constructed based on client and partner size; SAP technology and product; delivery specialization; and third-party product integration. There are currently nine distinct partner categories. For a listing, visit *http://www.sap.com/usa/ecosystem/partners/partnerwithsap/index.epx*.

From a customer's perspective, when exploring the possibility of working with an SAP outsourcing provider, there are several key SAP partner categories that should be of interest. The following are the high-level categories and their respective benefits to you as a customer.

The Customer's Perspective

9.6.1 SAP Services Partner

The SAP Services Partner accreditation is the most basic of all of the accreditations. At a minimum, unless there is an overwhelming reason not to do so, a client should only engage with an SAP outsourcing provider who has this credential. This recommendation is intended for outsourcing partners being used for full project or production support services. It is not necessarily applicable to clients looking to leverage outside SAP consulting services from independent consultants or staffing firms.

> **Note**
>
> A full suite of consultant-specific credentials exists — such as "Certified SAP Professional" — that SAP also uses to endorse quality.

There are three levels within the SAP Services Partner space. They include Services Partner, SAP Alliance Partner, and Global Partner. The distinctions between the various levels are based on consulting partner size (number of SAP consultants), geographic reach (regional, national, or international), and capabilities and breadth (SAP delivery focus areas). Regardless of what level of SAP services a client is interested in,

Levels of service partners

any one of these levels of SAP Services Partner category would suffice. As mentioned earlier, this accreditation type is less of a differentiator and more of a level playing field characteristic.

9.6.2   Business Process Outsourcing (BPO)

BPO is actually an SAP partner category. This SAP accreditation identifies the SAP outsourcing partners that excel within the SAP offsite delivery arena. From an SAP perspective, this group of partners is mostly associated with offshore delivery or "factory" capabilities. Typically meant to support large enterprise customers, this partner category provides clients with large pools of SAP talent for comprehensive delivery. In many cases, the areas of SAP expertise reside within the technical arena such as custom development (ABAP reporting, Java), NetWeaver Basis, or "heads-down" construction.

9.6.3   SAP BusinessObjects

In October 2007, SAP acquired BusinessObjects to strategically enhance its business intelligence portfolio. Now named SAP BusinessObjects, this acquisition greatly bolstered SAP's value proposition within this space, providing it with a much needed lift against the competition. Along with the software suite came a sophisticated BusinessObjects services partner ecosystem providing BusinessObjects consulting expertise. This original group has since laid the foundation for strong SAP Business Objects consulting services and stands as a unique accreditation meant to acknowledge leading SAP outsourcing consulting firms capable of providing best in class delivery.

9.6.4   Channel

Pre-configured installations

This SAP partner category provides clients (typically meant to service the $50 million — $300m revenue range) with the option of "preconfigured" industry-specific installations. These "All in one" (A1) partners provide organizations with market vertical-specific SAP ERP boxes enabling quicker and less expensive deployment.

There are currently a multitude of A1 versions ranging from high-tech to wholesale distribution; oil and gas field services to light manufacturing; and medical device manufacturers to professional services. The value proposition to clients is that theoretically, 70% of the configuration and delivery is integrated into the product from the get-go.

For an SAP outsourcing partner to be categorized as a channel partner, the respective consulting firm has to go through a rigorous approval and certification process validating that the proposed SAP product meets SAP's strict guidelines.

9.6.5 Education Partners

Focused on providing SAP training consulting services, "education partners" are another specialized SAP partner category. Although SAP itself does provide comprehensive SAP education courses across the world, it relies heavily on this partner group to address additional, client-specific SAP training requirements. As with many other partner categories across the ecosystem, SAP utilizes this partner group to deliver SAP education courses on behalf of SAP.

Client training

From a client perspective, the value proposition is cost (education partner services are typically more cost-effective than SAP direct education services), availability (partners will work completely around a client's schedule as opposed to fixed SAP education course dates), and convenience (partners provide services at the customer location as opposed to having the client go to an often remote training facility, which involves travel costs).

9.6.6 SAP Hosting

As a growing partner segment, SAP hosting service partners provide customers with the ability to outsource their physical SAP hardware to a certified SAP accredited third-party provider. This is a relatively recent partner category, and suppliers serve a key client need: a less expensive alternative hardware approach. Until recently, organizations installing SAP software did not have the ability or luxury to not purchase the necessary supporting hardware. Even for the most basic SAP landscapes, corresponding hardware costs could have potentially been cost prohibitive.

Outsourcing hardware

This is where the SAP hosting provider comes in. With this infrastructure alternative, customers are now able to rent the appropriate SAP hosting hardware resources needed for their entire SAP landscape. Furthermore, these partners have productized their services into commoditized options ranging from the most basic and limited to more complex and robust options. Alternatively, many SAP hosting providers also are capable of providing customized packages.

From a services perspective, all SAP hosting partners provide NetWeaver operational support services down to the database, networking, and operating systems level. The typical suite of services includes the daily "care and feeding" of the environment but typically do not extend much beyond this (e.g., NetWeaver activities include system tuning and patching but do not cover daily transports). However, many SAP hosting partners have expanded their service offerings to include additional SAP (and non-SAP) consulting services, ranging from additional NetWeaver Basis activities, development services, non-SAP system hosting (e.g., Microsoft Exchange or other applications), and additional non-technical SAP services.

9.6.7 Software Solution Partners (Powered by SAP NetWeaver)

Building specialized functionality

This group is one of the fastest growing partner categories. Aimed at "filling the holes" within the overall SAP landscape by providing focused third-party SAP bolt-ons, this group partners with SAP to further strengthen the overall SAP product suite for the end customer. Although SAP does provide tremendous breadth and depth in all of their integrated products, there is simply too much ground for any single vendor to cover. SAP understands this. In fact, SAP encourages this category group to design, build, and integrate specialized functionality that SAP does not address.

For instance, take the tax arena. SAP does not cover and does not wish to cover (as of the writing of this book), the ever-changing and complicated world of international taxation. As opposed to designing and supporting a software package that requires tremendous maintenance (e.g., yearly tax rate changes in Brazil, by region), SAP would rather leave that functionality to the "experts" and instead, integrate.

The process through which to receive this prestigious certification is both rigorous and difficult. After going through a series of technical reviews, demonstrations, review of design and coding, and heavy scrutiny from a designated SAP organization known as the SAP Integration and Certification Center (ICC), the product is finally blessed.

Certified add-on solutions

9.7   Screening Process

When partnering with external SAP outsourcing providers, it is imperative that your organization is provided exactly what it is looking for. For organizations that have extensive internal SAP skill sets and a long history of SAP experience, selecting from proposed candidates might be second nature. However, for those relatively new to the SAP world or dealing with either a bleeding-edge SAP technology or SAP area with which they are not familiar, this might be more difficult. Therefore, it is crucial that some form of SAP technical screening is performed (see Figure 9.4).

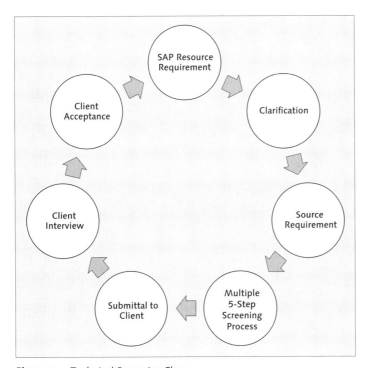

Figure 9.4 Technical Screening Flow

For some SAP outsourcing providers, a technical screening mechanism is built into the resourcing process. Whether this exists as an additional vetting step within the resourcing lifecycle or is performed internally within your organization, ensuring that a given resource's presented skill set accurately reflects what they truly know and have done should not be a "nice to have."

This screening process further mitigates the potential that the proposed candidate or candidates do not misrepresent their skill sets and are the proper fit on many levels (corporate culture, communication, presentation skills, etc.).

The ideal resourcing model to benefit clients that should be utilized by SAP resourcing organizations is discussed next. This model typically exists more within the SAP strategic staffing realm; however, true SAP service integrators should follow the basic principals whether providing one of their own resources or working with one of their trusted sub-vendors.

▶ **Initial qualification screening**
The vendor screening process begins by contacting the candidate by phone. At this time, the placement manager qualifies the potential candidate to make certain they meet the vendor's strict employment criteria by asking questions concerning current employment status and salary, employment authorization (visa), location/transportation and willingness to travel, availability, degree/certifications, and a brief skill set breakdown. The vendor records candidate information in some form of document.

▶ **Qualification skill set assessment**
Recognizing that there are numerous components that make up a match, the vendor engages the candidate in a conversation about the candidate's reasons for the current job search and about career goals and professional interests, and then reviews the current job requirement with the candidate. The vendor then screens the consultant, utilizing a pre-developed, pre-qualifying skill set questionnaire.

▶ **In-person interview**
The vendor conducts an extensive reference check utilizing an application for employment. Candidates are questioned about their

employment authorization, past and present employment and salary information, security clearances, willingness to submit to a drug test, history of prior felonies, educational history, and professional references.

▶ **Work history review**

The placement manager conducts an extensive review of the candidate's work history in chronological detail, noting technical experience and any odd patterns, such as job hopping, unexplained gaps between assignments, irrelevant work history, or a pattern of short assignments. Throughout the interview process, the vendor poses questions that relate to performance competencies and skill sets required for the position.

▶ **SAP technical screen**

The vendor performs an extensive SAP-centric, in-depth technical interview. The technical interview is performed by an SME who has the same skill set as the candidate being interviewed. This technical screen lasts, on average, approximately one hour and the proposed candidate is asked specific questions testing both his experience and knowledge. After the technical screening, the SME evaluates whether the candidate is the appropriate fit for the role and provides a written summary of the technical interview.

▶ **Client interview**

The vendor schedules the candidate for a client interview, as directed by the client. If the client prefers not to interview the candidate in person, only the candidate's resume is submitted to the client. In addition to the interviewing process, the vendor works with each client to understand any client-specific requirements and ensures the candidate meets these requirements.

You will find more details on the screening process in Appendix D.

This often overlooked process is an easy way to weed out poor candidates and save money in the long run. Do not assume that your SAP outsourcing partner has performed this important and valuable extra step. In many cases, it is overlooked by clients who have assumed that their SAP outsourcing provider has already performed this safeguarding activity.

Outsourcing technical screening process
Ironic as it may sound, a cottage industry has been created to support customers looking to screen third-party SAP candidates. If your organization does not have the needed internal SAP skill sets and wishes to outsource the technical screening to a trusted third-party, objective SAP expert, you have options. A myriad of SAP technical screening services exist in the marketplace, including online SAP technical screening questionnaires, formal interview services, and SAP specialty technical screening consulting firms. They have arisen to address this customer need.

9.8   Alternative Sourcing Models

Working with SAP outsourcing partners is not limited to either pure staffing or working with true SAP service integrators. On the contrary, many other partnering models exist and are used within the marketplace. (Of course, some are more widely leveraged than others.)

We will now look at several partnering alternatives that organizations can employ when looking to obtain SAP-specialized resources.

9.8.1   Contract-to-Hire

During high demand, low supply SAP markets, the contract-to-hire or right-to-hire model tends to be popular. This alternative SAP sourcing arrangement works exactly as it sounds: a resource is brought into an organization on a contractual basis and then is transitioned to a full-time employee after a certain set of conditions has been fulfilled. Various condition possibilities exist; however, the main conversion factor is usually timeframe (six months, one year, etc.) or customer discretion (the organization has the option to extend a full-time employment offer after six months if it feels that the candidate is the proper permanent fit and has the necessary funding.)

Clear terms and conditions!
When planning to use this practice, you must be very clear to the prospective SAP candidate or representing consulting organization that at the end of the contractual period, your organization is very serious about transitioning the consultant to a permanent employee. Although

this arrangement must be bi-directional, it is not an opportunity for either party to take advantage. Unfortunately, in some cases, consultants use this opportunity to take a job in the short term while having no real interest in converting to full-time employee status. Although this sourcing model does have real advantages, ensure that you have a candidate's documented interest in writing prior to bringing the candidate on board.

9.8.2 Build-Operate-Transfer (BOT)

"Build-operate-transfer" (BOT) falls smack in the middle between "internal outsourcing" and third-party vendor outsourcing. Conceptually this is a "rent to own" arrangement — an organization engages a third-party partner willing to build an outsourced organization on behalf of the client. Through a clearly defined contractual agreement, the third-party partner works in a vendor capacity until either a benchmark is met (number of users, support volume, etc.) or a given timeframe has elapsed (contract conversion length, number of months, etc.). After the threshold has been reached, these third-party resources become the organization's employees overnight. Although this is a gross oversimplification of the BOT model, it frames this rental-type arrangement and, in turn, inherently expresses its potential value.

For organizations interested in strategically building their internal SAP support capabilities, the "try, then buy" model might make sense. This model enables your organization to test the quality of the resources and then decide whether ownership ultimately makes sense. This is basically the "rent-a-center" SAP outsourcing option.

"Try, then buy"

9.8.3 Vendor Management Systems

For large organizations looking to consolidate their SAP outsourcing providers and, in turn, lower their overall outsourcing costs, vendor management systems and managed services providers might be another outsourcing alternative. Over the last 15 years, vendor management programs have gained favor in helping organizations more effectively manage their use of contingent labor. In the last three to five years, these programs have matured to a point where they can effectively help organizations manage their use of project-, deliverable-, or service level-based suppliers (including outsourced services). The extension to managing specialized services providers, such as SAP outsourcing, is obvious (an offering the market now refers to as services procurement management [SPM]).

A vendor management solution is a structured program that includes a dedicated program management team, optimized business processes, and an underlying technology that optimizes the workflow and captures key transactional information about the services. In this model, a managed services provider (MSP) is brought into the organization to coordinate procurement, sourcing, payment, and contract management functions between outsourcing SAP providers and the client. As part of this arrangement, the MSP leverages technology — a vendor management system (VMS) — to manage the entire process for the client. The MSP becomes the central point of contact and coordination for this activity, managing business rules and processes established by the client.

These programs can accrue significant value for the client. Among the benefits most often noted are the following:

▶ **Cost savings**
Drive cost savings through standardization of market rates, evaluation of best value, and optimization of activities supporting the management of these services.

▶ **Accountability**
Hold service providers, including SAP outsourcers, accountable for committed deliverables and/or SLAs.

▶ **Compliance**
Create a standard, streamlined process, greater transaction processing visibility, and enhanced control over spend levels.

In general, clients embrace the model due to the decrease in cost while the vendors often resist the model. This is because the reduction in cost is taken from the margin previously made by the suppliers and split between client savings and MSP profit.

Typically, this model is utilized by Fortune 500 organizations managing significant spend ($10 million and above) on project or services spend (including SAP outsourcing). This model — although attractive to all market space segments — has yet to be effectively utilized by smaller corporations given the need for economies of scale in delivery.

Case Study: TAPFIN Process Solutions

TAPFIN Process Solutions is an outsourcing provider focused in the area of resource fulfillment and vendor management services. TAPFIN's (*www.tap-fin.com*) background comes from the consulting and related technology services world. Likely, it is this background that has enhanced their ability to provide comprehensive vendor and services procurement management outsourcing, particularly in the areas of information technology spend management. MSP's offer integrated resource fulfillment, including managed services provider for vendor management, services procurement, and recruitment process outsourcing. Methodology-wise, TAPFIN utilizes a proprietary delivery methodology supporting program operations. Program deployment methodology has been certified under the ISO 9001:2000 standards. Implementation managers are trained under the PMI PMBOK process. No MSP should be delivered without a strong underlying technology under a tool-agnostic approach. TAPFIN uses a number of technology partners, including (listed alphabetically): Beeline, ClickCommerce, Econometrix, Fieldglass, PeopleClick, Provade. From a best practices perspective, Kip Wright, President of TAPFIN, offers the following: "Here are some best practices when considering the use of an MSP to manage your SAP outsourcers:

▶ **Internal culture**
These programs are only successful if they have full and complete executive sponsorship, willing to limit 'exceptions' for certain suppliers.

▶ **Key objectives**
The program should be structured with clear, defined goals and objectives. Make sure all involved understand exactly what your organization is looking to achieve through the program.

▶ **Performance management**
Know with which metrics you want to measure the performance of both the MSP and the various service providers (including your SAP outsourcers).

▶ **Right partner**
Find a provider who has proven experience in managing services spend, particularly that involving technology consulting and outsourcing providers.

▶ **Stay involved**
These programs don't run themselves, and the MSP should only be viewed as an extension of your organization."

9.8.4 Acquisition Strategies

Insourcing

In rare cases, the purchase or acquisition of an SAP consulting firm makes the most sense. Typically, these companies are large in scope and have long-term SAP resource requirements. Global companies running robust SAP environments with internal CCCs or COEs might find it cost-beneficial to purchase an existing and proven SAP consulting company with experienced resources. Instead of utilizing SAP outsourcing firms or attempting to cultivate the necessary skill sets in-house, this "just add water" approach — although potentially more expensive and an investment up front — allows an organization to hit the ground running immediately.

> **Case Study: Interesting role reversal: SAP outsourcing firm purchases client-internal IT department**
>
> In most instances of SAP expertise acquisitions, the customer or client acquires an SAP consulting organization to fulfill their SAP resourcing requirements. However, recently, a big-5 global consulting firm turned the traditional model on its head, thought outside the box, and purchased a company's entire internal IT department! If this wasn't "strange" enough, the story gets better. To add another twist, the consulting organization turned around to provide the client with SAP resources! Absorbing the client IT department into their consulting model, these resources switched "badges" and embarked on a major SAP implementation. Although this is obviously not common within the industry, for these organizations, it was a mutually beneficial arrangement, addressing their needs bi-directionally.

9.8.5 Direct Hire

The final alternative SAP outsourcing strategy is permanent placement. As opposed to looking at contingent SAP resources or contract-to-hire, in this scenario, your organization chooses to directly hire employees from the get-go as full-time employees.

Better cost structure

This resourcing strategy has multiple advantages. The first and foremost is cost. As a generalization, internal SAP resources cost less than external resources. This includes the additional burdened cost associated with benefits, insurance, 401k contribution, vacation, and so on. Another advantage relates to knowledge retention. As valuable organizational and SAP-specific knowledge is obtained, this information remains with the client as opposed to leaving when the outsourcing partner leaves.

From a disadvantage perspective, several drawbacks exist as well. Although cost is typically less for internal resources than external resources, as a generalization, candidates willing to become permanent employees tend to have less experience. (Again, this is a generalization that does not always hold true.) Another drawback with this approach is access to resources, especially for "hotter" or more specialized skill sets. If your organization is looking to obtain some of the more difficult SAP skill sets, the search might be more challenging. Typically, skilled SAP resources are comfortable with their consulting lives and not comfortable with a perceived reduction in salary.

One equalizing factor revolves around the market. Depending on the SAP market and the economy, SAP resource supply and demand can shift the advantage one direction or the other. In a tight economy (such as the 2008/2009 recession), customers are able to obtain higher quality talent and better prices. This is simple macroeconomics: more supply provides better pricing for customers and fewer options for consultants. Of course, the opposite holds true as well. In "hot" markets, clients will find it difficult to hire permanent employees.

9.9   Exit Strategy

When engaging an SAP outsourcing partner, the goal is to cultivate and build a long lasting relationship; one that provides both organizations with a mutually beneficial arrangement. (One-sided relationships where either the partner takes advantage of the customer or vice versa ultimately end in failure.) However, as with any engagement, there must be some form of exit strategy or back-up/back-out plan.

This exit strategy takes into account how your organization can "easily" replace the SAP outsourcing provider either with another third-party SAP outsourcing provider or with internal SAP resources.

To protect your organization's best interests, it is imperative that:

► A proper exit strategy is developed.

► The proper processes have been established.

► An outsourcing development methodology has been codified.

► Well documented integration and interaction processes exist.

Simply pulling the plug on your SAP outsourcing provider without performing any of these fundamental steps could prove to be catastrophic regardless of the level (or lack thereof) of competence.

Standardization is so important that an entire chapter of this book has been devoted to this topic. In Chapter 13 (The Value of Standardization), we discuss at length the importance of establishing a consistent set of methodologies and frameworks. The importance behind standardization lies in the criticality of easily understandable and well-defined processes. This fundamental outsourcing building block — when established and followed properly — can help facilitate the transition from one SAP outsourcing partner to another (or even facilitate the transition from external to internal). After setting up these constructs, your outsourcing partners can theoretically be easily replaced with other SAP outsourcing providers. Because the framework remains consistent and hopefully leverages a widely accepted set of IT operations or project methodologies (such as COBIT, ITIL, ASAP, Run SAP, etc.), your exit strategy should be "plug and play."

Again, this does oversimplify the vendor transition process and theoretically, your organization will lose value when transitioning from one partner to another due to loss of organizational knowledge and established working relationships, additional ramp-up time for the new partner, and so on; however, establishing a common set of IT processes and procedures can make the transition less painful.

You can't expect to meet the challenges of today with yesterday's tools and expect to be in business tomorrow.
— Unknown

Section 3: Best Practices, Insights, and Lessons Learned

This section rounds out the book by presenting insight and practical/actionable lessons learned behind some of the special areas regarding SAP outsourcing that might not be as obvious to larger clients. Distinct nuances between the different challenges faced by large companies as compared to midmarket companies will be featured in this section. Although outsiders may believe that this market segment has overwhelming advantages (and advantages do exist), it also faces unique challenges. This chapter will identify some of these challenges and provide resolution recommendations. Finally — similar to other sections in the book — this section will provide real-life client examples to further illustrate the concepts presented.

The way of the creative works through change and transformation, so that each thing receives its true nature and destiny and comes into permanent accord with the great harmony: this is what furthers and what perseveres.
— I Ching

10   Large Enterprise

The Fortune 100 and global organizations are afforded luxuries regarding outsourcing SAP operations that other organizations simply are not. For example, the role of BPO, its scope, location, integration, partner selection, and so on are all areas in which large organizations have more leverage, power, and control over their partner construct and the corresponding partner(s). This section will discuss BPO within the context of a large organization, focusing on the corresponding advantages, challenges, and areas of differentiation. Here are several of the main topics tackled in this section:

▶ Unique advantages for larger SAP clients including "deep pockets," stronger talent pool, and greater access to alternatives

▶ The role of SAP as a product in the large enterprise space

▶ Strong SAP alignment

▶ Bleeding-edge SAP product (alpha/beta) development

▶ Modelling: BOT and internal SAP COE models

10.1   Unique Large Enterprise advantages and their Maximization

Those who argue that size doesn't matter are either naïve or misguided (to put it lightly). As with anything in life, larger organizations — by plain definition of their size — have more influence and options when dealing with outsourcing partners than those outside of this market space. Due to their high consumption of SAP products and services — from both overall licensing and resourcing perspectives — these organizations have a great deal of leverage and opportunity, which they should (and can) use to their advantage.

> **SAPanese: Industry solutions**
>
> As part of its software product suite and value proposition, SAP has developed (and continues to develop) — in conjunction with their partner community — a set of "templated SAP software versions" geared toward specific market verticals. These versions of SAP software — commonly referred to as "IS-[solution] such as IS-Oil — provide industry-specific Best Practices, configuration, and developments. Currently broken into three main categories (Financial and Public Services, Manufacturing, and Service) and a host of sub-categories (Retail, Oil & Gas, High-Tech, Public Sector, etc.), there are over 60 distinct industry-focused offerings.
>
> These offerings' value proposition is to provide organizations with a more tailored product, specific to their unique business vertical and, in turn, minimize customization. Although the value proposition is strong and does "jump start" an organization's use of SAP software, it rarely exists as a silver bullet (i.e., additional configuration and development is often required).

10.1.1 Deep Pockets

Large budgets

Like bees to honey do SAP outsourcing firms flock to customers with large SAP budgets. As mentioned earlier, this market segment is afforded certain luxuries that smaller organizations are not, including the ability to utilize MSPs and VMS. As described in the previous chapter, evoking these resourcing alternatives provides previously unavailable discounts. This is all due to an organization's size and corresponding purchasing power, nothing else.

Longer project duration

Another typical advantage of large companies is their ability to provide longer SAP engagement opportunities to prospective partners. Stability is attractive, and due to an organization's size and longer-term engagements, SAP outsourcing firms are more likely to engage with a three-year proposed implementation as opposed to a three-month quick hit initiative. (This does not assume that all large clients always have longer term projects; however, although large enterprise clients might not always have extended project timelines, they typically do have multiple initiatives running concurrently.)

One of the world's leading telecommunication corporations based in Europe has been a heavy SAP user for many years. Due to its strong SAP strategic alignment, this multi-national identified an opportunity to maintain the same quality of SAP resources while simultaneously lowering its TCO from a services perspective. How did they do it?

From an SAP consulting perspective (i.e., working with SAP services integrators, including SAP Professional Services), this organization felt that the project pricing should reflect a quantifiable pricing model. The argument was presented that if the SAP outsourcing partner wished to participate in the project, they should have "some skin in the game." Because the services provided involved fully outsourced delivery and corresponding deliverables, upfront fixed-cost negotiation was employed. This strategy helped provide a clear understanding between the client and the consultant while at the same time lowering project expenditures.

From an SAP staffing perspective, this Telco felt that the resource needs requested were commoditized requirements. Whether concerning a heads-down ABAP developer, testing analyst, or functional CRM configuration consultant, the company felt that the pricing needed to reflect staffing prices as compared to the more expensive price modelling. In addition, to further lower staffing resource costs, the client chose to implement a VMS model, which enabled them to lower SAP staffing costs by 4%.

Both strategies assisted this Fortune 500 company in lowering its overall SAP services cost while maintaining the same level of quality — quite impressive, indeed.

Thus, the real question is this: How can your organization benefit from its financial position? Clearly, two aspects are leverage and buying power. Whether driven by long-term contract appeal or the prospect of multiple SAP engagements, your procurement department is well positioned to negotiate rate and quality of resource. Although one would hope that your SAP outsourcing partners would always provide the most cost-competitive pricing, this is clearly not the case. SAP consulting organizations charge what the market will bear. It is the responsibility of your procurement group to ensure the most cost-competitive pricing.

10.1.2 Deliverable-Based and Fixed Pricing

Although not necessarily unique to large enterprise organizations, the concepts of deliverable-based and fixed pricing are typically employed more frequently in this market segment than others. Many client organizations in the SAP world build their pricing models around time and material hourly rates. Traditionally, a given SAP outsourced resource would be paid an hourly rate of x dollars, multiplied by the total number of hours in a given pay period.

Definitive SOW needed — Alternatively, two other pricing models can be employed: deliverable based pricing and fixed price. Both of these models require that a clear understanding is defined, along with a definitive SOW. Loose requirements and ambiguous language are unacceptable in this model. (Working under these types of conditions not only heightens the potential for disconnect between partner and client but even worse, could derail an SAP initiative and cause potential financial ramifications.)

Deliverable-based pricing is based on the delivery of an agreed on product. This product could come in a multitude of forms. The following is just a small subset of examples:

▸ **Technical product**
An SAP technical end-product within a clearly defined scope and with specified expected results. For example, this could be a configured SAP system such as a GRC Access Controls installation with fully configured Fire Fighter and Compliance Calibrator functionality.

▸ **Analysis/recommendation**
A clearly defined and documented recommendation on how an organization can improve on a specific SAP area. For example, this could be an optimization recommendation as to how an organization could improve on its current month-end close financial process.

> **Tip**
>
> Construct an agreed on table of contents for any analysis product to ensure that a clear understanding is set for output results!

► **Documentation**

A clearly defined deliverable documenting a given functional business process, technical component, infrastructure landscape design, SAP Best Practice, and so on. For example, this could be an ABAP technical specification regarding an important interface for integrating SAP ERP Financials with a third-party payroll system.

► **Testing**

Test plans, test cases, testing strategies, and test results across a wide range of testing phases, including unit, string, integration, regression, performance, and user acceptance testing. For example, this could be a detailed, comprehensive testing plan for an Order-to-Cash process, including functional and technical test cases, and their expected and actual results.

10.1.3 Building Relationships

Due to the nature of the types of SAP initiatives in larger organizations, including their longer duration and higher number of ongoing or concurrent projects, this customer base has the unique opportunity to cultivate and build long-term relationships with consultants. This simple but powerful reality provides organizations with not only preferred pricing and locked-in rates but also the luxury of working with the same resources again and again. This model is invaluable, and although not limited to larger clients, it is more frequently realized in these organizations.

Think about how much time is spent at the beginning of each project, during ramp-up related to non-SAP activities. Logistical and administrative processes related to on-boarding requirements such as network ids, SAP logons, site badges, and so on all take time, which equates to cost. | Continuity

This does not even speak to unique organizational and client-specific knowledge. Unique business process understanding can take months — sometimes years — to obtain. Assuming your organization leverages standard SAP business processes, there is still a unique way in which your company carried out the implementation, and if your company designed unique business processes and built custom functionality, gaining an understanding of these can take quite some time. | Understanding of business processes

Working with the same consulting organization throughout the same initiative — and potentially across multiple projects — positions your organization more soundly when addressing project needs.

When dealing with global delivery and production support needs, continuity is even more crucial. Due to the nature of the outsourcing needs (operational longer-term sustainability), a strong, deep, and broad understanding is fundamental to successful delivery. Utilizing the same resources and retaining valuable system knowledge provides stability and access to otherwise lost SAP knowledge.

10.2   The Role of SAP in the Large Enterprise World

Strategic relevance   As a product and system footprint, SAP is often a very strategic — if not *the most* strategic — application in larger organizations, and when dealing with SAP as a system, large organizations tend to look at everything through SAP lenses. (This is based heavily on the corresponding corporate investment.) Because SAP systems play such a fundamental role in the corporate landscape and the corresponding corporate psyche, SAP resource requirements are treated with greater importance and in some cases, urgency.

Let's take, for example, a large multi-national oil and gas corporation. In every area of the corporation, SAP plays a fundamental role. In finance, this Fortune 50 company works with multiple SAP products, including SAP ECC 6.0 (new G/L), financial SCM, Business Planning & Consolidation, and BW, among others. In other functional areas in the organization, SAP is equally as prevalent.

Due to the pervasiveness and reach of SAP as a strategic product, resource requirements often receive higher priority. Furthermore, due to SAP's ubiquity, executive sponsorship and acceptance provides the much needed support required in driving SAP initiatives. This very important buy-in enables large organizations the ability to drive SAP projects.

Figure 10.1 SAP's Footprint Capabilities from a Business Process Perspective

Another key differentiating factor for large enterprise organizations as compared to smaller companies is tolerance to cost. As a generalization, SAP programs (whether large-scale initiatives such as complete SAP ECC 6.0 full-lifecycle SAP implementations, or smaller point solution initiatives such as BW 3.5 to BW 7.0 technical upgrades) require greater expenditures for software licensing and services integration. Although smaller organizations wince at SAP pricing, larger organizations are more familiar and less "shocked" by the bigger investments involved in SAP projects.

Tolerance to cost

All of these factors surrounding how SAP is viewed in the large enterprise space provide a distinct advantage to big corporations when dealing with SAP programs. Likewise, this higher visibility and corporate acceptance provide a strong framework for greater leverage over both SAP outsourcing companies looking to partner and internal executive challengers.

10.3   Strong SAP Alignment

SAP — the company — is involved in every SAP installation. Whether from an account executive or professional services perspective, it provides support, guidance, and account management services to customers, big and small. If this is not the case for your organization, then you have either chosen to not be actively involved with your SAP representatives, or your organization needs to change this immediately!

For large enterprises, however, SAP plays a bigger role. Depending on the size of your organization, SAP will be heavily involved in not only a consultant role for SAP-related strategy and product inquiries but also in working with executive management for a long-term roadmap vision.

Building your
IT vision
Many of SAP's strategic accounts — known as global strategic accounts (GSA in SAPanese) — work symbiotically with their customer counterparts, and from an organizational corporate strategy perspective, many customers work together with SAP to design their long-term (and short-term) IT vision.

Large enterprise companies that are tightly aligned with SAP as their strategic software platform have broad and deep access to SAP as a company. (Conversely, smaller organizations — based on their lower software demand and corresponding spend — do not have the same access as clients who spend millions of dollars a year.)

Influence on SAP
As part of this relationship, large enterprise companies have great influence over SAP and also greater access. Obtaining access to SAP specialists in dire times (or non-critical times), to SAP industry and technology specialists for deep-dives into existing or new functionality, or to resources for other atypical requests, is much easier for large enterprise organizations because of their tight alignment (and interdependency) with SAP.

10.4 Bleeding-Edge SAP Technology

Large enterprise organizations also have a distinct advantage over smaller size customers via their access to bleeding-edge SAP technology. Due to the types of initiatives on which large enterprise companies embark and their inherent complexities, SAP typically partners with large enterprise customers on newly developed SAP functionality. This unique access to brand new SAP products is offered only more often than not to large organizations because of their significance, recurring spend on SAP products and consulting, and strategic long-term partnership with SAP as a company.

One concrete and common example is SAP's "Ramp-Up" program. This invitation-only program provides clients with the opportunity to be part of a group of a select few who will have access to new SAP functionality and the corresponding technology. As part of this program, organizations accepted as "Ramp-Up" customers can view SAP's truly latest and greatest product enhancements or products. This gives organizations potential competitive advantages and a "head-start" on how to take their company to the next level utilizing new SAP software before general public releases are available.

Ramp-Up program

SAP strategically decides whom they accept into "Ramp-Up" groups, which includes deciding who will:

▸ Act as a reference to tout new SAP functionality

▸ Provide constructive criticism and recommendations on how to improve the provided functionality

This second point is crucial. By being part of the Ramp-Up program, large enterprise companies are able to help shape products as they desire them to be. This unique opportunity provides another potential competitive advantage to large organizations participating in this sought-after program. Per SAP's own explanation:

Helping to shape the product

> *"With SAP Ramp-Up, you benefit from accelerated support channels and dedicated coaches who have direct access to SAP product development and management. And you gain reduced cost, time, and risk, for both your SAP Ramp-Up implementations and your regular implementations. With*

SAP Services, your company can emerge as a first mover in your industry and your IT department as the strategic role model in your company.

SAP Services performs critical business bunctions: Project scoping analyzes solution scope against expectations and performs feasibility review to determine how we can meet requirements. Project coaching provides a dedicated expert in the SAP Ramp-Up back office so as to expedite channels of support and resolve issues quickly. Knowledge transfer selects highly skilled consultants — trained via programs involving innovative e-learning tools — and organizes communities that enable team members to capture and share knowledge."

Due to the program's competitiveness and desirability, only a minority of participation requests are granted. Therefore, large enterprise companies, due to many of the reasons described earlier, are much better positioned than their midmarket counterparts for program invitation and inclusion. Having the ability to intimately participate in bleeding-edge SAP products, recommend and shape yet to be released SAP functionality, and include these new features into the SAP landscape provides large enterprise SAP shops with much coveted possibilities.

Partnered SAP development

As if the "Ramp-Up" program were not attractive enough, some large enterprise organizations are provided an even more special and unique opportunity: partnered SAP development.

Due to the complexity and robustness of a typical SAP installation at a large enterprise client, the corresponding challenges and business process requirements do not always fit within the parameters of a traditional SAP-provided and standard SAP process. Whether industry-specific functionality regarding a unique industry vertical business practice (such as special customer service needs in the consumer packaged goods arena) or specialized non-SAP provided, canned core technical interconnectivity processes (such as PI/XI adapters needed for new system communication), large enterprise clients encounter custom development requirements not always available in standard SAP software.

In these cases, SAP is sometimes interested in pursuing a rarely exercised approach: partnered development. If SAP believes that a true marketplace need exists outside of this single client and there is revenue potential in the additional functionality, SAP will work with the client to co-develop the new requirement. As a rule of thumb, SAP does not support — let alone encourage — custom development. SAP's business proposition to the marketplace is that core SAP software is capable of meeting the majority — if not all — of your organization's business needs. However, if a customer (or SAP for that matter) identifies a market need, SAP will co-develop the new functionality together with the client. In particular, SAP will work closely with the large enterprise to analyze, design, build, test, and deploy the new features into the customer's SAP landscape.

As part of the arrangement, the customer agrees to allow SAP to include this new functionality into later SAP software releases. For both parties, this is a win-win relationship. From the customer's perspective, SAP provides subject matter expertise within the given product to assist in the design and implementation of brand new functionality and who knows the software better than SAP? From SAP's perspective, the customer is a real-life alpha customer providing industry-specific expertise to shape the most accurate functionality.

Integration into the standard

It is most often large enterprise organizations who are offered this opportunity; small and midmarket companies are rarely asked. Again, due to the size of the organization, spend, and — most important — complexity of business (resulting in important new business requirements), this market segment is the "squeaky wheel" that gets the coveted SAP grease.

10.5 Large Enterprise Consultant Modeling

Due to many of the reasons discussed previously, large enterprise organizations have more unique opportunities than smaller, less funded companies. This statement also holds true in the resource modeling arena. Larger clients can build certain SAP support mechanisms and pursue more investment-type consulting strategies than other market segments. Two specific examples include the BOT model and the COE.

10.5.1 Build-Operate-Transfer (BOT)

The BOT model was explained previously in Section 10.8.2. From a large enterprise perspective, this consultant model can be a unique consultant engagement and subsequent acquisition strategy not available to other market segments.

Economies of scale Because many large SAP enterprise organizations span the globe and thus have an end user base across multiple continents, time zones, languages, and business processes, these organizations' economies of scale provide a unique opportunity.

With the BOT model, large organizations can initially lease an SAP outsourcing firm in a "try then buy" model without having to make an upfront investment. Due to their size and available budget, this lets large enterprises "kick the tires" (or experience) a particular outsourcing firm; other (smaller) organizations do not have this option.

10.5.2 Global Center of Excellence

Another large enterprise SAP outsourcing consulting model is the COE. Although smaller organizations might also leverage a COE model, global corporations servicing a broad range of SAP functionality across a robust end user community have different challenges and, in turn, opportunities than their smaller counterparts.

Shared service The global COE model for large enterprises can act as a shared service. This shared service, supporting processes and technologies across the globe, can be implemented using a variety of methods. For example, a large enterprise might wish to outsource this service completely to an SAP consulting company. Alternatively — and on the other end of the spectrum — the organization might wish to build an internal COE. Or — lying somewhere in between — the organization might wish to use a hybrid model, leveraging internal employees and external resources to build a comprehensive SAP support structure.

> **Case Study: Global energy company and its COE**
>
> During the late 1990s, a global energy company began the momentous task of migrating from its distributed European SAP R/2 systems and non-SAP, legacy, home-grown products into a single SAP R/3 environment. After years of rolling out SAP software and systems across Europe — in over 20 countries spanning Western Europe, Eastern Europe, Central Europe, and Scandinavia — the core implementation team had gained such tremendous SAP knowledge and experience that the rollouts had become efficient and the process fine-tuned to the level of a well-oiled machine.

Based on the breadth and depth of the project team and the need for a comprehensive SAP support mechanism capable of servicing such a robust model, this global conglomerate chose to transition much of the project team comprised of both internal employees and external SAP outsourced resources into their European COE.

As opposed to fully outsourcing their COE services to a third-party SAP specialist or conversely fully supporting end users via a strong internal employee-based model, this large enterprise decided to construct a balanced mechanism leveraging both pools of resources. This model meant strong client presence (enabling knowledge continuity) and included external consulting to round out the team.

This COE exists to this day.

10.6   Summary

Regardless of the SAP outsourcing support services model used, large organizations have the advantage of having access to various SAP service options for supporting their organizations to which smaller companies do not have access. This is a clear differentiator based strictly on company size. Due to the very nature of large enterprises (deeper pockets, greater visibility with SAP and partners, brand recognition, SAP's more strategic role in the organization, etc.), this market segment is positioned differently than their smaller midmarket counterparts.

Although this market vertical's challenges are not drastically different from those of other market segments, their ability to address these challenges and the tools they have available to them most definitely are. Knowing this lets large enterprises more creatively navigate SAP outsourcing obstacles. Clearly, it is to this market segment's advantage to maximize their position and tackle all SAP outsourcing challenges with every arrow in the quiver. Remember, however: As with any discussion about SAP outsourcing generalities exist but the specific solution is always unique to the organization's given SAP initiative, environment, and needs.

Change does not necessarily assure progress, but progress impla-cably requires change. Education is essential to change, for edu-cation creates both new wants and the ability to satisfy them.
— Henry Steele Commager

11 The Midmarket Space

The midmarket — a much explored market segment very familiar with the SAP world and loosely defined as organizations with less than $1.5 billion in annual revenue — struggles with certain unique painpoints not faced by companies in the large enterprise space. Conversely how-ever, this market segment does have access to alternative solutions.

This chapter will focus exclusively on this organizational size and how outsourcing SAP operations can be best leveraged to maximize overall SAP initiatives and improve project efficiencies for companies of this size. This chapter will first present some of the common challenges faced by this market segment and then provide recommendations on how to effectively address these challenges. Although certain large enterprise solutions to outsourcing challenges (such as purchasing a BPO or invoking a BOT) might not be realistic options for midmarket compa-nies, other solutions (such as 100 % outsourced SAP consulting) might just do the trick strategically for the overall most cost-effective delivery for these organizations.

The following are several key areas unique to the midmarket space that will be explored in this chapter:

▶ Unique challenges for midmarket SAP clients such as limited resources and the difficulty to attract SAP talent

▶ The use of the SAP super-super user alternative (aka, the "master of all trades")

▶ How to stretch your SAP investment dollar: application management services and fully outsourcing SAP services

11.1   Unique Midmarket Challenges

Without question, the midmarket has unique challenges. Typically working with greater constraints than its large enterprise counterparts, this special SAP market segment is forced to think creatively. With challenges comes opportunity, and this group is blessed with access to many alternatives when addressing their outsourcing strategy. The following key challenges exist in these types of organizations:

▶ Limited resources

▶ Limited funds

▶ Midmarket multi-tasking

▶ Lack of market appeal

▶ Lack of executive management focus

▶ Unfamiliarity/inexperience

11.1.1   Limited Resources

Smaller companies naturally have smaller IT departments. Continuing with this logic, internal SAP-focused resources are even more limited in supply. Having these bandwidth challenges, midmarket customers often find it difficult to sufficiently support their business user base.

For midmarket companies, the user base — although comparatively small (less than 500 people) — still requires proper "care and feeding." Even in the most basic SAP environments, a bare bones SAP resource plan is required.

Minimum staffing Take for example an organization who has implemented standard SAP ECC, including its core components of SAP ERP Financials, SAP Logistics, and SAP NetWeaver MM. To provide executive-level reporting, the company has also chosen to implement an SAP business intelligence solution such as SAP BW 7.0 or SAP BusinessObjects. Table 11.1 shows the straw man resource pool *required at a minimum*. (This does not take into account some form of help desk mechanism, business process analysts, or project management components.)

SAP Area	SAP Product	Corresponding Resource Skill set
Financials (G/L, AR, and AP)	SAP ECC 6.0	FI/CO functional consultant
Logistics (SD)	SAP ECC 6.0	SD functional consultant
Materials Management (MM)	SAP ECC 6.0	MM functional consultant
Development	SAP ECC 6.0	ABAP developer
Infrastructure	SAP NetWeaver	Basis and Solution Manager administrator
Security	SAP ECC 6.0	Security administrator
Business Warehouse	BW 7.0 and/or Business-Objects	SAP BW developer

Table 11.1 Bare-Bones SAP Support Team for Basic SAP Installation

As you can see, for even the most basic SAP installation, a minimum of eight resources (including some form of designated production support project management) is required simply to keep the lights on!

Attempting to justify this full-time resource model (with potentially limited production support end-user requirements) to upper management will most likely be challenging.

11.1.2 Limited Funds

Although every organization ideally wishes to properly source their SAP resource needs, sometimes life simply does not allow for this. When limited SAP budgets come into play — whether for contingent SAP implementation-focused resources or longer-term COE production support needs — organizations regardless of size are faced with the challenging task of providing sufficient coverage with less than optimal reach. This challenge is even more of an issue for the midmarket.

Generally speaking, smaller organizations are more often than not faced with making their Dollar, Euro, or Yen stretch farther than larger organizations. Having one specialized resource per SAP skill set is usually not

One resource per skill set?

259

only a luxury but downright unfathomable. In fact, most midmarket IT directors or CIOs would view this SAP resourcing model (i.e., one resource per skill set to fully staff an SAP production support mechanism, for example) as "overkill" to the organization and as plain cost-prohibitive.

11.1.3   Midmarket Multi-Tasking

Another key differentiator in this market segment is the need for multitasking. For large enterprise organizations with armies of SAP resources, this is not an issue and individual client or consulting resources can focus on and specialize in a particular SAP area. This is not true in the midmarket.

Let's take for example a typical SAP implementation delivering on a standard SAP ECC 6.0 implementation. Most, if not all, SAP projects implement SAP ERP Financials. As part of base SAP ERP Financials, multiple subcomponents are also usually installed. These include G/L, AP, and AR. (This does not include some other relatively standard FI/CO areas such as Controlling and Treasury.)

In a large scale operation, each SAP skill set would be handled by a different specialized SAP resource. G/L would be handled by one individual, AP by another, and so on. Based on the large enterprise staffing model, in this scenario, five resources would be utilized (see Table 11.2).

Not so in the midmarket. Within this realm, resources are asked to cover more, with a broader focus and less depth. Based on the midmarket resourcing model (whether internal or external), a *single* resource would be tasked to handle *all* of G/L, from a to z. Table 11.2 shows an example.

SAP Resource Requirement	Large Enterprise Approach	Midmarket Approach
Financials G/L	Sally	Robert
Financials AP	Tom	Robert
Financials AR	Sandeep	Robert

Table 11.2 Midmarket vs. Large Enterprise Resourcing Approach

SAP Resource Requirement	Large Enterprise Approach	Midmarket Approach
Financials Treasury	Alex	Robert
Financials Controlling	Jennifer	Robert

Table 11.2 Midmarket vs. Large Enterprise Resourcing Approach (cont.)

Another common midmarket challenge involving multi-tasking is coverage of both SAP and non-SAP areas. For example, smaller IT organizations often leverage the same resource to handle SAP-related issues *as well as* non-SAP issues.

Both SAP and non-SAP coverage

For the infrastructure area, a single resource might be tasked to handle networking, Windows administration, database administration and other infrastructure-related non-SAP skill sets. But that's not all. From an SAP infrastructure perspective, the *same resource* might be charged with covering all NetWeaver Basis, security administration, and Solution Manager activities.

Although not impossible, this SAP resourcing approach can be not only daunting and challenging *but* also escalate risk beyond normal tolerance to unneeded levels. By placing too much responsibility on a single individual, your organization is more exposed to the "bus factor" (i.e., what happens if this resource is unexpectedly hit by a bus) by "putting too many eggs in one basket."

11.1.4   Lack of Market Appeal

When dealing with staffing and resourcing, we often forget that these "resources" are actually human beings, with human emotions. These emotions of course shape perception and an organization's ability to attract SAP talent.

From an external contracting perspective, attracting outsourced SAP talent is much easier and less complicated. Although not solely driven by pay rate, this certainly plays a large factor in deciding in which SAP initiative to participate.

When dealing with full-time resources, salary is only one factor of many. Other relevant decision-making factors — including an organization's location, their reputation with the marketplace, and an individual's perceived growth potential — all have considerable impact on a midmarket company's ability (or inability) to attract full-time employees.

These very real perspectives from prospective permanent employees have an impact for some midmarket organizations. This "lack of market appeal" or perception of being "less sexy" are serious impediments to an employer's ability to attract top talent.

11.1.5   Lack of Executive Management Focus

The midmarket focuses on lean operations and has extra sensitivity to the bottom line. Of course, running the business efficiently is a focal point for all organizations; however, companies with less of a financial "cushion" (such as organizations in the midmarket) employ greater scrutiny and have heightened sensitivity.

No strategic relevance

Because of this perspective, although it is still considered important, SAP as a strategic component within the organization does not have a greater value than any of the other applications used. Thus, in the eyes of executive management of smaller companies, home-grown legacy systems, SAP systems, non-SAP human resource applications (such as ADP or Ceridian), and others all carry the same weight.

Large organizations do not have this problem. Due to the significant investment and strategic nature SAP systems hold in a large enterprise's strategic vision, executives at this level not only understand the tremendous importance of SAP systems from an overall IT perspective but also the company's dependence on these systems. There is a distinctive difference between "lip-service" and true commitment. Large organizations — based on the great expenditures invested in the initial implementation and long term support — understand that if their SAP systems fail, there is a high likelihood that the business will also fail.

Conversely, because midmarket executive management often sees SAP as a product and less as a strategic organizational focal point, it is also viewed as less of a prized "commodity" in a midmarket organization's IT landscape. This attitude toward SAP provides it little leverage or criticality among the other IT applications and makes it difficult to highlight the need for SAP resources because executives do not share the same sense of urgency or importance.

11.1.6   Unfamiliarity/Inexperience

Furthermore, some midmarket organizations underestimate the necessity for top talent (internal or external) when dealing with SAP initiatives. When assigning resources for an upcoming SAP project, it is quite common that the core team consists of resources willing to be "given up" by management.

Again, because these organizations tend to run much leaner, managers in both business and IT are reluctant to provide key players who run their operations. Thus, instead of providing top talent to SAP initiatives (those who understand the business inside and out or system people with the strongest IT skill sets), managers volunteer lower performing resources.

This organizational underestimation can thwart the success of an SAP program. Lack of understanding or unfamiliarity with SAP's complexity, as well as a devaluation of strong resource need commitment, provide additional unnecessary challenges.

Having highlighted several of the common challenges confronted by the midmarket, let's now take a look at how to tackle them. Although the challenges can be daunting, many successful midmarket SAP shops have found ways to address their SAP needs via both leveraging internal employee strategies and outsourcing their SAP operations.

11.2   The SAP Super-Super User Alternative

Through evolution, mankind has adapted and found ways to persevere over every great struggle encountered. Fortunately, the SAP world is no different. Presented with the struggles of having so many areas to cover, a special set of individuals has stood up to the challenge.

Knowledge in
several SAP areas We all either know or have heard of these types of people in our SAP environments. They are individuals who have either been forced to or taken the opportunity to gain deep knowledge in multiple SAP functional and/or technical skill sets. This special breed is known as the "super-super user."

A "master of all trades," this individual is able to effectively support multiple SAP skill sets when others are not. This tremendously valuable type of resource is available across multiple market segments, independent of an organization's size. However, it is the midmarket that gains the most from this level resource.

The super-super user delivery alternative combats many of the challenges described previously such as limited budget/financial resources (which equates to a midmarket organization's inability to hire multiple resources) or limited internal manpower (which equates to a midmarket organization's inability to assign a single resource to a specialized SAP skill set). Taking the super-super user approach is equally as effective for SAP implementation efforts *and* ongoing SAP production support operational activities. The real challenge is finding the appropriate people.

Where to find the
appropriate people Several methods exist that have proven to be effective for finding this talent, as follows:

▶ **Cultivate internal resources**
One method for "finding" super-super users is internal organizational cultivation. If your organization includes individuals who have the aptitude, interest, and potential for becoming super-super users, it is possible to train such talent. Multiple methods exist that you can use for training, including official SAP certification classes, "bootcamps" held by leading SAP partner organizations such as Wellesley Information Systems (WIS), skill set mentoring/pairing with trained knowledgeable resources, or — as a last resort — self-training.

▶ **Permanent placement hire**
If your organization has the budget and ability to hire an already trained resource, this might be a wise decision. Selecting a trained multi-dimensional SAP resource that has extensive experience across the range of areas for which your organization requires knowledge and support immediately addresses your needs. Typically, a good

resource pool can be found in the consulting space. If you are lucky enough to find a "road-warrior" looking to get "off the consulting road," this could be a win-win situation. The permanent placement method often takes more time but is usually worth it.

▶ **SAP outsourcing**

As an alternative to hiring a full-time resource, you can leverage outsourcing services. This option theoretically provides your organization with a proven resource capable of meeting your SAP needs. Due to the readily available resource pool, this option allows you to be highly selective as to exactly the resource and corresponding skill set(s) you desire. Although more challenging to find than a brown squirrel, if you are looking for the "purple squirrel," SAP outsourcing is indeed an alternative.

▶ **Shared service**

The shared service SAP support model (another SAP outsourcing method), provides different and often more flexible options. Instead of paying for a single outsourced resource to be onsite full-time, with the shared service model your organization can pay into a pool of hours that can be applied across multiple resources. For example, if your SAP production support needs include multiple SAP functional skill sets across multiple SAP functional areas, the shared services model provides full SAP coverage. Not all shared services models are the same, however. Therefore, you might receive different support from different individuals on different days for the same SAP functional area. Nonetheless, this alternative is very cost-effective and flexible if you are willing to be accommodating.

11.3 Stretching your SAP Dollar: Outsourcing Options

As we have discussed, midmarket companies typically find themselves in more challenging financial environments than their large enterprise counterparts. Looking to provide the same level of support to their customer base as large enterprises, the midmarket must find creative alternatives via which to stretch their SAP investment.

Midmarket companies recognize this challenge and have in recent years been approaching their SAP purchases and supporting services in innovative ways. Also, SAP has been packaging its software in different ways over the past several years to find more effective ways for its products to resonate with this increasingly growing market segment.

Two very effective cost-saving methods have gained tremendously in appeal in recent times, especially in this market segment. These approaches include SAP Application Management Services (AMS) and fully outsourcing SAP operations. Let's look into these midmarket options.

11.3.1 Application Management Services

AMS as a vendor support mechanism has been around for quite some time. This holds especially true in the non-SAP space. Organizations looking to outsource their hardware (hardware platforms such as servers and networking equipment), underlying infrastructure software (databases such as Microsoft SQL Server), and related support services (database administration, network administration, and operating system support) have been able to go to AMS providers for many years.

With SAP's push into the midmarket — coupled with a greater acceptance for offsite managed infrastructure alternatives — midmarket SAP clients have begun to demand lower cost SAP hosting services and the market and vendor community have responded.

Past cost structures

In the past, if an organization chose to implement SAP systems, their TCO was not just related to SAP software licensing costs and the related implementation services; hardware capital expenditures were also required. For some midmarket companies, this additional investment was far too much. SAP licensing and related installation costs were already hefty expenditures for this market segment and with the additional hardware costs, organizations were challenged even more.

SAP hosting partners

Furthermore, the initial investment was not limited to hardware and software costs. System operators and administrators were also necessary to maintain the infrastructure operations. With the additional cost for a minimum of three full-time employees so that a midmarket company could maintain its own SAP environment and underlying dependent foundational systems, overall cost went over the top.

SAP and its vendor ecosystem recognized this challenge and quickly moved to provide a resolution. Because SAP understood that new sales were not just dependent on SAP licensing costs, the company needed to find ways to alleviate this obstacle. The solution: the SAP hosting partner.

Having this alternative to internal organization infrastructure installation available, customers were able to work with an SAP outsourcing partner focused on providing full application management services.

Leveraging the SAP AMS outsourcing model, midmarket organizations are able to benefit from numerous commoditized products in any number of combinations. The list that follows describes the support service options, beginning with the most technical level (infrastructure support) and continuing on to the more application-level suite of services:

▶ **Data center operations**
At its core, an environment must sit on top of hardware products that provide the foundation for the system. This data center layer and its corresponding infrastructure technical support services cover security requirements, data backup and disaster recovery needs, resource maintenance, and the electrical power supply.

▶ **Networking services**
On top of the data center reside all of the networking and connectivity devices. This layer provides midmarket clients with the ability to connect with the AMS provider. Issues concerning latency, networking system performance, and the like are dealt with by those responsible for this area.

▶ **Operating system administration**
Next comes the operating system. Different AMS and SAP hosting providers work with different operating systems depending on preferences and customer demand. In the SAP world, most SAP customers — whether midmarket or large enterprise — utilize Microsoft Windows or Linux. Although the vast majority of SAP customers work with Windows, there is a growing trend to use Linux. The associated AMS support services focus on maintaining high quality system performance and seamless operating system operations.

▸ **Database application support**
In the SAP space, most customers work with Oracle, Microsoft SQL Server, or (in some cases) MySQL. For smaller midmarket companies, MySQL service is a lower cost and sufficient database alternative. From an AMS support services perspective, this group provides database tuning while working alongside the NetWeaver Basis administration resources.

▸ **SAP NetWeaver administration**
The final standard AMS service typically provided by SAP hosting providers is SAP application layer or NetWeaver Basis support. This group and corresponding service provide the lowest level of SAP infrastructure support. SAP Basis services focus on NetWeaver activities such as system installation (setting up a new SAP environment/box), SAP system tuning and operational activities, hotpack/enhancement package application,, and other operational services. These SAP Basis services do not generally include the daily "care and feeding" activities such as transports, SAP Note application, and printer setup. (However, these types of services are available at an additional cost.)

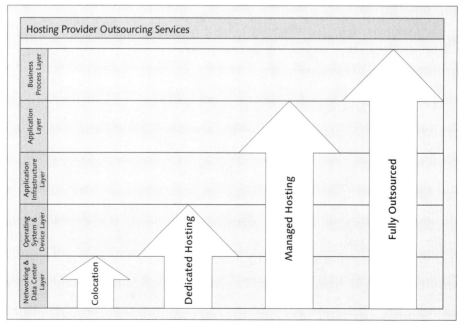

Figure 11.1 AMS Service Capabilities

As described previously, the traditional SAP hosting model does not typically include NetWeaver activities above and beyond the standard suite of operational activities. However, to provide a more enticing services offering, many SAP hosting providers have begun to provide additional NetWeaver activities. For example, some of the Basis activities discussed previously could be added as additional services to your SAP hosting model if you are interested in doing so. A cost/benefit analysis would need to be done but based on the amount of activity and agreed on SLAs, it might be worth your while.

Additional SAP support services

In addition, some in the SAP AMS world have also either begun or already fully established "upstream" SAP support services (as shown in the Application Layer and Business Process Layer in Figure 11.1). These technical SAP application-level services (ABAP custom development, security, etc.), along with SAP business process functional configuration support, now provide customers with a "one-stop-shop" scenario for your entire SAP support needs. Combining traditional SAP AMS services with SAP Global Delivery capabilities, midmarket organizations can now work with a single SAP provider from a to z.

For a listing of SAP-recommended AMS providers, refer to *http://www. sap.com/ecosystem/partners/partnerwithsap/hosting/amsproviders/index.epx*.

11.3.2 Full Service Application SAP Outsourcing

Another SAP support alternative that is becoming very popular in the midmarket space is full service application SAP outsourcing. This model has become extremely popular for customers dealing with post go-live production support needs. With this model, instead of attempting to build an internal SAP support mechanism with full-time employees, midmarket organizations are able to fully outsource their SAP needs (and sometimes their overall IT needs as well).

Many midmarket organizations who are not IT-focused feel that although SAP is a fundamental component in their overall system portfolio, they are not an SAP consulting organization and they have no interest in becoming one. Building a skill set and workforce to maintain their SAP environment is viewed as a diversion from core competence and would take the focus away from the organization's primary business objective.

Focus on core competencies

Therefore, instead of investing into the resources necessary to support an SAP environment, midmarket companies are turning to partners. Depending on the customer requirements and the SAP outsourcing vendor's model, midmarket organizations are able to partner with an outsourcing provider capable of meeting their business (SAP functional configuration such as controlling, production planning, project systems), technical (SAP security administration, SAP portal, SAP custom development), infrastructure (NetWeaver Basis, Solution Manager), business intelligence (SAP BW, BusinessObjects), and even help desk (level 1, level 2, level 3) needs.

Case Study: Novolyte and its fully outsourced SAP model

Previously part of a large corporation, Novolyte Technologies was spun off in the last quarter of 2008. Prior to the divestiture, all of Novolyte's production support needs were handled by an overreaching corporate-wide SAP production support COE. "Our SAP post-production services were handled internally when we were part of the greater organization. However, after the spinoff we were confronted with the decision as to how we will handle the SAP production support needs," remembers Rick Watkins, Novolyte Technologies' corporate controller. "It was a service that we took for granted in the past." Standing at a crossroads, Watkins and the company needed to decide which path to pursue for their 100 person user base: internal support or fully outsourced SAP Global Delivery. For Watkins, it was an easy decision. "Based on the amount of investment required to hire a full-time SAP production support team versus working with a partner for on-demand support, the decision was simple. It was a no brainer."

Thus, after becoming their own company (including an inherited SAP ECC 6.0 environment), Novolyte chose to outsource their entire IT functions across two outsourcing providers to support all infrastructure needs (both SAP and non-SAP) as well as their entire SAP application support services. Watkins and Novolyte Technologies as a whole are extremely satisfied with the result. "The outsourcing path we followed has provided us a cost-competitive alternative in which we are extremely pleased." Watkins would easily choose this option again and recommends his choice to other midmarket organizations of similar size.

Different models

There are just as many permutations of outsourcing models as there are SAP outsourcing vendors in the marketplace. However, a common set of models provided by outsourcing vendors to the midmarket does exist.

Each of the alternatives has its advantages and disadvantages related to various pricing models. The following are several of the primary fully outsourced SAP constructs:

▶ **Pooled resources (non-dedicated)**

Instead of having a dedicated SAP production support resource assigned to service your organization full time, with this model, your SAP needs are met by a pooled team of resources. Because of the nature of this model, this is typically one of the least expensive production support alternatives. With this model, any available skilled resource will work on the issue until a resolution has been found. Think of it as throwing an issue over a fence and whoever is available on the other side of the fence picks it up and works on it. Although pricing is typically an advantage with this model, support resource unfamiliarity can be a distinct (and major) disadvantage.

▶ **Pooled resources (dedicated)**

With this model, dedicated pooled resources are assigned to service your organization. This means that instead of random resources working on your issues (as is the case with the non-dedicated model), your organization will have multiple resources familiar with your account assigned to it. Although a given issue might not always be serviced by the *same exact* resource, it will be handled by one from a pool of dedicated resources. With this model, learning curves are shortened and organizational knowledge is cultivated (rather than lost).

▶ **Minimum number of hours**

Some SAP outsourcing partners require that clients commit to a minimum number of hours (and in turn, associated cost) per time factor. Constructs of this type typically revolve around either monthly or weekly periods of time. To ensure that client commitment exists and that the arrangement is beneficial to the vendor, the customer commits to a certain number of hours its organization will utilize. This minimum number can be either by skill set or across the entire SAP production support mechanism. In rare cases, these SAP production support outsourcing partners also provide "roll-over" features allowing companies to use unused hours from the previous month in the following month. Table 11.3 shows an example.

Resource	Hourly Rate	Minimum Monthly Hours	Estimated Cost
Integration Manager	$0	160	0
Offsite Production Support Manager	$0	160	0
Windows 24x7x365 Support (Level I)	Fixed monthly fee	N/A	$X
SAP 24x7x365 Support (Level I)	Fixed monthly fee	N/A	$X
HCM Support (Level II)	$X	40	$X
PP Support (Level II)	$X	40	$X
ABAP/XI Support (Level II)	$X	40	$X
Security Support (Level II)	$X	40	$X
FICO Support (Level II)	$X	40	$X
Total Minimum Monthly Cost			$X

Table 11.3 Minimum Number of Hours SAP Outsourcing Model

▶ **On-demand**

This "pay as you go" support model is the mobile phone equivalent in the SAP world. Instead of committing (and paying) for a minimum monthly amount of allocated SAP production support time per resource, your organization only pays for the actual amount of activity performed by the SAP outsourcing partner. This SAP production support model is very attractive to customers due to its pricing efficiency and the on-demand feature can also be combined with either of the two pooled resource models described previously.

▶ **"24x7x365"**

One of the most robust SAP outsourcing models is the "24x7x365" construct. Supporting an SAP organization 24 hours a day, seven days a week, 365 days a year is an outsourcing arrangement that is truly comprehensive. It should, however, only be utilized if the customer performs SAP operations around the clock and most midmarket organizations do not have this type of services requirement. However, if a company does require such a model, the associated costs are not usually as high as one would think. However, by employing this model, resource needs do increase three-fold to cover the additional two shifts.

11.4 Summary

As discussed in this chapter, the midmarket segment has special SAP support challenges not faced by the Fortune 500. Issues driven by company size such as limited resources and limited funds as well other factors cause midmarket companies to approach their SAP outsourcing obstacles with creative alternatives. With challenge also comes opportunity; and as discussed in this chapter, for every problem there is a solution.

A dose of common sense is worth a thousand consultant hours.
— Guillermo "Bill" Garcia (Altoviento Solutions)

12   The Value of IT Standardization

To most effectively leverage SAP outsourcing providers, it is imperative that both customer and vendor speak the same language. The standardization of IT processes, governance, integration, and engagement strategies all play a fundamental role in ensuring that you are getting the most out of your provider and, conversely, that your SAP outsourcing partner clearly understands your expectations.

The key to this is standardization.

Although the term "standardization" can have a myriad of meanings depending on the audience, for the purposes of SAP outsourcing, we will focus on the definition of business process standards. A business process is the way an organization does its work; it includes the steps followed to accomplish any given objective. Business process standardization deals with achieving a consistent way of executing these processes. When consensus is reached about the activities and flows that constitute a given process, the measurement of the process performance can begin.

Business process standards

Throughout the course of this chapter, we will explore several of the main components within IT process standardization and how standardization plays a fundamental role when dealing with SAP outsourcing operations and fine-tuning your IT mechanism. We will discuss the following:

- ▶ The value of IT business process frameworks
- ▶ Widely utilized IT business process frameworks such as Information Technology Infrastructure Library (ITIL) and Control Objectives for Information and related Technology (COBIT)
- ▶ High-level roadmaps on how to conduct a project to standardize IT processes

12.1   Why bother with standardization?

Over the course of the last few years, IT organizations have begun to explore the role of standardizing IT processes. Companies have gone through multiple cycles; eliminating silos; working on making their different organizations speak a common, industry standard language; and focusing on aligning IT services with business priorities.

Better position to negotiate

The results have been multi-fold. An organization with an ongoing process improvement process is on the right track to run IT as a business. However, the rationale or motivation does not end here. As part of the growing trend toward outsourcing SAP operations, organizations have begun to perform this activity in preparation for outsourcing their SAP initiatives/pursuits. Not only does standardization provide a baseline for vendor partnership but furthermore, it can provide more negotiating leverage during contract discussions.

But what can an organization do to improve its negotiation position if the current operations are not standard, are difficult to understand (perhaps even by internal customers), and are poorly documented? The can do plenty, for example the following:

▸ Define and initiate a process of documentation and continuous improvement

▸ Build a strategy aimed at improving the communication between different IT areas

▸ Facilitate the work with consultants charged with the task of understanding the current operation

▸ Develop and support the construction of an outsourcing proposal

But the question still stands… why bother?

Lower TCO

The answers to this question are many. Getting the house in order, so to speak, before outsourcing commences reduces the TCO of your outsourced process. When SAP service providers quote services, they often calculate fees based not only on the ongoing costs to provide the service (plus a margin) but also on the transition costs from the current operation to the outsourced model.

Even in deals that include setup (one-time) fees, the ongoing rate may include a margin of safety, which is likely going to be in direct proportion to the ambiguity of the current state of your SAP processes.

If your IT operation still exists as a set of silos that are poorly integrated and difficult to understand, your organization could greatly benefit from a focused initiative (sometimes even a project) aimed at documenting key processes, making your operation as transparent as possible, and initiating a continual improvement activity that will eventually facilitate the integration of existing processes with the outsourced operation.

Any progress your IT organization achieves before engaging potential SAP outsourcing service providers to analyze your operation and quote services will ultimately result in a more competitive quote at the end of the evaluation process.

12.2 Implementing Strong IT Practices — IT Process Frameworks, Industry Standards, and Other Tools

There are many approaches an organization can take to standardize its IT operation and to improve its processes, ranging from continuous improvement to business process reengineering. (That discussion is a book in itself!) Therefore, the objective of this section is not to present any complex methodology or the proposal for a multiyear strategy. Rather, we will discuss one "quick and dirty" approach — a simple, no-nonsense alternative you can initiate in a very short period of time: a process documentation and continuous improvement initiative.

If your organization has the time and resources to initiate a major project, it is highly recommended to do so. However, if you are looking to improve your operation in small steps utilizing your current resources and tackle the low hanging fruit of better understanding your operations and adopting a common set of standards, this section is for you. It will provide practical, common sense, and proven ideas applicable within even the most stringent resource constraints.

277

There are several bodies of knowledge than can facilitate the standardization and simplification of an IT operation. They include ITIL, COBIT, Capability Maturity Model Integration (CMMI), Project Management Body of Knowledge (PMBOK), and several others. The following are several of the most widely known and accepted industry standards and models for the documentation, standardization, and continual improvement of IT practices and processes:

ITSM   IT Service Management (ITSM) encompasses the disciplines required for making IT work. It includes, among others, incident management, configuration and asset management, change management, capacity management, availability management, service level management, IT service continuity management, security management, and financial management for IT services.

Global de-facto standards for ITSM such as ITIL allow an IT organization to align its operation to the priorities of the business. It also:

▸ Simplifies the work and delegation of activities. When everyone works from the same page of the same book, job roles are consistent and performance measurement becomes straightforward.

▸ Facilitates resource assignment and increases accountability.

▸ Allows IT areas to understand the scope, responsibility, and processes of their fellow areas.

▸ Enables integration and reduces the likelihood that critical tasks are overlooked.

▸ Simplifies the vendor management and service level management processes, facilitating setting service delivery expectations with contractors, service suppliers, and outsourcers.

▸ Facilitates the documentation of key processes and the definition of performance measures.

▸ Expedites the transfer, deployment, and replacement of staff.

ITIL   ITIL is the most widely used collection of best practices in IT service management. It was developed by the United Kingdom's Office of Government Commerce (OGC) and is supported by several publications and an international user group. The best practice processes promoted in ITIL both support and are supported by standards BS15000 and ISO 20000.

COBIT is an IT governance and process framework that provides a generic process model for a typical IT function, creating a bridge between what operational managers need to execute and what executives need to govern. It was created by the Information Systems Audit and Control Association (ISACA), and the IT Governance Institute (ITGI) in 1992.

COBIT provides managers, auditors, and IT users with a set of generally accepted measures, indicators, processes and best practices to assist them in maximizing the benefits of the use of information technology and in implementing appropriate IT governance and control in a company.

It facilitates, among others, to:

▶ Organize IT activities into a generally accepted process model.

▶ Link business goals to IT goals.

▶ Efficiently leverage IT resources.

▶ Define the management control objectives, necessary for the successful delivery of IT services.

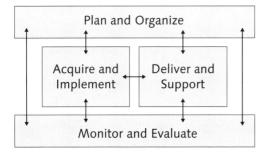

Figure 12.1 COBIT Domain Framework

As shown in Figure 12.1, COBIT defines IT activities in a generic process model within four domains. These domains map to the traditional IT areas of plan, build, run, and monitor:

▶ Plan and Organize (PO) — provides direction to the other processes in line with business priorities.

▶ Acquire and Implement (AI) — provides the solutions and passes them on to be turned into services ("solution delivery")

▸ Deliver and Support (DS) — takes control of the solutions and makes them available to end users as IT services ("service delivery")

▸ Monitor and Evaluate (ME) — monitors processes to ensure that the direction provided is followed

Process maturity models

Many questions can be addressed when trying to evaluate how IT is being managed and IT's effectiveness supporting business goals. For example:

▸ What are your peers doing, and how are you doing in relation to them?

▸ What is an acceptable industry good practice, and how are you placed regarding these practices?

▸ Is your organization doing enough?

▸ What do you need to do to reach an adequate level of management and control over your IT processes?

A good place to start is to establish a baseline, based on the current status (or maturity) of the IT processes. Understanding a relative measure of where the IT organization is, can help determine where to go and the level of maturity desired in a set timeframe, and help define a tool for measuring progress against the goal.

A method for measuring process maturity was originally introduced by Carnegie Mellon's Software Engineering Institute (SEI) to measure the maturity of software development capability. This Capability Maturity Model (CMM) later evolved to become Capability Maturity Model Integration (CMMI), a process improvement approach to guide organizations through their process improvement efforts. CMMI helps integrate traditionally separate organizational functions, set process improvement goals and priorities, provide guidance for quality processes, and provide a point of reference for appraising current processes.

Since the introduction of CMM in the early 90s, several maturity models have emerged as a means to measure the relative maturity of a process. COBIT also introduces a basic maturity scale that can easily be applied to IT processes, as shown in Table 12.1.

Maturity Level	Description
0, Non-existent	Non-identifiable process.
1, Initial/ad hoc	No standardized processes; instead, ad hoc approaches that are applied on a case-by-case basis. Management is disorganized.
2, Repeatable	Repeatable but intuitive. Similar procedures are followed by different people undertaking the same task. No formal training or communication of standard procedures, and the responsibility is left to the individual. High reliance on the knowledge of individuals (therefore, errors are likely).
3, Defined process	Processes and procedures have been standardized and documented, and communicated through training. Following these processes is mandatory, although deviations are not easy to detect. The procedures are not sophisticated but rather a formalization of existing practices.
4, Managed and measurable	Compliance with procedures is monitored and reported. Management takes actions where processes appear to not be working effectively. Processes are under constant improvement, and automation and tools are used in a limited or fragmented way.
5, Optimized	Processes have been refined, based on the results of continuous improvement efforts. Technology is leveraged, providing tools that improve quality and effectiveness. Processes are resilient, easy, and quick to adapt.

Table 12.1 CMM Maturity Levels

COBIT provides guidelines to perform a process maturity assessment, describing the characteristics of the IT processes as they evolve from a non-existent to an optimized maturity level. These attributes can be used for assessing and documenting the current state (taking a snapshot of the as-is state) and for defining maturity goals (to-be state). After the as-is and to-be states have been determined, the IT organization can pro-

Process Maturity Assessments

ceed to perform a gap analysis between the two states — actual and desired — to determine what it would it take to get to the desired state and to initiate a process improvement initiative.

The dimensions used by COBIT for determining the maturity of a process are as follows:

▶ Awareness and communication

▶ Policies, plans, and procedures

▶ Tools and automation

▶ Skills and experience

▶ Responsibility and accountability

▶ Goal setting and measurement

Later in the chapter, we will also mention some of the ITIL-based tools that enable process maturity assessments of IT service management processes.

PMBOK A PMBOK guide is regarded as one of project management profession's most essential resources — a de facto standard for the project management practice. It can help project management practitioners prepare for credential examinations, or assist organizations in creating and shaping their project management system and methodologies.

Theory of Constraints (TOC) TOC is a continual process improvement philosophy, originally introduced by Dr. Eliyahu Goldratt in his book "The Goal. Beating the Competition" (Gower Puplishing 1986). It provides guidance to improve processes and organizations by focusing on very few issues: the constraints to ongoing profitability.

The TOC views organizations as systems consisting of resources, linked by the processes they perform. The goal of the organization is the primary judge of success. A constraint is defined as anything that limits a system from achieving higher performance relative to its purpose. The interdependencies between the activities in a process makes the analogy of a chain (or network of chains) very descriptive of a system's processes. In the same way that the strength of a chain is determined by its weakest link, the performance of a process is determined by a few constraints that are affecting the throughput (or efficiency) of the process.

TOC proposes a systematic and focused approach to continual process improvement:

1. Define the system and its purpose (goal).
2. Determine how to measure the system's purpose.
3. Identify the system constraint.
4. Decide how to resolve the system constraint.
5. Resolve the system constraint. When a constraint is eliminated, go back to step three and identify the next constraint to resolve.

12.3 A Simple, Common Sense Approach to IT Process Standardization and Improvement

Process improvement methods can provide a big return on a modest investment. A no-nonsense approach to process standardization and continual improvement includes the implementation of a continual improvement program that combines tools for the following:

▶ Creating a process improvement discipline (e.g. Deming method [plan, do, check, act], TOC)

▶ Determining a baseline and goals for process improvement (CMMI)

▶ Straightforward process redesigns (good practices process frameworks such as ITIL or COBIT)

In this section, we will include an example of how to take a process from an "initial" level to the point where key processes are — at least — "repeatable" or even better, "defined."

12.3.1 Adopt an IT Service Management Framework and Start Speaking a Common Language

The benefits of speaking a common language within your organization are immense. To explain this, it helps to ask people to list the number of terms used in a single organization to refer to an IT incident. ITIL defines an incident as "an unplanned interruption to an IT service or reduction in the quality of an IT service". In different organizations an "incident" may be referred to as a "ticket," a "call to the help desk," a "problem," or an "issue." Conversely, ITIL defines a "problem" as "the root cause of one or more incidents."

Consistent terminology

Wouldn't it be beneficial if all the incumbents in the IT lifecycle used the same terminology for the same terms? Guaranteed, it would. Otherwise, you're using too many terms — just multiply the possible variations of the meaning of a term by the number of terms and the participants in the communication process and you'll see how this is a problem. Using ITIL is helpful because it is the de-facto standard for IT service management (ITSM) in companies and any major outsourcer understands and speaks this "language." You can also benefit from this by improving the chances to effectively communicate with your counterparts and service providers.

Multiple courses exist that provide the fundamentals for ITIL and ITSM. Among the key training providers are Pink Elephant, Hewlett Packard, and Computer Associates. Two and a half days of training provided to your IT leads followed by a certification exam at the end of the training may be all your organization needs to understand the benefits of ITIL and to get motivated to learn more and, hopefully, adopt some of the guidelines.

This training, along with management support and sponsorship, is a great starting point.

12.3.2 Initiate a Project to Adopt a Common Approach to IT Service Management and Document Key Processes

After your key leads go through ITIL awareness sessions to introduce the idea and benefits of adopting a process framework and get certified in ITIL foundations, the organization is better positioned to adopt a common language. This common vernacular sets the reference framework (including your outside SAP Services providers) in which to begin the selection of key management and infrastructure staff to form the core driving forces behind project definition and implementation.

Documenting key processes

Your first step on this project would be to document key processes, starting with those likely to be SAP outsourced.

ITIL provides a good frame of reference to document and redefine IT service management processes. In this area, you may need the expertise and tools of someone who has gone through a similar process before. If your company has a quality program such as QS9000 or Six Sigma, you could leverage their process documentation standards and tools to document your IT processes. Remember to "keep it simple," documenting enough detail to be able to communicate and evaluate improvement opportunities but leaving the documentation high level enough so that documentation doesn't become an endless exercise.

A good process document should contain at least: Contents

1. Purpose

2. Scope

3. Definitions

4. Roles and responsibilities

5. High level process flow

6. Additional notes and comments

7. Key performance indicators (KPIs)/metrics

8. References/source materials

9. Document revision record

10. Approval

11. Appendix and addendums

12.3.3 Assess your Organizational Process Maturity Level

A key activity in the process is to determine the level of process maturity of your key processes. To do this, you can use a frame of reference such as ITIL or COBIT (or a combination of the two) and a process maturity model similar to CMMI. Many SAP consulting companies provide these services at a low cost — especially when there is the possibility to provide additional services — helping you take advantage of "quick hits" and "low hanging fruit," as these opportunities are often called.

To determine the current state of your IT processes or take a snapshot of   Tools
your current state (as-is) with an IT maturity assessment, you can also

285

pay for a self assessment tool such as Pink Elephant's PinkScan (a very good start for the do-it-yourself crowd).

An accurate assessment of the current situation is important to:

▸ Build a business case for introducing best practice IT service management to your organization.

▸ Understand the hot spots that will provide the most visible and high impact results for your business.

▸ Develop benchmarks for evaluating the success of the best practices implemented.

▸ Determine the quick hits and the order of implementation for the range of good practice processes.

12.3.4 Determine Process Maturity Goals

The next step is determining where the organization envisions itself in the future and when this can be attained. This process requires:

1. Prioritizing your process improvement needs

2. Selecting which processes to tackle/improve first

3. Developing an implementation plan

After you understand where your organization or business processes stand, you need to define where you want to be, and when. You can do this using the same maturity scale and the criteria used to evaluate your as-is state. With a clear evaluation tool, you should be able to determine not only the level, but also the steps that will get you there.

Using this information, you can create a roadmap to achieve the next level of maturity and to take advantage of "quick hits," documented in the previous phase.

At this point, and to define your target maturity and goals, you may decide to compare your processes with industry benchmarks or other organizations' data. However, in the interest of keeping it simple, you can rest assured that the basic goal of improving your processes continuously, one step at a time, will result in enormous benefits over time and will help you improve the maturity of your organization.

12.3.5 Identify Improvement Initiatives and Define an Implementation Master Plan

After you have determined the capability levels you want to reach for selected processes, you need to determine how to get your processes to the expected level of maturity.

To achieve this, you will need to define an implementation plan aimed at closing the gaps between the current state of your processes and the desired state. This plan will look more like a portfolio of initiatives rather than one isolated project. At this point, you will also execute plans to collect the low hanging fruit; the short, low-effort and relatively high return projects you envisioned in the previous phase.

12.3.6 Launch Improvement Projects and Execute

For the purpose of illustrating the case for process standardization, we will oversimplify matters in this section. However, that does not mean that any initiative in the IT world can be taken lightly. Structure and consistency are fundamental to success when running initiatives or executing projects, and a good project management approach is the best way to achieve stated goals. The world of best practices — or "good practices" as they are referred to now — provide de facto standards for project management, such as PMBOK and Projects in Controlled Environments (PRINCE). However, because we decided to keep this illustration simple and thus are assuming minimum process maturity, a short time frame, and limited resources, we will mention an — again — oversimplified approach, in this case, to manage these initiatives.

When you know what initiatives you are going to undertake, list them all in spreadsheet or project management software. Then, list the ten major things that need to happen to implement each of the initiatives. Next, estimate activity duration and sequence the tasks, considering priorities and dependencies. After you complete the prioritization and sequencing of your portfolio of initiatives, you need to verify resource availability and adjust your plan if necessary.

List, prioritize, sequence

Execute Good project management does not require expensive tools and complex processes. Furthermore, considering the elemental nature of the initiatives in our example, we will only include a few tool recommendations to control and run projects effectively.

You can start by defining a project charter. This document describes the project basics, including objectives, approach, and scope. Important sections in a project charter are as follows:

- Executive summary
- Problem statement
- Business vision, goals, and objectives
- Measurable objectives
- Assumptions
- Constraints
- Methodology/approach
- Risks
- Roles and responsibilities
- Scope (in scope/out of scope)
- Deliverables
- Milestones
- Benefits
- Costs
- Interdependencies
- Metrics/success factors
- Stakeholders
- Approvals
- Appendix

Another important tool is the project work plan that lists key activities, duration, dependencies, and responsibilities. Although a spreadsheet can be used for this, the recommended tool is project management software.

Also, track action items, issues, risks, and agreements in a project management log. Tracking these items facilitates control and enforces accountability. Key fields to include in a "project management log" (also called "PMLog") are shown in Table 12.2.

Key PMLog Item	Description
PMLog item #	The ID number automatically assigned to the action item
Type	Specifies whether the record refers to an action item, a project issue, an agreement, or a risk
Phase	Identifies the project phase for the action item or project issue
Short name	A short name or category that identifies the action item
x-Ref	ID of other record(s) with which this PMLog item has a dependency
Reported date	The date on which the PMLog item was recorded
Reported by	The person reporting the PMLog item
Priority	High, medium, or low
Description	A detailed description
Responsible	The person responsible for resolving this action item or issue
Due date	The date by which the action item or issue needs to be resolved
Accept (Y/N)	Specifies whether the responsible person has been notified and accepted the assignment
Status	(C)losed, on (H)old, in (P)rocess
Date	The date when the action item or issue was resolved or closed
Solved (Y/N)	Specifies whether the action item or issue was resolved
Comments	Additional comments

Table 12.2 PMLog Fields

As you complete your initiatives, do not forget to evaluate the results. Successes are your best tool to get your organization to support subsequent initiatives, and the lessons learned will help you improve your project management practice and capabilities.

Close and measure results

12.3.7 Compare Results Against Original Objectives and Start Again

The process described previously is a point of reference, not a methodology. There are many ways to address the challenge of process standardization and this chapter presents one proven, simple set of steps to better understand the kind of activities that need to happen to get your organization speaking the same language and following standard processes. Subject matter expertise is certainly crucial when defining a project like this; however, executive sponsorship is one of the most important success factors.

After you implement the first set of processes with concurrent in-depth training and certification of key staff, assess the success of the first stage of the venture.

At this point, you are ready to start again, assessing your new organizational process maturity level.

12.4 Standardization in SAP Environments

In Figure 12.2, SAP presents an interesting combination of best practices. Components from Run SAP, ITIL, project management, and application management are combined to illustrate a best practice approach to IT service management in an SAP environment. Your SAP outsourcer will likely get your organization close to a similar model but the more you advance in that direction before the transition, the greater the likelihood that you will obtain better rates.

In this chart, SAP presents an service management environment comprised of three core areas: application management, which is responsible for the support and continuous improvement of the SAP applications landscape; integration processes, which are responsible for the integration of new capability into the production environment; and service management based on the ITIL framework, which is responsible for the overall support and delivery of IT services and operation.

In this section, we will introduce an IT process framework based on ITIL that will help you understand the extent to which core processes can be documented to facilitate the understanding of the current state, the definition of process improvement goals, and the communication with outsourcing providers.

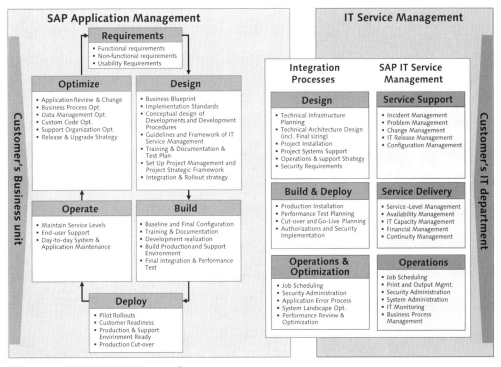

Figure 12.2 SAP IT S&AM Framework

In contrast to model in Figure 12.2, the chart shown in Figure 12.3 presents the SAP Service Management processes in a context that includes ITIL, Run SAP, and the SAP Applications Management frameworks.

In this figure, the green bubbles underline ITIL's service delivery processes, defined to support long-term planning and optimization of an IT environment. Underlined in blue are ITIL's service support processes, which focus on short term incident resolution, controlled management of changes, and an effective and efficient management of infrastructure assets. The yellow circles represent processes defined in the Run SAP methodology for the adequate management of an SAP production environment and operation. Finally, the processes underlined in red present a typical applications management environment, with cycles starting in the documentation of business requirements, ending in the transition of the new functionality to production (SAP operation), and including a well defined and ongoing process improvement and optimization initiative to continuously drive value to the business.

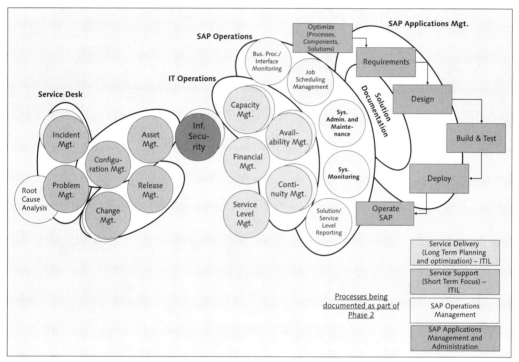

Figure 12.3 Service Management Chart, Mapping ITIL, Run SAP, and Applications Management Frameworks

12.5 IT Processes — Where to Start

Several process frameworks exist that provide a structure to prioritize the processes you need to document and perhaps standardize. Three good examples include COBIT, ITIL, and American Productivity Quality Center's (APQC's) process classification framework. These frameworks assist in laying the necessary foundation for standardization. Each of the organizational functions and processes — when properly defined — enable your IT group to maximize your IT functions and, in turn, enabling better SAP outsourcing return!

12.5.1   IT Processes — Context Diagram

To better understand the context of IT processes, let's take a look at a high level representation of an IT organization from the process standpoint.

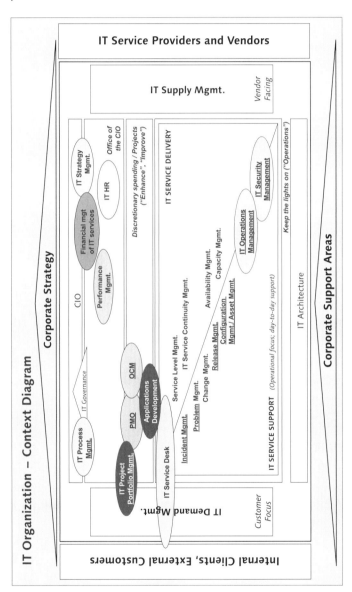

Figure 12.4 IT Governance Context

The graph in Figure 12.4 shows key process areas in an IT organization:

1. IT management
2. Demand management
3. Supply management
4. IT portfolio and project management or the management of discretionary spending
5. IT service management or the processes to run IT or "keep the lights on"
6. Support processes such as IT architecture

Another representation of an IT operation and its key processes is shown in Figure 12.5.

This figure shows key process areas in an IT organization:

1. IT management
2. Demand management
3. Supply management
4. IT portfolio and project management or the management of discretionary spending
5. IT service management or the processes to run IT or "keep the lights on"
6. Support processes such as IT architecture

This framework, or a similar one, is a great start to understand the context of the services that could potentially be outsourced and to determine the scope and priority of the outsourcing endeavor.

12.5.2 IT Process Documentation

In this section, we will include a brief description of a few key IT processes, developed based on ITIL, and intended to illustrate an adequate level of detail and a starting point for initiating a process documentation initiative.

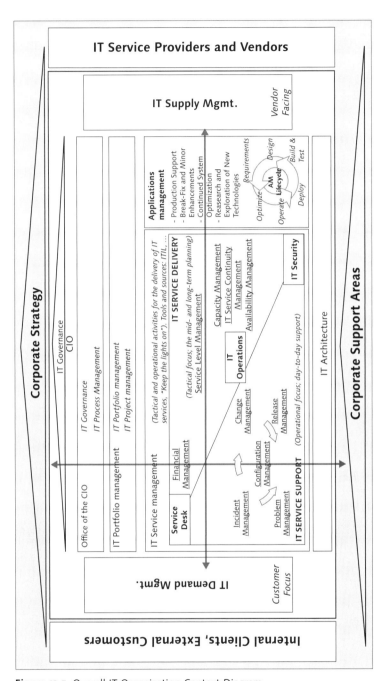

Figure 12.5 Overall IT Organization Context Diagram

The list that follows is a summary of core IT processes for documentation and standardization purposes:

- IT process framework
- Strategic planning
- IT governance
- Performance management
- Project portfolio and project management
- Organizational change management
- Change management
- Incident management
- Problem management
- Release management
- Asset and configuration management
- Security management
- Manage information systems (IS) operations
- Service level management
- Applications development
- Human resources management
- Risk management
- IT procurement and vendor management
- Data management
- Financial management of IT services

SAPanese: The SAP standardization tool — SAP Solution Manager

Much has already been said about Solution Manager (Chapter 7) and its features; however, this powerful multi-faceted tool should also be mentioned again when discussing process standardization. Solution Manager and many of its components allow an organization to build common processes around IT functions. Whether internal technical features such as CSA and CSM; implementation-related components such as Project Administration; or "client-facing" functionality such as Service Desk — all provide a standard method of performing repeatable functions.

When dealing with SAP outsourcing providers, such common processes (especially because they are performed via SAP tools) provide the correct framework for IT services.

You can use this list as a baseline for prioritizing the core processes in your IT area: potential targets for standardization and continual improvement. Some definitions are as follows:

► Service level management — defining, negotiating, and monitoring agreed service performance

► Availability management — ensuring services are available when, where, and how they are required

► Capacity management — ensuring that capacity exists to support service delivery

► Service continuity management — planning for service delivery in the event of a disaster

► Incident management — restoring services as soon as possible

► Problem management — diagnosing and eliminating problems that result in service outage

► Change management — controlling changes to the service supporting infrastructure

► Configuration management — managing the data related to the service supporting infrastructure

► Release management — managing releases of key service components

► Financial management — managing IT budgets, cost models, and charge-back models

12.6   Other Tools for IT Process Standardization

Creating a service catalog is a critical step in ensuring that IT services align with business needs. It helps establish a standard set of IT service offerings, with associated service levels and costs. A service catalog, created with the internal customer in mind, provides the basis for a balanced, business-driven discussion on trade-offs regarding the cost and

IT services catalog

quality of the services offered. It enables a continuous, win-win discussion between the customer and the service provider that ensures higher customer satisfaction, optimized costs, and SLA compliance.

Once in place, a service catalog can drive changes that will both reduce costs and improve service quality. The ability to accurately measure the value and performance of service delivery enables IT to adapt to changing business conditions and apply resources — whether internal or external to the company — in an optimal way.

Service catalogs can provide the means to:

▶ Define IT services and SLAs that align with business needs.

▶ Manage service delivery and adapt to customer demand.

▶ Ensure efficient service delivery by automating fulfillment and monitoring service quality.

▶ Communicate the value that these services represent to the business.

A service catalog also facilitates the balancing act between the demand and supply of SAP services. A focus on the demand can lead to runaway costs, whereas a focus on the supply can lead to poor alignment. A service catalog brings balance by facilitating the continuous monitoring of the balance between demand and supply, by enabling process-based accountability, and by tying metrics and goals to results instead of work.

A service catalog is:

▶ *The* definitive source for all approved IT services.

▶ A primary point of interaction with customers.

▶ The system of record for the fulfillment of service requests.

▶ A tool to measure IT and vendor performance.

A service catalog, however:

▶ Does not replace other means of interaction between IT and its customers.

▶ Is not a portfolio management tool.

▶ Does not replace a help desk tool.

Some of the key benefits of implementing a service catalog include streamlined communication between IT and its customers, effective management of client expectations regarding the service they are buying, enabling clients to create customized service portfolios, helping IT to translate service offerings into supporting product and infrastructure requirements, and serving as a key component of an IT portfolio management and governance strategy.

ITIL/service level management defines an SLA as an agreement between an IT service provider and a customer. It describes the IT service, documents service level targets, and specifies the responsibilities of the IT service provider and the customer. A single SLA may cover multiple IT services or multiple customers.

SLAs

In contrast, an operational level agreement is defined as an agreement between an IT service provider and another part of the same business that provides services to them.

Finally, an "underpinning contract" is a contract with a third party that supports delivery of an IT service by the IT service provider to a customer. The third party provides goods or services that are required by the IT service provider to meet agreed service level targets in the SLA with their customer. The topic of SLAs is discussed in much greater detail in Chapter 15.

ITIL/configuration management defines a configuration management database (CMDB) as a database used to manage configuration items (CIs) throughout their lifecycle. The CMDB records the attributes of each CI as well as relationships with other CIs. A CMDB may also contain other information linked to CIs, for example incident, problem, or change records. The CMDB is maintained by configuration management and is used by all IT service management processes.

Configuration management database (CMDB)

Configuration management is the process responsible for maintaining information about CIs that are required to deliver an IT service, including their relationships. This information is managed throughout the lifecycle of the CI. The primary objective of configuration management is to underpin the delivery of IT services by providing accurate data to all IT service management processes when and where it is needed.

A CI is any component that needs to be managed to deliver an IT service. Information about each CI is recorded in a configuration record within the CMDB and is maintained throughout its lifecycle by configuration management. CIs are under the control of change management. They typically include hardware, software, buildings, people, and formal documentation such as process documentation and SLAs.

The aforementioned tools are a great complement to an IT process documentation and standardization effort, aimed at making the operation of an IT area more transparent. There is a lot of information to cover with reference to this area but if this chapter generated enough interest for you to learn more about how to standardize your IT operation, the objective has been fulfilled.

12.7   Summary

The contents of this chapter can help IT organizations develop a process-oriented and customer-focused methodology to assist in the alignment of technology services to business priorities and to enable the continuous improvement of the delivery of information services.

Some of the benefits you can derive from this activity are as follows:

▶ Having a standardized method to prioritize SAP investments. This includes the management of the collection of projects in which a company invests to implement its strategies and the processes to identify, prioritize, authorize, manage, and control projects.

▶ Having a standard process to perform changes to the technical environment with minimum disruption to IT services.

▶ Having an incident management process to return IT services to customers as quickly as possible and to minimize the adverse impact on business operations.

▶ Having a consistent environment for continuous improvement.

▶ Improving customer satisfaction through better and measurable availability and performance of the IT service quality.

▶ Improving communication and information exchange between IT personnel and their customers.

Through the implementation of world class methods and standards, an IT organization can set the stage for a successful update of the SAP environment and for an improved delivery of overall information services. Companies can become more customer- and service-oriented and will be able to continuously improve their effectiveness as they consistently deliver world class services to the business they support.

Aside from preparing the organization for an easier, smoother, and more effective transition to an outsourced environment, and increasing the likelihood of reducing transition costs, the following is a list of other potential benefits from a process documentation, standardization, and continual improvement initiative:

- ► Align IT with the organizational goals and strategy
- ► Raise the profile of IT
- ► Implement compliance
- ► Help convert strategic goals into IT projects
- ► Perform project and portfolio management/gain increased project visibility
- ► Minimize IT risk
- ► Perform IT strategic planning
- ► Measure performance
- ► Embed IT into the organization's culture
- ► Manage demand for IT services
- ► Optimize IT operations
- ► Balance supply and demand (of IT services)
- ► Increase cost transparency

Success, remember, is the reward of toil.
– Sophocles

13   The Role of the Integration Manager

Most SAP outsourcing models build some form of onsite or integration management structure and presence. The extent to which the chosen BPO partner is assimilated depends on multiple factors. In the past, organizations did not treat their BPO partner as an extension of their organization but instead as more of a "pitch it over the fence" disconnected service.

However, as part of the new integration models and as outsourcing has become more readily accepted, alternative options have arisen, including full-time integration management, onsite consultant integration, and hybrid products.

Very few positions in an SAP organization hold as much influence and power as that of the integration manager. Part gatekeeper, part oracle, part politician, part navigator, and part conduit (to name just a few), the integration manager's unique role transcends multiple skill sets and, in turn, requires a special type of person.

Multiple skills required

For organizations that understand the importance of this critical position, leveraging an integration manager the correct way can help steady the SAP (production environment) ship, deal with ever-changing currents, and still maintain the proper course. The integration manager, if empowered and supported by a support control advisory board (CAB), can maximize an organization's SAP investment while continuing to grow its value in the business.

This chapter will discuss the nuances behind integration management and cover the following key points:

- The role of the SAP integration manager
- The key characteristics needed by the integration manager
- The integration manager's relationship to the delivery mechanism and CAB
- What an integration manager sees and thinks (an insider's view)
- The necessity of having an integration manager

13.1 The Integration Manager: A Definition

For organizations unfamiliar with the role of the integration manager, the position might seem foreign and its definition might be unknown to them. Conversely, some organizations may believe that they understand the role's definition, although in reality, they do not. Thus, the initial step in understanding why an integration manager is best-suited to assist your organization in optimizing your SAP initiatives is to first clearly define what the role is and what it is not. Only then can a true understanding of its value to the greater SAP production support mechanism be appreciated.

Integration as a challenge

By definition, we all understand that SAP as a product is heavily integrated. Its tight interconnectedness is both a benefit and potential liability to an SAP installation. Modification in one area — although seemingly independent from other SAP functionality — can not only have an impact but could actually cause damage in another.

Thus, understanding both the integration and complexities involved in SAP is fundamental to maintaining its integrity, maximizing its functionality, and minimizing any unneeded disruption. The solution: the integration manager.

Responsibilities

The integration manager is charged with several primary responsibilities:

- **System protector**
  Acts as the guardian/gatekeeper/bulldog of productive SAP environment(s)

- **Referee**
  Reviews and vets proposed SAP modifications and changes to the system

- **Oracle**
  Understands the SAP functional and technical "touch points" across the system

- **Super connector**
  Brings together all key stakeholders, owners, and appropriate parties involved in discussing proposed SAP changes

In essence, the integration manager is responsible for stewarding your SAP environment.

Sumit Manocha of TRM consulting — a seasoned SAP veteran with over 10 years of experience, who has acted as an integration manager numerous times — has a strong opinion based on his personal experience and business process focus. He writes:

> "A successful integration manager is someone who can keep day-to-day issues under control, provide effective resolutions in a timely manner, guide all concerned parties (business users, support staff) and manage business expectations."

Although the integration manager holds many responsibilities and "titles," this role is not and should not be a "dumping ground." Also, the integration manager should not be expected to be a master of all SAP knowledge (clearly an impossible task). All specific SAP application expertise (both functional and technical) still clearly remains the responsibility of the respective application owner(s). Likewise, the application ownership remains the responsibility of those dedicated resources (as part of the overall COE model), along with the corresponding work activities.

What the integration manager should not do

Vlad Eydelman of Reditech Incorporated — an experienced SAP integration and project manager for over 12 years — stresses this point:

> "The integration manager [should] manage the project timeline, scope, and deliverables and ensure a quality product... [but] don't have the integration manager focus on executing the solution. This takes away from the value an integration manager offers."

Some organizations rely too heavily on their integration managers because of this person's broad SAP knowledge. Furthermore, some integration managers fall into the trap of accepting this responsibility for a number of reasons (e.g., their ability to deliver, guilt/embarrassment, unwarranted sense of responsibility, to expedite issue resolution, etc.) Although the integration manager should be familiar with all of the SAP puzzle pieces, the specific details must reside with the experts. Failing to delegate could ultimately lead to less than ideal results and backfire.

13.2 An Integration Manager's Persona: Characteristics and Attributes

The integration manager is human. However, based on all of the needed characteristics one might assume that an integration manager comes from a distant planet populated by super humans. Although this is not the case, a successful integration manager must have certain characteristics and emulate a specific persona. As the saying goes, "it's not what you say, it's how you say it," for this role, style is just as important as substance.

Navigating through highly passionate, emotionally charged, and important SAP environment issues takes a confident leader able to earn (demand) the respect of implementation colleagues as well as understand how to best maneuver in tumultuous waters. Unfortunately, issues of corporate politics, hidden (and not so hidden) agendas, and incompetence all exist as potential obstacles.

Independence   Therefore, it is fundamental that an integration manager not only is open-minded but also presents himself as objective, independent, and fair. Failing to be perceived as such and, in turn, unwilling to listen to all parties could promote an unhealthy environment and hamper the integration manager's ability to get things done.

Beyond political acumen, a successful integration manager must be respected. Due to the attention focused on this position in any of the SAP outsourcing delivery mechanisms (such as a COE, production support, or implementation model) as well as in the organization at large, the integration manager must be seen as a competent team player focused on the organization's success. Perception is reality. If the integration manager is perceived as power-hungry, self-serving, politically motivated, or inept, his ability to effectively initiate change will be compromised.

As with any position in an SAP organization, respect must be earned and not demanded. Due to this position sitting squarely at the crossroads of many SAP business units, technologies, organizational departments, and so on, it is imperative that the integration manager behave in a way that will be respected, hoped to be emulated, and ultimately admired.

Finally, with such responsibility and attention, confidence is key. If team members smell uncertainly or weakness, the integration manager's role could be jeopardized, nullifying any authority. Exuding a strong understanding of the issues, their integration points, and who from the greater SAP outsourcing delivery model should be involved in any given discussion all must be displayed to promote faith in the integration manager and trust in the process.

Confidence

At the extreme end of confidence lies arrogance, which could be debilitating. Being perceived as a "know-it-all" or as condescending prevents the integration manager from building cooperation and collaboration. Regardless of ability, if an integration manager is seen as difficult to work with, his effectiveness is lost. Therefore, the thin line between cockiness and confidence should never be crossed.

13.3 The Role of the Integration Manager and the Relationship to the Control Advisory Board

The integration manager holds a special role in the overall context of the SAP outsourcing delivery mechanism. The integration manager is not only the primary protector of the SAP environment but also its gatekeeper. In the gatekeeper role, the integration manager leads the organization's CAB (see Figure 13.1).

When dealing with change requests either during an SAP project or after an SAP installation has been successfully implemented, these major modification requests to the system must be reviewed in a systematic process via a defined review board. In many organizations, this review governance board is known as the control advisory board (CAB).

Control Advisory Board

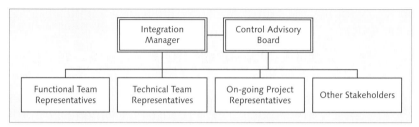

Figure 13.1 The Integration Manager and the Relationship to the CAB

Regardless of group title, most organizations have an advisory group comprised of key stakeholders and technology and business process owners who review proposed changes to the SAP productive environment. Whether formal or informal, every organization should have some review mechanism ensuring environment integrity.

This review board, which includes the integration manager, should only be engaged for significant modifications to the system. (Although this injects some subjectivity to the process, every organization is different and has different thresholds. It is therefore the responsibility of the organization to define the tolerance level and at what stage the CAB review process must be engaged.)

SAPanese: Change management in the SAP realm

Change management in SAP projects is perhaps one of the greatest challenges, if not the greatest challenge. Regardless of how well designed and implemented your SAP environment may be, if your internal customers do not embrace the system, all will be lost. Therefore, the role of the integration manager also includes strong ambassador skills.

Furthermore, well designed and executed training must be provided to the end user community (your clients) to ensure that they not only understand the system's features but also feel a part of the process. Although the emotional aspects are often underestimated and overlooked, they are just as important as the technical SAP activities!

Although day-to-day issues should be addressed by either the implementation delivery team or the production support mechanism (such as a COE) directly via help desk and tracking tools, major modifications to the system and enhancement requests should be addressed via the CAB mechanism.

Comprised by all of the necessary stakeholders and subject matter experts, the CAB is led by the integration manager. The CAB's role is to address any enhancements, major modifications, or significant change requests to what has already been delivered or designed. For productive SAP environments — and depending on the role of the COE — this may even include additional projects (both small and large) to your SAP system.

Led by the integration manager

As the "chairperson" of this review board, the integration manager works with the CAB to facilitate healthy, constructive, and productive discussion. Utilizing his needed characteristics as described previously, the integration manager ensures that the proposed changes presented to the CAB are clearly articulated by the presenters, rationalized and justified, and thoroughly vetted.

Typically, the CAB meets frequently (daily, weekly, or bi-weekly) to hear and discuss proposed design changes. During this standing meeting, representatives from the delivery team and other vested individuals (external project team members, etc.) present requested changes to the CAB. During the requestor's presentation, the CAB is able to ask questions to fully understand the scope and rationale for the requested change.

In a sense, the CAB sits as a court to hear, interpret, analyze, and judge the requests. After hearing all of the requests in a given session, the CAB approves or rejects the proposals. Approved proposals are assigned a priority in conjunction with any existing change requests and are subsequently worked on by the appropriate SAP delivery team members.

Because not all CAB members are technology savvy, in some cases the integration manager must act as an interpreter, translating SAP terminology and functionality into layman terms. Based on personal experience, Sumit Manocha notes:

> "Apart from being able to understand technology, [the] integration manager needs to understand the core business and be able to talk to the user community in their language."

Also, when presenting modifications to the advisory group, the integration manager must ensure that all relevant parties are included in the discussion; this translates into the respective presenting parties (if it is a cross functional/technical discussion) and the affected stakeholders/ business users. The integration manager chairs the review process, challenges when necessary, and assists in prioritizing approved SAP functionality (or technology) changes.

However, the integration manager does not act as royalty, sitting in a throne simply blessing proposed SAP system modifications. As an extension of the SAP outsourcing delivery model, the integration manager must also act as a SAP outsourcing advocate. Whether representing outsourcing requirements to the CAB or the organization, the integration manager is figuratively the elected representative of the SAP delivery mechanism.

Therefore, it is imperative that the integration manager also place the overall organization's interest first. Furthermore, because the integration manager serves the greater SAP environment, he must also set aside personal opinion if it conflicts with the better interest of the delivery team. Clearly, this role takes a special character, temperament, and demeanor to fill. That is, not everyone is capable of being an integration manager.

Based on their position in the organization and their unique role, integration managers are afforded a different perspective into the inner workings of an organization's SAP environment and how companies can best maximize their SAP investment. Sumit Manocha believes that integration managers should be focused on three key core tasks:

> *"One, to make sure, all existing processes are running smoothly and to iron out any issues in a timely manner on a daily basis; Two, to fine tune and enhance current processes to optimize the organization's returns on investment; [and] Three, based on past experiences, to suggest and implement solutions that will create value for the organization in the long run, overriding all initial costs."*

Project management skills
Beyond providing SAP-specific guidance and knowledge, integration managers feel that strong project management skills are essential. Eydelman could not emphasize this enough based on her personal experience. In fact, she ranks strong project management skills over SAP application knowledge:

"The most important component is sound project management skills. Again, the integration manager needs to know how to manage the relationship between the client and the team and deliver a solid product/solution that follows solid project management methodology."

Although understanding the SAP application suite and technology is important, effectively managing change, prioritizing properly, managing aggressive schedules/deadlines, and focusing on reducing cost all take precedent.

This highly influential and critical position is, of course, presented with challenges. Sumit reflects:

"The biggest challenge an integration manager faces in today's global environment… is the dispersed nature of its business operations across the globe. Whether it's the business users, the support staff, or the third-party partners, the fact that they all are spread across different time zones sometimes makes it difficult to resolve an issue in a timely manner."

However, in his experience, this challenge has likewise provided opportunity:

"The same challenge sometimes works in favor of the integration manager by having part of the support staff on the other side of the globe so that when the business community is done for the day, the support staff is working on the issue to be resolved before users come back the next morning."

Vlad agrees and highlights another common challenge: balancing the client's needs and demands against the skill sets of the delivery team:

"During the ramp-up phase, most of the knowledge of custom code/processes lies with either the integration manager or the former project team. It takes time for the [delivery resolution] team to come up to speed. So, the integration manager has to balance the learning curve with client expectations and managing cost."

13.4 Necessity versus Nicety

In the early heyday of SAP and with the "best of breed" philosophy (i.e., when different leading software packages were selected by an organization per distinct functionality), the SAP product suite and corresponding footprint was less comprehensive. This is no longer the case.

Driven by an externally focused acquisition strategy of purchasing leading software products such as BusinessObjects, Virsa, Outlooksoft, Lighthammer, and so on, coupled with an aggressive internal development effort to expand the SAP product reach, SAP is now well positioned to capture a strong percentage (if not all) of a business' strategic needs.

Multiple SAP products

Thus, there is now a higher probability that organizations are leveraging multiple SAP products in a company. Therefore, understanding how SAP works, its touch points, and its integration is all the more crucial to the success of an IT organization. This is the role of the integration manager. Lacking a "global" SAP picture and failing to appreciate the interconnectedness could severely damage an environment and compromise day-to-day business.

Many businesses are now choosing a single ERP provider. Often, that ERP provider is SAP. In turn, SAP as a product suite is becoming more and more a strategic business decision for organizations. As the organization continues to consume more SAP functionality (whether this functionality is internal to SAP ECC/ERP or includes non-ERP components such as CRM, BW, BusinessObjects, etc.), its dependency on understanding SAP grows as well.

Ensuring that a champion, system owner and protector, and strategic visionary exists is paramount to long-term success. These are all responsibilities of an integration manager.

An integration manager is crucial regardless of organizational size

When it comes to the need for an integration manager, organizational size or the size of an organization's SAP footprint or IT organization doesn't matter — that is, all organizations need an integration manager. Typically, larger organizations understand the need and rarely dispute its justification; this is not, however, always the case with smaller organizations. To the contrary, smaller IT organizations often challenge the need for the integration manager role. However, this stance does not make sense because all of the reasons that larger organizations require an integration manager hold true for smaller companies as well. To be exact: smaller SAP footprints also require a champion and oversight because all SAP environments have to have ownership assigned.

One alternative for smaller organizations struggling to justify this position is "doubling up." This means that perhaps the integration manager position and another delivery team position could be held by the same individual. Depending on bandwidth and organization environment, this model can be successful. The bottom line is that the role of the integration manager is no longer a luxury but a necessity.

13.5   The Integration Manager from your Offsite Partner

Regardless of the delivery model, whether internally driven or leveraging an SAP outsourced vendor, the integration manager is crucial. However, when dealing with an SAP outsourcing partner, the role is even more important. (Note that there should be only *one* integration manager in an organization. This section is meant to highlight some of the specific nuances unique to the integration manager's role if he is provided by your SAP outsourcing provider.)

Because your SAP partner's "eyes and ears" are those of the onsite integration manager, this role should be part of any offsite delivery model or vendor proposal. Therefore, the vendor's integration manager sits at the crossroads of many processes within offsite delivery.

Because of the sheer number of so many moving parts, the vendor integration manager must ensure that everything is being driven properly. Activities, including work efforts being designed and developed across time zones; business workshops being conducted to gather end-client business requirements; executive and project management demanding delivery status; and so on all require attention to detail and strong customer interaction.

The vendor integration manager must remain on top of all of this activity. This role requires a person who can juggle multiple activities and who can multi-task effectively. Of course, a comprehensive understanding of SAP products and technology is crucial, that is, understanding how the SAP components, products, and technologies interrelate is paramount.

Responsibilities

If your assigned integration manager fails to cover any of these responsibilities, *replace him*! There is no time for learning on the job or failing to meet your requirements — this role is truly the most important role when partnering with an SAP outsourcing provider. There is little room for error due to the large responsibility that sits on top of the integration manager's broad shoulders.

However, although the partner integration manager is the onsite representative of the offsite SAP delivery team, he (just like an internal integration manager) should not be expected to be a master of all SAP knowledge. Specific SAP application expertise (both functional and technical) and overall ownership remains the responsibility of the respective offsite delivery team members (as part of the overall SAP outsourcing delivery structure), along with the corresponding work activities.

Some organizations also rely too heavily on their partner integration manager (because of his broad SAP knowledge) or have unrealistic expectations of the integration managers' responsibilities. Unfortunately, because of the pressure partner integration managers are under and because of their sensitivity to client perception, some of them fall into the trap of accepting this responsibility. This can happen for a number of reasons, for example, their ability to deliver, guilt, embarrassment, unwarranted sense of responsibility, or perhaps a need to expedite issue resolution.

Delegation   Although SAP partner integration managers should be familiar with all of the SAP puzzle pieces, responsibility for specific details must reside with the respective experts. Failing to delegate could backfire, leading to less than ideal results.

With delegation, however, comes responsibility and again, the partner-assigned integration manager must understand and support this. The responsibility for delivery resides with the offsite model and regardless of the model used, the offsite delivery arm is responsible for acting as the arms and legs of the integration manager. Therefore, when leveraging an SAP offsite model, the SAP consultants supporting the organization should perform all delivery work, whether technical (e.g., SAP NetWeaver Basis system monitoring, ABAP development of custom objects, and design and modeling of security profiles) or functional (e.g., G/L account creation, sales order type modification, and plant extensions).

13.6   The Integration Manager's Counterpart: The Offsite Delivery Support Manager

The integration manager in any model does not work alone. Although he is the "face man" for the offsite delivery organization, an army of resources exists supporting and delivering what has been committed. One such managerial resource worth noting is the offsite delivery support manager.

This important role is pivotal to the overall success within an offsite delivery engagement. Organizations usually employ an offsite development or production support manager, depending on the organizational model and the amount of effort involved.

When the amount of effort and activity is too much for an integration manager to track, this offsite manager acts as the primary point of contact for the onsite integration manager. The support manager oversees all offsite development work, escalates any delivery issues to the integration manager, and provides accurate and timely updates regarding the status of outstanding delivery work. This person is essentially an onsite extension of the integration manager offsite.

13.7   Summary

The role of the integration manager provides an SAP organization and the respective SAP environment with a dedicated focal point responsible for maintaining both corporate SAP vision and system integrity. Lacking this type of oversight, integration, and facilitator can lead to the unraveling of your SAP environment and eventual rework of the system (i.e., wasting time and money).

Understanding the relevance of this fundamental position — along with addressing the key points in this section — can help solidify a firm and stable course for your changing SAP environment. Conversely, ignoring the need for an integration manager can damage your organization's ability to navigate the inevitable change or even worse, cause your SAP environment to be compromised.

*Peak performers see the ability to manage change as a necessity
in fulfilling their missions.*
— *Charles A. Garfield, American peak performance expert,
   researcher, trainer*

14   Service Level Agreements

The standard to which an organization holds their BPO partner is paramount to its overall success. Service level elements such as response time, risk, escalation management, change control, communication protocol, and so on all must be defined, established, and mutually agreed on by both customer and partner. This chapter will speak to these important benchmarks, the generally accepted rules, common business practices, and recommendations unique to various models.

When working with an SAP outsourcing partner, clear expectations must be set between both parties to ensure that there is no disconnect. Miscommunication or misperceptions are fatal when working with any partner; this is even truer when adding a distance factor.

Clear expectations

In this chapter, we will explore several of the primary factors involved in establishing, fostering, and maintaining a fair and comprehensive suite of vendor SLAs. High level SLA factors include the following:

▶ How to establish clear, fair, and comprehensive SLAs

▶ SAP tools to use in managing SLAs (Solution Manager's Central System Administration and Service Level Management tools)

▶ The appropriate SLA guidelines and determining factors for SAP environments, SAP technologies, and SAP business scenarios

14.1   Establishing SLAs

Defining the SLAs, response times, and hours of operation (if applicable) are fundamental in ensuring that clear expectations exist between your organization (the client, SAP end users, and the business) and your chosen SAP outsourcing provider. Setting clear, well understood, and agreed on expectations ensures that there is no misunderstanding on what defines the various levels of severity and how quickly issues will be resolved. Few things can be worse for an organization on either an implementation or production support initiative than a disconnect between how the production support team is meant to support the business.

It is imperative that all of the necessary stakeholders (project sponsor, project managers, integration manager, IT director, CIO, etc.) are involved in defining all of the service-related criteria. Including all of the correct players from the beginning ensures management commitment and project team "buy-in."

14.1.1   Primary Components

Three primary technical components are needed when establishing SLAs, as follows:

- Vision and purpose
- Services performance
- Terms and conditions

All three categories must be clearly defined by the partner and agreed on by the customer to ensure the proper foundation for delivery.

Vision and Purpose   A solid direction must be established from the onset, identifying what purpose the agreement is meant to serve. Similar to a corporation's vision statement, this purpose declaration documents why an SLA exists and what purpose it serves. An example vision for an SLA could be as simple as that outlined in the box "SLA sample vision."

SLA sample vision

The purpose of this SLA is to establish a clear understanding of how ABC SAP Consulting (ABC) will provide SAP production support outsourcing services to XYZ Customer (XYZ). This SLA will:

- ▶ Outline services to be offered and working assumptions between ABC and XYZ
- ▶ Quantify service level expectations
- ▶ Establish quantitative metrics with which to measure the quality of service provided
- ▶ Define escalation procedures and levels of severity
- ▶ Provide a method for resolving conflicts

This purpose statement provides direction to the service provider from day one. All additional requirements are driven from this vision statement, and therefore, it is important to concisely and concretely identify the reason for the SLA's existence.

The next major component in SLAs is services performance. This includes key metrics and the respective rules of engagement. Different SAP outsourcing models can have different initiative-specific key metrics or KPIs. However, typical metrics exist that many organizations use, especially in the SAP production support space. These include:

Services performance

- ▶ **Hours of operation**
  This defines the hours during which your SAP outsourcing provider will provide delivery services. An infinite number of possibilities exist such as normal client hours of operation (e.g., 9am to 5pm); 24 hours a day, seven days a week, 365 days a year (24x7x365); or on demand. These parameters provide the framework for when your organization has agreed on support.

- ▶ **Scope**
  For what is the SAP outsourcing vendor providing services? This detailed definition should clearly articulate exactly what SAP components and versions, levels of support, and so on will be covered by the partner. This section in the SLA document should also clearly identify what is out of scope. No assumptions should be made. Everything understood should be covered and highlighted.

- ▶ **Severity levels**
  This subsection states the various levels of severity along with their respective definitions. Typically the levels start at low and move up in severity through medium, high, and finally, critical. Each of the sever-

ity levels is allocated a respective definition. For example, critical severity is typically defined as causing the business to lose revenue.

▶ **Response time**

As part of the agreement between customer and vendor, specific response times must also be defined. Response time is the amount of time in which the vendor must respond and acknowledge that the given issue exists. It does *not* equate to resolution time. (That is a separate metric.) Response times are based on severity levels. If a given severity is deemed of higher criticality, the response time provided is typically faster due to the higher urgency.

▶ **Resolution time**

Along with response time comes the time in which an issue must be resolved. This key metric is also based on the level of criticality, with more urgent issues requiring quicker resolution.

▶ **Service levels**

If your organization is using an SAP service provider for multiple "levels" of delivery, these layers must be defined. Levels include bands of support, effort, or experience that are provided as distinct SAP services. For example, if your organization is employing a third-party SAP Services provider for both help desk and medium experience SAP configuration support, your organization would likely want to define two service levels: level 1, SAP Service Desk, and level 2, SAP functional configuration experience.

▶ **Process flow**

Finally, the given method for support must be documented in the SLA document and agreed on. This process flow defines the methods in which the provider and customer will engage as well as the tools (see Figure 14.1). For example, to clearly document issues, provide service level statistics, and optimize outsourcing services, a third-party tracking tool such as Remedy might be utilized. Furthermore, the process flow might also be provided within a flowchart to clearly show the customer to vendor interaction, along with their dependencies.

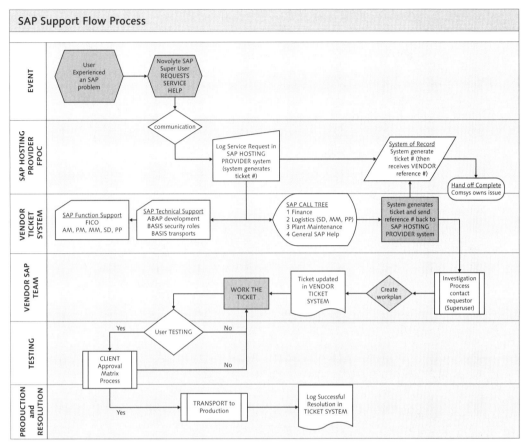

Figure 14.1 Sample Process Flow (SAP Production Support Example)

The final component in the SLA is specific engagement terms and conditions (T&Cs). T&Cs provide yet another contractual agreement between the two parties, ensuring that there are no assumptions or disconnects.

Terms and conditions

T&Cs frame some of the administrative and logistical nuances that define the relationship. Examples might include the tools that are utilized (ticket tracking-related, work effort management, and statistical and metrics-based reporting), escalation methods, key contacts, review procedures, and other key administrative areas of interest not covered by the other SLA sections.

14.1.2 Defining the Correct SLA Amount

After understanding the various aspects of an SLA, the next step is defining what is specifically required for unique engagement and specific needs. That is, it is imperative that SLAs are appropriately "sized."

A careful balance must be struck between too much and too little. Failing to define — upfront — the proper amount of SAP outsourcing support can prove to be debilitating to your organization and too much SAP support can prove to be a waste of money.

The process through which to appropriately define your SAP outsourcing SLA levels is more of an art than a science. For organizations that have "been there, done that" in this space, the process is much easier because it can be based on metrics, previous knowledge, and experience.

For organizations that have never been through this process before it can be not only a daunting challenge but could result in a costly mistake.

The following are several key areas to think about when constructing an SLA for the first time (or any time for that matter):

Use an RFP
Assuming that your organization has yet to choose a partner, open up the opportunity to multiple partners using an RFP. As part of the RFP process (see Section 10.4.3 on how to create an RFP), require that your vendors provide SLA proposals.

Even if you believe that a given partner is the correct one to choose and there is no need to "shop the RFP around," it is still highly recommended to test the waters. The RFP process, along with the provided deliverable, will not only help educate but will likely also promote more competitive pricing.

This valuable step will also allow you to compare various approaches and assist in shaping the best SLA(s) for your scenario. Assume that prior to the RFP process (if you originally did not see the need to take this to market), you had a favorite or front runner. By engaging additional vendors in the RFP process, you now have the luxury of comparing the other vendor responses against that of your favorite. Without going through this process, you would not have had this free-of-charge "apples to apples" comparison, which just might turn out to show that a different vendor can meet your needs better, perhaps even at a better cost.

Similar to the point made previously, leverage the information and experience your vendors can provide. If you choose not to take your SAP outsourcing opportunity to the marketplace, request (or better yet, require) that your vendor provides a detailed SLA to use as the foundation for discussion.

Leverage your vendors

Remember that you are in control of the negotiations and it is your organization that defines what your needs are. However, your SAP outsourcing partner is also supposed to be the subject matter expert in this space and it is the SAP outsourcing partner's responsibility to help provide guidance and recommendations if your understanding is not accurate. Although you might not always agree with a vendor's perspective, being provided with candid and constructive feedback is the responsibility of a true partner. Sometimes what you don't agree with is exactly the message you should listen to.

Everything equates to cost. This is especially true when you are dealing with SLAs and SAP outsourcing agreements. It is only logical that the higher the level of service, the higher the associated cost. Therefore, when deciding the appropriate level of SAP services and support, remember that cost is impacted.

SLAs and pricing

14.2   SLA Supporting Tools

The primary tools utilized in the SLA world are similar to some of the tools previously discussed in earlier chapters of this book. Tools such as SAP Solution Manager's Central System Administration; ticketing tracking tools such as Heat, Remedy, and Peregrine; and work management and development tools such as VersionOne can all be leveraged equally effective in this space. Because the different tool categories have been discussed at length already, this section will not rehash previous material but merely state that they should also be considered when dealing with SLA's.

Beyond some of its components discussed previously, Solution Manager has a dedicated sub-component that focuses exclusively on SLAs and reporting. It is appropriately called Service Level Management (SLM).

Per SAP, SLM is explained as follows:

> *"Solution monitoring — SAP Solution Manager performs centralized, real-time monitoring of systems, business processes, and interfaces, which reduces administration effort. It can even monitor intersystem dependencies. Proactive monitoring helps you avoid critical situations, whereas automatic notifications enable fast response to issues."*

In layman's terms, SLM provides proactive service level tracking functionality (configurable specific to an organization's given processes and requirements) to ensure that the agreed on levels of support are provided to the appropriate parties. Whether for internal SAP production support users, COE management, SAP end users, or other dependent parties, SLM provides the framework in which to gauge the effectiveness of your outsourced SAP provider.

As part of the configuration and setup process, Solution Manager guides you through a series of "best practice" documents used to form the needed SLM teams, document your "customer's" SLA requirements, and configure these SLA requirements within SLM. (Customers could be end business users, internal SAP COE team members, or management.)

The next step is establishing the proper intervals used in SLA reporting. Specific to the given process and corresponding resolution, SLA intervals are defined and then assigned to the proper responsible party to link the metrics needed in service level reporting (SLR).

Within SLR, all compliance metrics can be analyzed to assess the effectiveness of your SAP outsourced provider. These running compliance levels — including the KPIs established as important — enable your organization to leverage Solution Manager for SLA monitoring and reporting. See Figure 14.2 for an SLA report example.

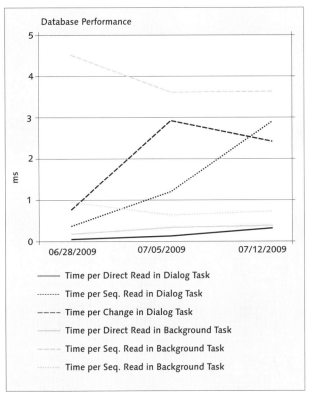

Database Performance

Figure 14.2 Example SLR

14.3   SLA Guidelines and Determining Factors

In the SAP space, guidelines exist that can provide a framework for how an organization can establish meaningful SLAs across a wide range of areas. As with any guideline, they are meant to serve as a reference to be consulted, not a "hard and fast" edict.

We will discuss several of the primary areas where SLA best practices should be utilized.

14.3.1   SAP Landscape

Different SAP landscape components may require different service level needs.

A simple example of this is based on the specific SAP "box." For some SAP environments within the larger system landscape, system availability is not as crucial to business needs as for other environments. For example, your production environments are much more important than your sandbox environments; therefore, system availability must be kept at a higher level as you move closer toward your production environment (see Figure 14.3).

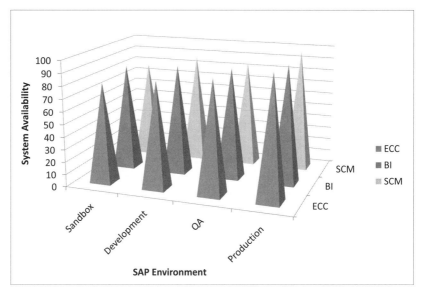

Figure 14.3 SLA System Availability Requirements Based on System Environment within the System Landscape

In this example, if your organization is partnering with an SAP outsourcing provider focused on SAP NetWeaver Basis operational services, it would be imperative that for specific systems (e.g., development, quality assurance, etc.), system availability metrics are clearly defined.

Think about your own SAP landscape. Is system availability business-critical across your entire SAP landscape? Likely, if your organization is similar to most SAP customers, the availability of your sandbox system is not as important as that of your production environment. Is this sandbox system then required to have the same set of SLA standards as the environment where you generate revenue? Of course, the answer is no.

14.3.2   SAP Technologies

Likewise, SLA "up-time" requirements might also be different across specific SAP boxes. No one questions the necessity for system availability. However, business criticality — as defined as the ranking of importance from a business and revenue generation perspective — should be the determining factor when defining SLAs.

For example, although important to the business, your business intelligence environments (BW, SEM, BusinessObjects, etc.) are typically not as business-critical as your core operational environments (R/3, SAP ECC, CRM, etc.) Being able to generate a monthly report from BW is clearly not as relevant to the overall success of your company as the ability to create a production order in SAP ECC.

Business intelligence

SAPanese: Business intelligence

The definition of the term "business intelligence" in the SAP world was much simpler several years ago. Prior to SAP's acquisition of BusinessObjects in 2007, business intelligence equated to SAP Business Warehouse. After BusinessObjects (referred to "on the street" as BOBJ, pronounced Bob-J) was brought into the fold along with several other strategic business intelligence and enterprise performance management (EPM) tools such as Cartesis and Outlooksoft, the term became much more fuzzy in the SAP world.

At the time of this writing, SAP's overall strategic business intelligence approach is to utilize "heritage" SAP NetWeaver Business Warehouse (SAP NetWeaver BW) as the data source foundation and then leverage Business Object's more robust suite of reporting tools such as Xcelsius (executive dashboarding), Crystal Reports (enterprise static reporting), Web Intelligence (sexier, more interactive, analytical reporting), and so on.

14.3.3   SAP Business Scenarios

External facing business-to-business (B2B) or business-to-company (B2C) processes might also require a different set of operational standards. If your organization extends its vendor facing functionality to SAP's Supplier Self Service (SUS), any system downtime could potentially result in your inability to fulfill your customer's urgent orders.

B2B and B2C processes

When leveraging an SAP outsourcing partner in general, a wide range of SLA factors are related to business scenario. Working with an SAP partner for level 1 SAP Service Desk (help desk) needs might require stringent (i.e., immediate) service level response time in some organizations, whereas in others, a 24-hour response time might be sufficient.

Case Study: Scorpion Offshore and its SLA shift

When initially establishing an SLA for their fully outsourced SAP environment, Scorpion Offshore Ltd. chose a comprehensive and stringent model. As part of the outsourcing model, Scorpion established a 24 hours by seven days a week by 365 days a year requirement for all of its level 1 SAP help desk needs. "We went into our SAP production support model believing that our SAP requirements would be 24x7," remembers Pam Thompson, Scorpion's corporate controller and SAP champion. Scorpion's core business is deep ocean oil and gas exploration and drilling. Via satellite, each oil rig was equipped with an SAP terminal for capturing work orders. Oil rig workers were responsible for the creation of these work orders and sometime required assistance. The original SAP outsourced production support model provided level 1 services designed to support these remote employees in common activities such as the resetting of SAP logon passwords and the creation of work orders. However, after several months of activity, Scorpion realized that this level of service was no longer required. "After the initial 'growing pains,' our remote workers quickly got the hang of their activities. Our original SLAs no longer were required and we felt that a less stringent set would be sufficient." Thompson restructured the SLAs to meet the reassessed needs and hasn't looked back. "Resizing some of our SLAs both up and down across all of our production support services has allowed us the ability to accurately match services with requirements. The model, for us, has been outstanding."

14.3.4 Type of Initiative

Another SAP environmental component related to SLAs concerns the type of initiative. If your organization is embarking on an implementation, specific SLAs might be different across various SAP applications or different phases within the project.

For example, as mentioned before, your sandbox SLA requirements are obviously not as stringent or urgent as those of your quality assurance box (or production environment for that matter).

Prototyping   Additionally, production support SLA requirements might also be very different for your various SAP initiatives. To illustrate this point, let's assume that your company is interested in prototyping a new functionality such as identity management. At the same time, your SAP environ-ment is in production mode and has been live for two months (this would still be a relatively new environment in most cases). If your orga-nization is leveraging the same third-party SAP outsourcing partner for delivery on both initiatives, you would most likely require different SLAs for these two areas.

Business-critical production environment SLAs require a more strict set of response times than those for a prototyping initiative. Therefore, even though you are utilizing the same delivery mechanism for multiple SAP outsourcing purposes, the specific SLAs would differ dramatically from one another.

Therefore, the specific metrics related to all of the examples described previously could be unique per environment (sandbox vs. production), component in your SAP landscape (BusinessObjects vs. SAP ECC), and determined based on both the internal SAP infrastructure team and end-user business process requirements.

14.4   Summary

Establishing fair and agreed on SLAs is a fundamental step in ensuring that your SAP outsourcing provider understands exactly what services they are to provide and, in turn, that you have something in hand against which to measure your provider. To augment this, the key rela-tionship between customer and vendor should always be one steeped in mutual respect, understanding, and partnership. An "us against them" mentality is counter-productive and destructive.

Established and mutually accepted SLAs provide the proper framework for working effectively together. Of course, the ultimate goal for any organization is to successfully deliver. The only way to ensure that the organization meets its own internal client (i.e., the business) needs is by clearly documenting and holding accountable their SAP outsourcing partner. Otherwise, if the SAP outsourcing partner fails, the organiza-tion fails as well.

Life is change. Growth is optional. Choose wisely.
— *Karen Kaiser Clark*

15   Conclusion

The subject of outsourcing SAP operations can provoke strong opinions and passionate ideas. Arguments on both sides of the discussion are based on valid concerns and corresponding advantages and disadvantages. To complicate things further, the number of models available to address this topic is nearly endless, with a corresponding infinite number of service possibilities.

Throughout the course of this book, we have attempted to approach this pervasive service offering in a structured and disciplined manner. By first covering the four "w's" of who ("Which organizations are potential candidates for SAP outsourcing?"); why ("Why might an SAP shop benefit from SAP outsourcing?"); what ("What exactly is SAP outsourcing?"); and when ("When is the right time to leverage SAP outsourcing?"), we have provided the framework for strategically analyzing its applicability and viability specific to your SAP scenario.

Strategic approach: The four "w's" of who, why, what, and when

The next step was to shift our perspective from the strategic to its practical application. The people in the field responsible for the work (and doing all of the "heavy lifting") must understand the how of outsourcing. These tactical discussions regarding the various delivery mechanisms such as the SAP implementation, its operational production support, and comprehensive SAP global delivery helped you understand how the actual work is performed. Furthermore, the tactical and fundamental building blocks regarding how to effectively select a partner and then maximize your organization's interaction with the partner rounded out some of the "do's and don'ts" of effective SAP outsourcing and its execution.

Tactical approach: How does it work; selecting a partner; engagement construct

Best practices, insights, and lessons learned The section on best practices, insights, and lessons learned explored some of the more specific areas of interest for different organizations and their special features. We discussed some of the challenges and nuances in leveraging SAP outsourcing associated to an organization's size. Large enterprise companies face distinctly different obstacles than their smaller counterparts and we looked extensively at these specific situations. Furthermore, we delved deeply into the unique advantages midmarket organizations experience, and into their areas of opportunity. We looked at both market segments (large and small/midmarket enterprises) from an organizational perspective and addressed how SAP outsourcing works most effectively for these organizations.

Finally, several additional key areas were covered, including the importance of program level and project level standardization; the often overlooked and/or misunderstood role of the integration manager; and the necessity for strong SLAs. Each of these key areas plays an important role in the partnership between client and SAP outsourcing provider. Hopefully, our exploration provided both valuable insight and actionable tasks, allowing your organization to grow.

If your organization chooses to leverage external SAP consulting for any of your initiatives, it is important for you to understand the fundamental concepts that have been discussed in detail in these chapters.

Key takeaways/ "golden nuggets" Important "golden nuggets" exist as opportunities through which to maximize your SAP outsourcing relationship. These might not always be obvious to the uninitiated and include items such as:

▸ The selection process, including the RFX lifecycle

▸ The role of the integration manager

▸ How to leverage valuable productivity tools (both SAP and non-SAP) such as ticket tracking systems, Solution Manager, and work management tools

▸ The value of strong and documented communication

▸ How to standardize your organization from a methodology, process, and structural perspective

Leveraging some of these key takeaways can help your organization navigate many of the inherent challenges associated with outsourcing SAP initiatives. Nonetheless, many over-budget and missed deadline project horror stories have provided a great deal of fodder against implementing SAP. Furthermore, some have also voiced strong opposition because of the challenges involved in implementing SAP and in working with external SAP providers. These stories have influenced a negative perception of SAP outsourcing.

Although some of these market viewpoints are founded and warranted, you shouldn't throw away the baby with the bath water, so to speak. Simply remember that if your organization chooses to leverage an SAP integrator for an SAP initiative, your end results will only be as good as your provider's grasp of the software's capabilities; their understanding of your specific technical and business requirements; and your organization's embracement of the initiative, so choose your partner wisely.

Choose your partner wisely

In the end, SAP is a software product. Nothing more, nothing less. It will not solve the world's problems or end hunger on the planet (unfortunately). Furthermore, too many of us have too much faith that SAP will magically resolve all of our business issues, all by itself. Although implementing SAP can make our businesses run smoother, help increase our revenue, and cause our technical environments to sing, it is a team effort consisting of implementer, customer, and SAP.

Another common theme presented throughout the book is change. For some organizations, the SAP outsourcing concept itself is a paradigm shift — a major rethinking of delivery alternatives. This major modification in approach requires an open mind and thinking in different, perhaps previously unexplored, areas.

Change is not easy but often worthwhile

Change is never easy. This is especially true for successful organizations that have driven SAP projects on their own for years. However, growth is only possible by exploring new alternatives. Although SAP outsourcing might not end up being the approach or answer to your SAP delivery question, by at least exploring it with an open mind, you might learn a few things you did not yet know and perhaps it will end up being the answer for you after all.

I have refrained from sharing any personal "war stories" throughout the book, concentrating instead on those from the field. However, I would like to share one experience that highlights and synthesizes one very important message and theme around outsourcing SAP operations.

On one of my very first SAP implementations back in the mid-1990s, my client was embarking on a major SAP initiative. One of the first true global SAP rollouts, this Fortune 50 international energy market leader was looking to upgrade many of their European affiliates from R/2 to R/3 while also bringing all of the non-SAP affiliates into a single R/3 templated instance. This ominous and awesome task covered 30 countries, over 20 languages, and more than 20,000 end users. To make things "worse" — and if the challenge wasn't great enough — Y2K loomed in the near future; the Euro was to be adopted; and a multi-billion dollar merger was taking place. A perfect storm, so to speak.

During the very first "all hands" meeting, the client program manager and consulting program manager stood side by side on the podium. "This project will only be successful if we — as [client] and [consultant] — work together in partnership." From the onset, the project was co-driven with a "we all sink or we all swim" mentality. Of course, there were challenges along the way; however, the message was clear and all parties were committed. I am proud to say that implementation after implementation was successful, with strong user adoption and both timelines and budgets met. It was one of the best experiences of my life and I know it was the same for many of my client and consultant colleagues.

The point is that whenever we discussed working with SAP outsourcing providers in this book, we used the term "partner." This word was chosen very deliberately. The concept of partnership is crucial to outsourcing success. Too many SAP projects are poisoned with unneeded challenges as a result of an "us versus them" mentality. When working with your chosen SAP outsourcing provider, the goal for all parties is successful delivery. SAP projects are challenging enough and there is little room for hostility, resistance, or conflict. I strongly urge you to embrace your partner for everyone's benefit, especially yours.

As we also discussed in this book, there are a myriad of outsourcing models. Each model has different advantages and disadvantages which must be weighed specific to your unique scenario. There is no silver bullet. Anyone who tells you differently is either misinformed or trying to take advantage. With every outsourcing opportunity, the appropriate due diligence must be carried out to best ascertain whether it makes sense and if so, how to go about it.

Outsourcing SAP is an art and not a science. It is my hope that this book has shed some light on the art of SAP outsourcing and on working with external SAP partners. This book is neither intended nor capable of acting as a "how-to-guide" covering every SAP outsourcing scenario. However, the information and concepts on the different topics discussed in this book will hopefully provide you with vision how to best drive your SAP initiative.

Outsourcing SAP is an art, not a science

Although working on SAP implementations and initiatives is usually not easy, often challenging, and sometimes painful, when done properly, the results can be amazing. Properly implemented SAP projects can drastically improve organizations, making the effort (all the blood, sweat, and tears) entirely worthwhile. For those who have experienced this, you know what I mean.

I am certain that with the right attitude, right approach, carefully chosen outsourcing provider, and hard work you will be successful.

Best of luck on your next SAP initiative.

Appendices

A   Sample Request For Information Document

#	Question	Answer
1	Statement of Confidentiality: Information as used herein, "information," shall mean both (i) written information received from the other party which is marked or identified as confidential, and (ii) oral or visual information identified as confidential at the time of disclosure which is summarized in writing and provided to the other party in such written form promptly after such oral or visual disclosure.	
	Each party may use information received from the other party hereunder, and may provide such information to its parent corporation, if applicable, and their respective employees or any subcontractors, (including proposed partner[s]) for their use only in connection with the evaluation and execution of this RFI. Each party agrees that, for a period of two (2) years from receipt of information, such party shall use the same means it uses to protect its own confidential and proprietary information, but in any event not less than reasonable means, to prevent the disclosure and to protect the confidentiality of the information received. The foregoing shall not prevent either party from disclosing information which belongs to such party or is (i) already known by the recipient party without an obligation of confidentiality, (ii) publicly known or becomes publicly known through no unauthorized act of the recipient party, (iii) rightfully received from a third party without obligation of confidentiality, (iv) independently developed by the recipient party without use of the other party's information, (v) disclosed without similar restrictions to a third party by the party owning the information, (vi) approved by the other party for disclosure, or (vii) required to be disclosed pursuant to a requirement of a governmental agency or law so long as the disclosing party provides the other party with notice of such requirement prior to any such disclosure.	

#	Question	Answer
2	Client Ownership: It is Client's intent that all product descriptions, specifications, reports, data, ideas, discoveries, inventions, and systems that are developed, modified, and created by the respondent pursuant to the definitive agreement which results from this RFI will be deemed work for hire, and Client shall have sole and exclusive rights of ownership therein. All such items shall be treated as confidential and proprietary information of Client. The respondent shall execute and cause any subcontractor, if any, providing the services to execute any and all assignments and other transfer documents which are necessary, in the opinion of Client, for Client to retain all right, title, and interest in such items.	
3	Failure To Perform: The bidder will in all instances be responsible for the performance of all its contractual obligations relating to this RFI and will not be relieved of responsibility in the event of nonperformance by its subcontractors.	
4	Media Release: Except for any announcement intended solely for internal distribution by the bidder or any disclosure required by legal, accounting, or regulatory requirements beyond the reasonable control of the bidder, all media releases, public announcements, or public disclosures (including, but not limited to promotional or marketing material) by the bidder or its employees or subcontractors including the name, trade name, trademark or symbol of Client shall be coordinated with and approved in writing by Client prior to its release. Bidder shall not represent directly or indirectly that any service provided by the respondent to Client has been approved or endorsed by Client or include the name, trade name, trademark or symbol of Client on a list of respondent's customers without Client' express written consent.	
5	Volumes: Client does not guarantee, nor will be contractually bound to, specific volumes of goods or services.	
6	Confidential Information: Does your company have a documented policy to ensure proper handling of confidential information and materials? Please provide details in the "additional information" box.	YES/NO

#	Question	Answer
7	Response Team: Provide the names of the primary and backup contacts in your company who have decision-making and participation authority with respect to this RFI.	Name* Title* Address 1* Address 2* City* State/Province* ZIP/Postal Code* Country* Telephone Number* Mobile Telephone Number* Fax Number* E-Mail Address*
8	Company Information: Please provide the following information.	Local Office — Company Headquarters — Parent Company Legal Name* Address 1* Address 2* City* State/Province* ZIP/Postal Code* Country* Telephone Number* Fax Number* VAT Number* Registration / License Number* D & B Number* Web URL*
9	Company History: Provide a brief description of your company history. Be sure to include: ▶ Ownership. ▶ The year your company was founded. ▶ The number of employees employed globally.	
10	Supplier Diversity: Indicate whether your company qualifies for any supplier diversity classifications. If so, please list.	

#	Question	Answer
11	Financial Stability: Provide your company's financial data (In USD $000)	
12	Current Relationship With Client: Does your company currently provide services to Client? If so, describe the scope of work and value for each year.	
13	Customer References: Please provide three (3) customer references.	Company Contact Name, Title Telephone Number E-mail Address Description of Work Performed May Client Contact?
14	Market Share: List your company's top three (3) competitors in terms of percentage of market share.	Competitor Regions/Counties Competitor Operates In Percent of Market Share 18 Month Trend (Market Share Gain/Loss Percentage)
15	Top Three (3) Customers: List your company's top three (3) customers and percentage of sales.	Customer Name Industry Percent of Your Company's Global Sales
16	Conflict Of Interest: Are you aware of any apparent conflict(s) of interest that may exist between your company, any employee or owner of the company (or any member of the immediate family of the employee or owner), and Client or any party that your company contemplates using to provide services.	YES/NO
17	Describe your global reach in EMEA, the Americas and Asia Pacific. Include the number of training consultants you have in each country. Additional supporting information may be uploaded as an attachment using the "Attachments" button on the main page of this RFI. Please be sure to reference the question number in the Saved-As title of your document(s).	
18	List the locations of your main offices.	

#	Question	Answer
19	Material Litigation: Is your company currently involved in any material litigation? Are there any petitions, claims, actions, judgments, or decisions pending that are likely to adversely affect your company's performance of the work? If so, please provide a description.	YES/NO
20	Legal Actions: Are there any petitions, claims, actions, judgments, or decisions pending that are likely to adversely affect your company's performance of the work?	YES/NO
21	Bankruptcy: Has your company ever filed for bankruptcy?	YES/NO
22	Contract Termination: Have you had any contract terminated for default or cause during the last five (5) years?	YES/NO
23	Child Labor: Do you have practices in place that adhere to child labor laws?	YES/NO
24	Government Citation: Has your company been cited for any violations by any governmental agencies? (e.g. OSHA, EPA, ATF, HAZMAT, etc.) If "Yes," provide details on any citations received in the last three (3) years.	
25	Insurance Carrier: Who is your insurance carrier, and what is the level of coverage held?	
26	Insurance Certificate: Please attach a copy of your insurance certificate here.	
27	Third-Party Staffing: If additional capacity is needed to meet Client requirements, do you contract with a third party?	YES/NO
28	Standards: Do you hold your third-party temporary staff to your organizational standards?	YES/NO
29	Educational Requirements: What is the minimum educational requirement for your SAP training staff?	No Formal Education* Associate's Degree* Bachelor's Degree* Master's Degree* Other: (Specify under "Add'l info")*
30	Initial Consulting: What is your company's training process relative to initial training of personnel?	

#	Question	Answer
31	Integration: How will your company integrate Client's standards of service?	
32	Management Structure: Describe your management structure for your operations. Be sure to include the duties and responsibilities of onsite management and regional supervision/management, with qualifications.	
33	Strategy and Principles: Provide details regarding your marketing strategy, operating principles, and values.	
34	Customer Service Center: Does your company maintain a 24/7 customer service center?	YES/NO
35	Hours of Customer Service: If your company does not maintain 24/7 availability, provide the hours it maintains for its customer service center.	
36	Customer Issues: How are customer issues resolved?	
37	Process for Resolving Customer Complaints: What is your company's process for resolving customer quality issues?	
38	Dedicated Account Manager: Does your company provide a dedicated account manager to support strategic customers?	YES/NO
39	Multilingual Services: Do you offer multilingual services? (Check all that apply.)	English Spanish Portuguese French German Italian Mandarin Cantonese Japanese Hindi Other: (Provide details under "Add'l Info")
40	Describe your relationship and trading arrangements with SAP. Additional supporting information may be uploaded as an attachment using the "Attachments" button on the main page of this RFI. Please be sure to reference the question number in the Saved-As title of your document(s).	

#	Question	Answer
41	Describe the tools you provide to produce tailor-made internal training documentation in an accelerated manner.	
42	Do these tools have the ability to produce multi-lingual screenshots and related material directly from the Client's configured SAP system?	YES/NO
43	Provide details of your provision of SAP consulting materials and SAP training courses in a number of languages, including English, German, French, Spanish, Portuguese, and Italian.	
44	What consultancy and tools do you provide to: ▸ Conduct an SAP Consulting needs analysis ▸ Design the training approach ▸ Develop SAP training materials ▸ Conduct SAP "Train the Trainer" training ▸ Conduct SAP end user consulting as required ▸ Provide ongoing performance support	
45	Outline your ability to provide best practice consultancy for the setup and running of an SAP client consulting center.	
46	Outline your ability to prototype key training deliverables for review with Client.	
47	Describe the types of SAP Consulting course materials you provide.	
48	Describe how your training approach aligns with the phases of SAP Solution Manager's ASAP methodology.	
49	Describe your ability to provide a document repository for training material to be accessed via, for example, SAP Help.	
50	Describe the types of training you can provide, including details of: ▸ Traditional classroom-based instructor-led consulting ▸ "Train the Trainer" programs ▸ Super user/cascade consulting ▸ Technology-based consulting, for example, online web-based (internet/intranet), eLearning, and CD-ROM	

#	Question	Answer
	▶ Virtual classrooms, webinars, online coaching, mentoring and tutoring ▶ PDA handsets ▶ Application-based context sensitive help	
51	Current Quality Control Program: Do you have a quality control program in place? If so, please describe in the "Add'l Info" box.	YES/NO
52	Audits: Do you have external and internal quality audits? Explain in the "Add'l Info" box.	YES/NO
53	Metrics Tracking: Does your company track the following metrics? (Check all that apply.)	Customer Service Conformance to Service Level Agreement (SLA) Work in Progress (WIP) Order Backlog Other
54	Targets and Achievements: What are your company's service level targets and achievements?	
55	Certifications and Awards: Has your company received any of the following certifications/awards? (Check all that apply.)	ISO 9001 : 2000 ISO 9004 : 2000 QS9000 Malcolm Baldridge Award (MBNQA) ISO 14001 : 2004 Other?

B   Sample Request for Proposal

Request for Proposal

SAP Production Support

August 1, 2009

Maya Mats, Inc.

123 Main Street

Anytown, ST 12345

1 Introduction

1.1 Maya Mats, Inc.

Maya Mats, Inc. is a leading provider of yoga lifestyle products. Maya Mats launched its service in January 2009 and has quickly established itself as one of the fastest-growing business yoga lifestyle companies in the Midwest. In addition, Maya Mats' product line has been critically acclaimed in parts of the far east, including Nepal and Cambodia.

1.2 Purpose of Request for Proposal

The purpose of this Request for Proposal (RFP) is to provide the requirements and guidelines that will be used to select a partner to assist Maya Mats, Inc. in the day-to-day production support of its existing SAP environment. The RFP is part of a competitive partner selection process that helps serve Maya Mats' best interests. It also provides vendors with a fair opportunity for their services to be considered. Maya Mats reserves the right to negotiate with multiple vendors to arrive at a mutually agreeable relationship. The purpose of this RFP is to provide basic information to assist partners in responding to this SAP production support services request.

1.3 SAP Implementation and Support Partner

Maya Mats seeks to build a strong working relationship with a strong SAP production support partner that will facilitate the attainment of the company goals on time and within budget. Maya Mats is looking for a proven SAP production support partner who has previously successfully supported an ECC 6.0 environment as the prime contractor, preferably in the yoga lifestyle industry; has a strong knowledge base and can bring valuable, practical experience to the team and can provide full SAP systems support; is qualified and experienced in the technical aspects of an SAP ECC 6.0 environment; will provide continuity of SAP resources throughout the duration of the contract; will provide for a thorough transfer of knowledge of configuration and technical architecture; can assist in the development of end-user training and documentation; brings enthusiasm and optimism to the team; works well with other external service providers (e.g., other SAP consulting firms, vendors, software vendors, hardware vendors, and consultants); and will work with Maya Mats in successfully supporting the fast-paced growth and business model.

1.4 Qualification of Vendor

A potential vendor must meet certain minimum qualifications as specified in this section. Vendors who do not meet these minimum qualifications will not be considered for further evaluation.

The minimum vendor qualifications are as follows:

▶ The implementation vendor must be a certified SAP Services Partner.

▶ The implementation vendor must be a certified Run SAP provider.

▶ The vendor must have acted as the prime contractor for a successful implementation of SAP ECC 6.0 (FI/CO, SD, MM, PP, WM), and BW/BusinessObjects.

▶ The vendor must have proven experience and skills in project management and governance and must be able to provide consultants who are certified and experienced in the Run SAP operations methodology.

▶ The vendor must be able to provide qualified consultants.

▶ The vendor must agree to a fixed monthly support cost.

A statement indicating that the vendor is willing to provide a performance bond equal to the amount of the proposal is requested.

2 Production Support and Project Scope

2.1 Information and Assumptions for Proposal

2.1.1 Objectives

The overall objective of bringing on a production support partner is to maintain and potentially enhance Maya Mats' SAP footprint. The objectives include:

- Supporting day-to-day business operations by ensuring that production tickets are addressed in a timely manner, providing secure and reliable system for day-to-day business operations and reporting.
- Ensuring maintenance of appropriate internal controls in the SAP system to address SOX compliance
- Providing additional business functionality to assist Maya Mats in analyzing SAP capability for the purpose of evaluating and deciding on alternative solutions.
- Assisting with business process-related projects that require enhancements in the SAP system to support the processes.
- Transferring knowledge to allow the internal staff to support and maintain these systems on an ongoing basis.

2.1.2 Assumptions

Maya Mats currently adapts its business practices to those supported by the configuration of standard SAP software with limited programmed extensions. Only where standard functionality does not exists within the SAP software will programming support be considered to support business processes.

For the fixed price proposal, the vendor should assume a contract review period of 12 months.

The vendor proposal should provide for a continued SAP presence and involvement with the project throughout the period of the contract.

2.1.3 Project Methodology

Maya Mats anticipates that each vendor will propose a proven implementation methodology.

2.1.4 SAP ECC Components Implemented

Maya Mats is currently using SAP ECC 6.0 or greater. The following components have been implemented in varying degrees: ECC FI/CO (AR,AP,G/L), SD, MM, PP, WM, IM, and BW, including BusinessObjects Crystal Reports.

2.1.5 System Sizing Attributes

The following estimates are provided for evaluation and proposal purposes:

▶ Anticipated enrolled SAP users: 50

▶ Anticipated concurrent SAP users: 25

▶ Chart of account numbers: 600

▶ Overall employees: 300

▶ Active vendors: 1,500

▶ Annual G/L entries: 50,000

2.1.6 Technical Architecture

Maya Mats' SAP ECC system has been implemented on an HP Proliant DL 380 server running Windows and using Oracle 10 as the relational database management system. Communications with system users will be via TCP/IP over both the local area network and using Citrix for remote access. Currently, the system landscape includes development, quality assurance, and production computer environments that have been established in support of the system and projects.

2.1.7 Maya Mats' Commitment

2.1.7.1 Project Team Organization and Staffing

Maya Mats' management team is comprised of the CIO, IT director and SAP financial system manager.

2.1.7.2 Project Team Staff Commitment

The functional project teams will work on as needed basis to support the completion of projects.

2.1.7.3 Infrastructure/Technical Support

Network technical support will be provided by Maya Mats' IT department. SAP project management and functional support will be provided by Maya Mats' staff. However, technical support for ABAP programming, NetWeaver Basis, integration, training, best practices, and possibly more advanced functional needs will have to be provided by the selected vendor.

2.1.8 Project and Production Support Completion Criteria

The completion criteria for project and production support issues are as follows:

▶ Documentation of requirements and business processes, end-user procedures, and end-user training completed.

▶ Plan and process owner sign-off for all implemented changes obtained.

▶ Functional and technical specifications documents created.

▶ The DEV->QAS->PRD testing and rollout strategy followed.

▶ System interfaces completed and tested.

▶ Legacy data conversion (if any) process completed and tested, and made auditable and reconcilable.

▶ Documentation of the system/component roll-out/go-live plan completed.

▶ Adequate transfer of knowledge carried out, to allow Maya Mats to independently manage, upgrade, and enhance the SAP ECC system.

2.2 Consulting Services Requirements

2.2.1 General Requirements

The vendor must recognize that Maya Mats is relying on the vendor's expertise to assist in the production support of the existing SAP environment and, therefore, must certify that each consultant provided by the vendor is an expert in the tasks and functions to be performed.

The vendor must ensure that adequate knowledge transfer occurs to allow the Maya Mats to independently manage, upgrade, and enhance the SAP ECC system.

2.2.2 Vendor Project Management

The vendor shall provide a full-time, onsite, SAP integration manager (IM) for the duration of the contract. This role will assist the Maya Mats' SAP production support manager and acquire and schedule the vendor's consulting resources. The vendor IM will consult with and advise Maya Mats' production support manager on planning, implementation methodology, scope definition, SAP ECC functionality, best practices, training, and all other matters necessary to ensure Maya Mats is successful in the completion of project/production support issues. Additionally, the vendor project manager will immediately alert Maya Mats' production support to any observed perils. The vendor IM must work at the direction of Maya Mats' production support manager. Maya Mats "owns" the production support environment, and Maya Mats' project/production support manager will direct — with the assistance of the vendor project manager — all production support activities.

Because management continuity is important, the vendor must agree that — unless directed otherwise by Maya Mats — a specific vendor manager will remain with Maya Mats' project for the duration of the contract, subject to his continued employment with the vendor. The vendor project manager must be experienced in managing production support environments of comparable size and complexity to that being proposed. The vendor IM must have experience in the yoga lifestyle industry (yoga teachers are greatly appreciated.)

The vendor's proposal must identify the specific individual(s) suggested as the IM, and provide that person's resume, qualifications, background, and references. Maya Mats reserves the right to accept or reject any proposed or assigned project manager, without cause, without regard to assignment, and at any time within the duration of the project.

2.2.3 Functional Consultants

Functional consultants must be represented by the vendor as experts in the tasks and functions to be performed. They will work with the production support teams in specifying Maya Mats' business process requirements, configuring SAP components to meet these requirements, testing the components, and mentoring Maya Mats' staff in the configuration of SAP components. They will consult with and advise team members on component functionality and configuration, best practices, testing procedures, and on all aspects of SAP system implementation, including specifications for data conversion and mapping, needed system extensions, and reports.

Functional consultants must be experienced in the functional areas in which they will consult, and in the configuration and implementation of the related components. The vendor must provide Maya Mats with the resume of each individual, including each person's certifications and experience, prior to the person's assignment to the project. Maya Mats reserves the right to accept or reject any proposed or assigned consultant, without cause, at any time within the duration of the project.

The vendor proposal must include a functional staffing plan, indicating the number, characteristics, and schedule for the consultants proposed to support the ongoing project.

2.2.4 Specific Functional Consultant Responsibilities

Functional consultants will work at the direction of Maya Mats' project manager and collaboratively with the project team to:

- ▶ Consult and participate in planning and managing the project.
- ▶ Consult and participate in blueprinting and specifying all system functionality, business processes, policies, and procedures.
- ▶ Consult and participate in specifying all system requirements, including those for legacy data conversion and required system extensions.
- ▶ Participate in configuring the SAP software to meet Maya Mats' needs and mentor Maya Mats' staff in this process.
- ▶ Consult on unit, integration, and acceptance testing.
- ▶ Support the development of end-user documentation, training materials, plans and programs.
- ▶ Ensure knowledge transfer from the vendor to the project team.

2.3 Mandatory Vendor Requirements

2.3.1 Project Milestones, Measurable Deliverables, Progress Payments

The vendor must agree to establish mutually agreeable, measurable project milestones and deliverables for the project, with progress payments to the vendor tied to the accomplishment of these milestones and deliverables.

2.3.2 Continuity of Work during Disputes

The vendor must agree that no work stoppage, interruption, or delay will be permitted should any dispute arise between the vendor and Maya Mats or any of the vendor's subcontractors during the course of this project or during the resolution (by whatever procedural or legal means) of the dispute.

2.3.3 Ownership of Work

All software, documentation, processes, procedures, or other intellectual properties that may result from this project beyond delivered SAP products are and will remain the sole property of Maya Mats.

2.3.4 Confidentiality of Information

Subject to the open records laws of the state, all data and information revealed or accessible to the vendor or its subcontractors concerning Maya Mats' contracts, staff, systems, processes, and procedures shall be held in strict confidence by the vendor. Vendor should agree to sign a mutual non-disclosure agreement.

3 Production Support Proposal

Vendors must submit proposals that include responses to all items listed in this section.

3.1 Executive Summary

The proposal must include an executive summary of the vendor's proposal. This executive summary should concisely convey what the vendor sees as the most important messages of the proposal, the factors that differentiate the vendor's offering from the competition, and the critical points for Maya Mats to consider in its production support.

3.2 Production Support and Project Implementation Proposal

3.2.1 Qualifications and Experience

In the proposal, with respect to qualifications and experience:

▶ Provide at least three references from organizations with which the vendor has been involved in SAP production support over the last five years.

▸ Describe the scope, in detail, of the services provided.

▸ Provide a contact name, title, and phone number for each reference.

▸ Detail how many of the vendor's own employees worked on each project, including their responsibilities and length of involvement.

▸ Provide additional comments about the vendor's participation in the project (if needed) to clearly describe the vendor's involvement in the implementation.

3.2.2 Methodology

In the proposal, with respect to methodology:

▸ Identify and describe the methodology proposed for SAP production support implementation, production support, and project management.

▸ Describe the vendor's experience with the proposed methodology.

3.2.3 Typical Project Plan (for New, Non-Production Support Initiatives)

In the proposal, with respect to the project plan:

▸ Provide the hierarchical outline (work breakdown structure) for major activities included in the project.

▸ Explain how the progress of the project will be tracked and how progress is measured.

▸ Describe how the vendor will manage the scope of the project.

▸ Describe the process for proposing changes to the project plan that were not covered in the original scope of work (change orders).

▸ Describe the role the vendor will play in defining specifications for extended functionality and reports.

▸ Describe how a plan for the development and delivery of training and documentation is incorporated into the vendor's project plan.

3.3 Proposed Staffing

In the proposal, with respect to staffing:

▸ Provide a proposed functional staffing plan indicating the number, characteristics, and schedule for the consultants proposed to support the contract.

▶ Provide a proposed technical staffing plan indicating the number, characteristics, and schedule for the consultants proposed to support the contract.

▶ Describe how the vendor's staffing plan provides for a continued SAP presence and involvement with the project throughout the contract.

▶ Identify the specific individual that will be proposed as project manager, and provide that person's resume, qualifications, background, and references.

▶ Describe the process by which the vendor requests the removal of a consultant from the project.

3.4 Price Proposal

In the proposal, with respect to pricing:

▶ Provide a fixed price proposal to deliver the services described in this RFP.

▶ Include a detailed description of the items included in the fixed price.

As part of the fixed price agreement, Maya Mats will retain the right to continue to use all tools, processes, and procedures used in the production support activities and implementation of projects.

▶ Maya Mats prefers that vendor provides local resources; if non-local resources are required, include a separate price proposal for travel-related expenses and the rates and assumptions.

▶ Itemize any cost items that are not included in the fixed price proposal.

▶ Provide a matrix of hourly rates for the vendor's functional and technical services at various skill levels. This matrix will serve as the maximum rates for negotiated work and services beyond the scope of the vendor's proposal, and for additional contracted programming services, if needed. Specify the cost differential between local resources and resources from off-shore locations.

4 Evaluation Criteria

After all qualifying proposals have been evaluated, Maya Mats will select one or more vendors with whom to conduct negotiations. Price will be taken into consideration, but does not have to be the determining factor. After negotiations have been concluded, Maya Mats will select one vendor and will award the contract to that vendor.

The evaluation will be based on the following factors:

- Qualifications and experience — 10%
- Technical approach (methodology and project plan) — 10%
- References — 30%
- Proposed staffing/support model — 20%
- Price proposal — 30%

Proposals will be evaluated based on information gathered from RFP responses, vendor presentation, reference contacts, and additional research.

5 Proposal Preparation and Submission

The RFP timetable and the guidelines for the transmission of proposals are defined in this section.

5.1 RFP Schedule of Events

Maya Mats will adhere to the following timetable in evaluating vendor proposals:

Event	Date
▸ Issue RFP	▸ August 1, 2009
▸ Deadline for written response	▸ August 15, 2009
▸ Vendor Presentations	▸ Week of September 1st, 2009
▸ Contract award date	▸ September 20th, 2009

5.2 Vendor Presentations

Vendors will be required to give a presentation of their proposal at the Maya Mats corporate office. Maya Mats will notify vendors of the date and time for these presentations. Presentations should not exceed two hours and should be focused on the proposal submitted by the vendor.

5.3 Proposal Format Requirements

Proposals should be prepared simply and provide a straightforward, concise description of the vendor's capabilities to satisfy the requirements of this RFP. Emphasis should be on completeness and clarity of content. However, vendors should include anything they deem essential to the successful implementation of the requirements of this RFP that is not covered in this document.

6 Terms and Conditions

6.1 Maya Mats Contact Person(s) for this RFP
Name: Orly Shivananda

Phone: 123-456-7890

Fax: 123-456-7891

Email: orly@mayamats.com

Please send all responses to the contact provided.

6.2 Proposal Errors
Vendors are liable for all errors or omissions contained in their proposal.

6.3 Right to Negotiate
Upon evaluation of the RFP, Maya Mats reserves the right to enter into negotiations with one or more vendors (not necessarily the vendor with the lowest deliverable price submission) that appear to have submitted a proposal that meet the needs and requirements of Maya Mats.

6.4 RFP Amendment and Cancellation
Maya Mats reserves the unilateral right to amend this RFP in writing at any time.

6.5 Right of Rejection
Maya Mats reserves the right, at its sole discretion, to reject any and all proposals or to cancel this RFP in its entirety.

6.6 Payment Schedule
A schedule of payments will be negotiated with the successful vendor. Payment will be based on performance of the successful vendor and correspond to acceptance milestones that will be negotiated. In no case shall any payment be made simply upon contract execution.

6.7 Period of Contract

The contract — when awarded — will cover the period from the date of award to a date to be mutually agreed on for implementation completion, with a provision to extend — by mutual agreement — for additional periods of one year each for continued support and consultation.

6.8 Contract Award

Maya Mats reserves the right to enter into a contract with the vendor whose proposal most closely conforms to the needs of Maya Mats as described in this RFP. Maya Mats also reserves the right to award a contract to a vendor other than the lowest price vendor.

6.9 Contract Format

This RFP document, the vendor's proposal submission, and the vendor presentation will be the basis for developing a contract. The contract will incorporate — by reference — all of the requirements, terms, and conditions of the solicitation and the vendor's proposal, as negotiated.

C   Sample Statement of Work

Statement of Work

Submitted to: Snake Enterprises

August 1, 2009

Presented by:

NIMBL LLC

Yosh Eisbart

Scope

In this proposal, NIMBL has outlined several aspects of the project, given what we know about Snake Enterprises' current environment. Our depth of experience and capability in managing SAP landscapes ensures that we can meet Snake Enterprises' project objectives. The purpose of this proposal and statement of work (SOW) is to partner with Snake Enterprises as an SAP solution services integrator for the duration of their SAP ECC installation.

It is understood that the high-level objectives of this project are to:

▶ Install two instances of SAP ERP 6.0 to facilitate Snake Enterprises' global rollout of SAP.

▶ Implement SAP ERP 6.0 while conforming to policies and standards currently in use at Snake Enterprises.

It is understood that the high-level scope of services of this project are to:

▶ Provide project management oversight involved in project scoping, resource planning, implementation management, issue escalation, and so on.

- Source all project resources as deemed necessary by Snake Enterprises, including but not limited to, one SAP senior Basis administrator consultant.

Objectives

The goal of this effort is to provide Snake Enterprises with two additional installations of SAP ERP 6.0 to support the existing ERP implementation. One installation of SAP ERP 6.0currently exists and the aim of this project is to review the current installation, determine desired patch levels, install two new instances of SAP ERP 6.0, complete baseline Basis configuration of the installations, setup daily/weekly/monthly Basis maintenance jobs, and provide integration into an existing Central User Administration (CUA) system.

NIMBL is proposing a three week engagement to complete the objectives listed above, including one week onsite and all remaining weeks spent working offsite. The objectives of this project can be broken down into two main functional areas. The activities for each area include:

- Review the existing environment
- Verify the existing installation of mySAP ERP 2005
- Review and determine the desired patch levels
- Install any missing component add-ons
- Review the post-installation configuration
- Transport the landscape definition
- Perform SAP router configuration
- Configure a solution landscape directory entry
- Maintain job schedules
- Install SAP ERP 6.0
- Perform a complete installation of a new QA system
  - Validate software requirements
  - Review system sizing
  - Define Oracle instance names
- Perform a complete installation of a productive system
  - Validate software requirements

  ▹ Review system sizing

  ▹ Define Oracle instance names

▸ Patch the installed systems

▸ Patch the existing systems with Maintenance Optimizer

▸ Install any plug-ins needed by remote monitoring

▸ Perform baseline configuration

▸ Configure work processes

▸ Modify default profiles

▸ Set system defaults

▸ Configure online help

▸ Schedule Basis maintenance jobs

▸ Perform integration into Solution Monitoring

▸ Add to Polyvision landscape on S01

▸ Modify the Project Administration project landscape

▸ Configure entries in CCMS, SDCCN, EWA

▸ Perform integration into the CUA system

▸ Generate an RFC

▸ Modify the CUA configuration to include new systems

▸ Perform integration into STMS

▸ Determine the domain controller (propose S01)

▸ Configure transport routes

▸ Configure QA worklist

▸ Perform additional tasks

▸ Create system documentation

▸ Document installation procedures

▸ Create an administration checklist

Assumptions and Risks

This SOW is based on but not limited to several assumptions as outlined in this section. If these assumptions are not met, project cost, schedule, and the overall solution may be impacted. Impact and change orders, if required, will be handled by the NIMBL project manager and Tom Jones, Snake Enterprises' executive sponsor.

The work, resource plan, and timelines specified in this proposal are based on preliminary information gathered during a telephone conference with Tom Jones at Snake Enterprises.

Snake Enterprises will provide NIMBL with access to the necessary personnel with the domain, business process, and system expertise required to assist with performing the Solution Manager implementation.

Snake Enterprises will allow NIMBL resources to access all appropriate system and business documents related to this project.

For any work performed at Snake Enterprises' facilities, NIMBL staff will be provided with an adequate work environment for the activities being performed. This will include work areas, supplies, telephone, and so on.

The goals and objectives of this project are based on the understanding that the proposed SAP ERP 6.0 systems have been appropriately sized for their desired use. This includes but is not limited to processor, memory, and usable disk space.

Delays in completion of activities that are the responsibility of Snake Enterprises and its staff may impact the scope and terms of this proposal and SOW.

Snake Enterprises will respond within two (2) working days to any NIMBL request for review, input, or information. If such request is for a review requiring Snake Enterprises' acceptance of NIMBL's work, and Snake Enterprises does not reject the work within the two (2) working days notice, this will constitute Snake Enterprises' acceptance.

The ability of consultants to work remotely depends on the setup and configuration of a standalone desktop to be used for the installation. The desktop will need Windows XP, Microsoft Office Standard, Adobe Acrobat Reader, an SSH client, an SFTP client, an X-Windows server, Oracle administration tools, and internet access. The desired remote administration application requires the consultant to be an administrator on the local machine.

Each installation will require a minimum of two (2) hours of support from the onsite oracle DBA. The required time frame for this support will be submitted prior to the activity, and it is requested that the appropriate DBA be made available during this time.

Project Staffing

NIMBL recognizes the importance of providing the correct skill sets and personnel during the SAP ERP 6.0 installation. Therefore, a specialized NIMBL consultant will be provided for this project.

Based on the initial phone discussion, a senior SAP NetWeaver Basis consultant is proposed as part of the project team to design, implement, test, and perform the work specified in this SOW. The initial project timeline created during the initial scoping exercise is included as an attached exhibit.

In addition to the staff identified above, NIMBL conducts an internal quality assurance review of all deliverable documents. Furthermore, NIMBL will provide an engagement manager at no additional cost to Snake Enterprises.

Deliverables

The list that follows identifies the proposed key deliverables specified in this proposal and SOW. This list of deliverables is based (at a high level) on the typical Accelerated SAP (ASAP) project methodology deliverables.

- Project Preparation
  - Create project plan
  - Document current technical infrastructure
  - Determine target release and patch level
- Blueprint
  - Create "to-be" landscape design (CCMS, TMS, SLD, and SMD)
  - Define landscape configuration
  - Determine maintenance and testing strategy

- ▸ Realization
  - ▹ Install/patch non-productive mySAP ERP 2005 instance
  - ▹ Complete baseline Basis configuration
- ▸ Final preparation for cutover
  - ▹ Install/patch productive mySAP ERP 2005 instance
  - ▹ Prepare documentation and perform training
- ▸ Go-live and support
  - ▹ Perform final configuration of production landscape components
  - ▹ Validate the configuration
  - ▹ Perform project review and closure

Project Timeline

In the attached appendix, refer to the Microsoft Project plan for detailed breakdown activities.

Costs

This section describes the financial terms and conditions of this SOW. This is a time and materials price engagement based on the current understanding of the scope and level of effort required. The projected cost is based on market consulting rates multiplied by the estimated projected hours, excluding overtime. These figures are meant to act as an estimate and are not meant to imply that Snake Enterprises is obligated to pay for any services not rendered.

The sections that follow cover pricing strategy, travel, and other non-labor costs, project control, and invoice and payment terms.

Pricing Strategy

The projected hours represent a +/- 10 % accuracy at the present time. After key phases within the overall project, the projected hours may change based on updated information, and a re-forecasting/re-estimation may be performed.

RESOURCE: Sr. NetWeaver Basis administrator

PROJECTED HOURS: 112

HOURLY RATE: $150

PROJECTED COST: $16,800

Non-Labor Costs

Any non-labor and non-travel related costs shall be submitted for approval through the appropriate Snake Enterprises official, prior to incurring the expense.

Travel and Related Costs

Travel costs are not included in the prices quoted above. Travel and related costs are handled as follows:

▸ Any travel costs, including but not limited to, airfare, ground transportation, lodging, and meals for NIMBL team members while traveling to and from Snake Enterprises will be billed to Snake Enterprises at cost.

▸ All travel will be approved by Snake Enterprises.

Project Control

Potential requests for changes to the project scope will first be identified using the issues management process. If the nature of the issue leads to a recommendation for a change request, then a NIMBL change request form should be completed. NIMBL and the client assess the proposed change and approve it by signing this form.

Based on the change request form, the project team will assess the request to determine the impact of the change on the project objectives, scope, deliverables, schedule, and budget. These changes and the impact assessment will be documented on the NIMBL change request form. The NIMBL change request form will be used to obtain the proper client reviews and approvals to determine whether the change should be implemented.

Invoice and Payment Terms

NIMBL invoices monthly. Accordingly,

▸ Snake Enterprises agrees to accept and pay the invoice submitted monthly for hours worked and approved expenses.

▸ Additional terms and conditions not expressly outlined in this proposal and SOW will default to those outlined in the contract between NIMBL and Snake Enterprises.

Acceptance Terms

Upon award, additional contract terms and conditions typically required by this type of work may require negotiation by and between NIMBL and Snake Enterprises. Such terms may include but will not be limited to provisions relating to representations and warranties, ownership and licensing, events of default and termination, delay, change management, acceptance, taxes, licenses, force majeure, financial considerations, and limitation of liability. NIMBL will enter into good faith negotiations with Snake Enterprises upon award regarding the negotiation of any such additional terms and conditions, provided, however, that the parties' failure to come to mutual agreement on such additional terms will not constitute a default under any contract. The prices and cost estimates quoted herein are valid for sixty (60) days and are subject to change, pending: 1) the discovery of factors during negotiations, the prior knowledge of which would have altered the assumptions set forth by NIMBL in this proposal for the scope of work, cost, level of effort, or schedule as set forth herein, or 2) actual changes to the underlying scope of work that would necessitate either a decrease or increase to the cost or level of effort as set forth herein. This proposal is not intended to create a binding contract or commitment and may not be relied upon as a basis for a contract by estoppels or otherwise. In no event will either party be liable for consequential, incidental, punitive, exemplary, or indirect damages in connection with the subject matter of this SOW or any contract that is executed thereto.

D   SAP Screening Process

Step 1 — Pre-Qualification Screening

The screening process begins by contacting the candidate by phone. At this time, the placement manager prequalifies the potential candidate to make certain they meet the client's strict employment criteria by asking questions concerning current employment status and salary, employment authorization (visa), location/transportation and willingness to travel, availability, degree/certifications, and a brief skill set breakdown. The placement manager records candidate information in a candidate submittal form.

Step 2 — Prequalification Skills Assessment

After the candidate meets step 1's criteria, the placement manager moves on to step 2 of the phone-screening process to determine the potential match between the candidate and the job requirement. Recognizing that there are numerous components that make up a match, the placement manager engages the candidate in a conversation about the candidate's reasons for the current job search and about career goals and professional interests, and then reviews the current job requirement with the candidate. The placement manager then screens the consultant, utilizing the pre-developed prequalifying skill set questionnaire. If the placement manager determines that there is a match, the consultant is scheduled for the step 3 in-person interview.

Step 3 — In-Person Interview

Step 3 of the screening process, the in-person interview, begins with the placement manager conducting an extensive reference check utilizing an application for employment. All candidates are required to sign the application for employment, certifying the accuracy of the information they have provided. Candidates are questioned about their employment authorization, past and present employment and salary information, security clearances, willingness to submit to a drug test, history of prior felonies, educational history and professional references.

The placement manager conducts an extensive review of the candidate's work history in chronological detail, noting technical experience and any odd patterns, such as job hopping, unexplained gaps between assignments, irrelevant work history, or a pattern of short assignments. Throughout the interview process, the placement manager poses questions that relate to performance competencies and skill sets required for the position. Each candidate is ranked on a scale from one to five, where a rank of one equals entry level and a rank of five equals expert.

Step 4 — SAP SME Technical Screening

An SAP subject matter expert (SME) is then engaged to perform an in-depth technical SAP interview. The technical interview is performed by an experienced SAP consultant who has the same skill sets that are being resourced. The interview typically takes between a half hour and one hour during which specific applicable questions are asked to determine the level of expertise of the candidate. After the technical interview, a technical summary is crafted for the placement manager to document the proposed candidate's interview results.

Step 5 — Client Interview

After completion of the SAP SME technical screen, the placement manager determines whether the candidate meets the technical and professional needs of the job requirements and if so, schedules the candidate for a client interview, as directed by the client. If the client prefers not to interview the candidate in person, only the candidate's resume is submitted to the client. In addition to this interviewing process, the placement manager works with each client to understand any client-specific requirements and ensures that the candidate meets these requirements. For instance, some clients request that employees take specialized tests or meet other specific criteria before they are selected for assignment.

E   The Author

Yosh Eisbart is a founding principal of NIMBL LLC (*www.benimbl.com*) — a nationally recognized SAP premier consulting firm. Since beginning his SAP career in 1995 as an Ernst & Young ABAP developer, he has been part of countless global implementations and production support operations in a multitude of capacities (developer, architect, team lead, project/program manager, integration manager, etc.) on projects for some of the world's most prestigious clients, including SAP America, ExxonMobil, BP Amoco, and Nestle. He holds multiple certifications, both SAP- and project management-focused. As part of NIMBL, he is responsible for the company's strategic vision practice, empowering both Fortune 500 and midmarket clients to optimize their SAP investments and maximize their return on investment.

Index

T

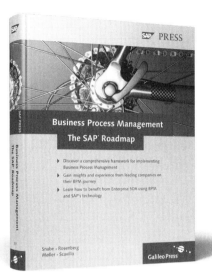

Discover a comprehensive framework for implementing Business Process Management

Gain insights and experience from leading companies on their BPM journey

Learn how to benefit from Enterprise SOA using BPM and SAP's technology

Jim Hagemann Snabe, Ann Rosenberg, Charles Møller, Mark Scavillo

Business Process Management - the SAP Roadmap

This unique book finally sheds light on Business Process Management - a term often misunderstood and misused. It explains what BPM is, how to implement it in your company, and it gives real-life examples of BPM implementations. The authors explain the phase model and the building blocks of the BPM approach (both, for the business and the IT perspective), and they also cover the important topic of aligning BPM and SOA concepts.

411 pp., 2009, 69,95 Euro / US$ 69.95
ISBN 978-1-59229-231-8

>> www.sap-press.com

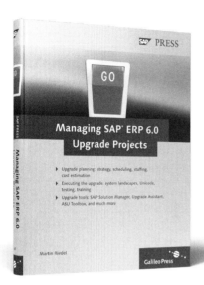

Upgrade planning: strategy, scheduling, staffing, cost estimation

Executing the upgrade: system landscapes, Unicode, testing, training

Upgrade tools: SAP Solution Manager, Upgrade Assistant, ASU Toolbox, and much more

Martin Riedel

Managing SAP ERP 6.0 Upgrade Projects

This book is the consultant's and project team's guide to smooth and successful SAP upgrade projects. It guides you through all phases of the project and gives insight on project management approaches, best practices, possible errors, resources and tools. After explaining how to determine the value of an upgrade, the authors start covering the individual phases of an upgrade: You'll learn how to plan for, how to manage, and finally how to execute the upgrade project in detail. A chapter on the upgrade tools, including coverage of SAP Solution Manager, rounds off this unique resource. The many tips, tricks, checklists, and best practices presentend in a reader-friendly and practical style will make this book your ultimate resource while preparing for the project.

362 pp., 2009, 69,95 Euro / US$ 69.95, ISBN 978-1-59229-268-4

>> www.sap-press.com

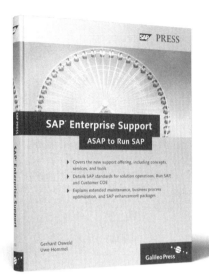

The new support offering, including concepts, services, and tools

Details SAP standards for solution operations, Run SAP, and Customer COE

Explains extended maintenance, business process optimization, and SAP enhancement packages

Gerhard Oswald, Uwe Hommel

SAP Enterprise Support

ASAP to Run SAP

This book provides IT managers and decision makers with a detailed guide to SAP Enterprise Support. Using a top-down approach, the book begins by explaining why Enterprise Support was introduced, and then details the concrete benefits and concepts of Enterprise Support. It teaches you how and why to use Enterprise Support and covers the new services that have been incorporated. This is the one book you need to really understand how SAP Enterprise Support can work for your organization.

339 pp., 2009, 59,95 Euro / US$ 59.95
ISBN 978-1-59229-302-5

>> www.sap-press.com

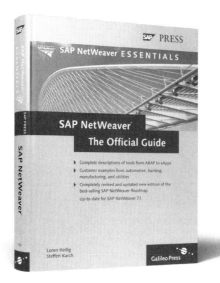

Complete description of tools from ABAP to xApps

Customer examples from automotive, banking, manufacturing, and utilities

Completely revised and updated new edition of the best-selling SAP NetWeaver Roadmap

Up-to-date for SAP NetWeaver 7.1

Loren Heilig, Steffen Karch, Oliver Böttcher, Christophe Mutzig, Jan Weber, Roland Pfennig

SAP NetWeaver: The Official Guide

This book is part of our SAP NetWeaver Essentials series and explains the concepts behind SAP NetWeaver for consultants and IT managers. Using four extensively documented customer examples from the automotive, banking, oil and gas, and manufacturing industries, the book provides you with important insights into how to optimize and redesign business processes with SAP NetWeaver. Further, coverage of technology aspects has been significantly expanded in this new edition: You'll get an introduction to enterprise SOA and to NetWeaver as an integrated technology platform, and you will learn all there is to know about architecture and the most critical technical aspects of the individual NetWeaver components. An additional chapter addresses lowering IT costs with SAP NetWeaver, and re-structuring your IT budget so you can spend more on innovation.

495 pp., 2. edition 2008, 69,95 Euro / US$ 69.95, ISBN 978-1-59229-193-9

>> www.sap-press.com

Interested in reading more?

Please visit our Web site for all
new book releases from SAP PRESS.

www.sap-press.com